BEHIND THE STORE

Stories of a First-Generation Italian American Childhood

::

VINCENT ROMEO

iUniverse, Inc.
Bloomington

Behind the Store
Stories of a First-Generation Italian American Childhood

iUniverse books may be ordered through booksellers or by contacting:

iUniverse
1663 Liberty Drive
Bloomington, IN 47403
www.iuniverse.com
1-800-Authors (1-800-288-4677)

ISBN: 978-1-4620-0219-1 (sc)
ISBN: 978-1-4620-0220-7 (dj)
ISBN: 978-1-4620-0221-4 (ebook)

Library of Congress Control Number: 2011903923

Printed in the United States of America

iUniverse rev. date: 03/17/2011

…dedicated to my father, Vincenzo and my mother, Rose, who gave me life then gave me the life I wanted…

"We can bear any grief if we put it into a story."
— Isak Dinesen

CONTENTS

::

PREFACE

I spent the year after my father died with my mother in their home in Hollywood, Florida. Not being a golfer or interested in the horses or jai alai and needing something to do with my extra time, I decided to pull together my mother's recipes—some written down, most of them in her head—and leave them as a legacy to her grandchildren. I was sure they would want to have them. And I didn't want her legacy lost—that everyday constancy of the many years of her wonderful, good, simple, and healthful food, which served as the base and center, the altar, if you will, of our life ... all of which she accomplished while running our neighborhood grocery store.

While collecting the recipes and thinking of anecdotes to go along with them, the persistence of memory took over, and soon the stories and scenes of our family life became the main subject of the book while the recipes were relegated to the background. Then in another evolvement, these stories, which were mostly fond and humorous stories about my father and mother, began to touch on deeper, more painful, and forgotten family remembrances.

At the same time, I made the discovery one day of a medium-sized cardboard box that I had forgotten existed while cleaning out closets in preparation to sell my parents' home. In it was all that remained of the physical evidence of my childhood that I had thought important enough to save. It was my Proustian madeleine. There were the usual mementos: my report cards with their congratulatory notes from my wonderfully supportive teachers all through my school years, my high school graduation diploma, a copy of my rather negative commencement speech (why had our principal allowed me to deliver it?), honor roll certificates, and beautiful letters from my favorite high school teachers telling me they were sure I had a wonderful future ahead of me. There were my first theater programs, most from my discovery of the Broadway road companies that played the Hanna Theater in

Cleveland. There was a surprising gift that had been given to me on the night of my senior prom by my prom date's mother: the small self-help book *As A Man Thinketh*. I had saved two full-page photos from *Life* magazine. One was of a very beautiful sixteen-year-old Elizabeth Taylor dressed in a revealing low-cut green dress. I was happy to be that boy who had so obviously been smitten. The other picture was of a young, obviously in love couple, walking hand in hand in the woods. I remembered it as soon as I saw it, for it was the image I most hoped for myself in my future life, that of being half of a happily married couple. Most surprising of all was a letter written by my uncle John while he was fighting in Europe during WWII. When I reread it, some fifty years after it had been written, it brought back a rush of sad memories, of a painful part of my youth.

Through these items I began a journey of surprising discoveries, a journey fueled by the importance of the particular items I had saved. They would lead me to know the person I was as a young boy and teenager. I had never articulated anything I felt as a young person. We were, after all, the "silent generation." And though childhood is only a prelude to life, a short time compared to the true life that comes after, it is the time when life's fresh images and memories are most deeply imprinted in the tabula rasa of the heart and soul. I knew I had strong feelings in my early years, for I still remembered in bright light the moments that had deeply imprinted themselves on the greedy mass of my brain. But as a young person I had never connected the dots; I had never put it all together. And though the real life and its necessities, needs, and desires soon took over my life, pushing down the childhood memories, the important moments always remained accessible to me. They were a daily subtext under the working life, with the painful ones often forcing themselves brutally up to the surface. Now in my midyears, with hopefully more consciousness than I had as a child, maybe I could sort them out and understand them better. I also reminded myself not to ignore the good memories of my childhood, for there were many of those too. As a youngster I was full of life, full of curiosity and audacity, and I had a strong desire to create.

Another realization was the importance of place and time in my identity. I would notice for the first time the difficulty of growing up first generation in an Italian American family. I would also solve some mysteries of my childhood, of which there were many. Equally important to me in this process was that I would come to a better understanding of my father, who had always been the major problem for me. Most importantly, I would learn to forgive … both others and myself. And that, it seems to me, is what memoir is for: to rediscover the past so that one may change the present, thereby allowing oneself to be rescued from the past. And in doing that, one can, like acting, turn the private anguish into art, make some sense of it, and get the better of the past by using it. But can we ever truly escape the past?

We are our memories. The very essence of humanity is memory, for without them we are not human. And we must honor our memories. It is one way we make meaning out of our lives. Memories are not only valuable to ourselves but they can also connect us to others, for we are all more alike than not, our experiences more similar than separate, and they have the power to break down the barriers of prejudice that often exist between us. Most of all we all need someone to know us as we are … and to forgive us. Finally, I write to get it right.

CHAPTER 1

Hot Bread with Olive Oil and Cheese

::

Our kitchen table was an ordinary one. Porcelain topped with simple lathe-turned knobby wooden legs and a single drawer on one side that held the family's eating utensils, it was always covered with a freshly laundered and ironed simple blue or yellow linen tablecloth. Mom had no time for a fuss. There was a matching set of six round-backed, spoked wooden chairs that were painted white. As I said, ordinary. But like many inanimate objects when I was a boy, that table was alive, and it held a great mystery for me. The porcelain top could be revolved a quarter of a turn and then, wonder of wonders, opened up into a wooden-topped table that was twice its original size! I knew it was a double-topped table; I could see the hinges. So that part was easy. What I couldn't figure out was how it turned. What inner mechanism did it have, I constantly wondered, that allowed it to be rotated so precisely and yet keep its place?

Born into this world as a new soul, it was my purpose as a boy to figure out the mysteries of the physical world. My eyes and ears, my mind and my heart would be forever curious, for since it was all new to me, I had everything to learn. And as a young boy, my powers of observation were keener than at any other time of life. So whenever opportunity allowed and the table was opened up to its full size to be used for big family parties or for making sausage, I always crawled under it to find out its secret, for what was hidden had to be revealed. But my search would always be in vain. There were no gears to be seen nor any tracks that the table followed. And I would never discover how the table accomplished its magic. When my father found me under the table during one of my searches he would say, "VINCENZO! WHAT'S THE MATTER WITH YOU! COME OUT FROM UNDER THERE!"

But I persisted. When alone in the house I would pull out the utensil drawer and, with a flashlight, search its dark inner depths. I could still see nothing that shed any light on this major mystery of my young life. So I had to assume that there was a concealed inner mechanism. If only I could see that mechanism! I would have happily taken the table apart just to know its secret, as I had done with many of my playthings, almost all of which, eventually, when the initial fascination had worn off, became scientific experiments. The engine of my windup train, one of my very few toys, had become a farm machine as I tried to grind grass in its inner workings. But I knew that the kitchen table was off-limits to my scientific boy's mind.

As I grew older I saw that there were two different powerful mysteries in the world: those of the physical world, the how-does-it-work mysteries, which were the first to hold me captive; and then the more intriguing mysteries that pertained to the "big people," a world more hidden and much more complex. And it was this world, the world of the "big people," that would eventually become my passion. Forever vigilant, my eyes and ears constantly attuned, watching and listening, even snooping if I had to, I had to know what made the big people tick. Why did they act the way they did? Why did they make the choices they made in life? This child's work was, in a sense, the beginning of my life's work, for the work of the actor is the examination of the human soul, its character, and its motivations. A holy calling, one might say, and an obsession.

I prayed and hoped for any scraps of knowledge that might fall my way. The adults would say, when telling a story only meant for themselves, "Look at big ears over there." But that never stopped me. I was insatiable, desperate to organize this strange world I'd come into and place it in some kind of learned order and sense. I never questioned whether I was getting it right; I just watched and listened. It seemed obvious to me that the adults were privy to all the answers; their very casualness and total lack of interest in all the mysteries that surrounded me clearly told me that. And I also understood from their attitude that they were not about to explain any of the more interesting mysteries to me, some of which were definitely off-limits to a little boy, which made them even more interesting and mysterious. This work was a fearsome responsibility because I realized that it was all up to me to solve the mysteries.

One of the best times to solve the many mysteries in my life was in the early evening, when my father, my mother, my sister, and I were all gathered together around our magical kitchen table. At those times it was the heart of our house—the family altar on which the simple and healthy food my mother prepared that nourished and sustained our family was served and honored. It was also where we had our eyes opened to all the rest of life: politics, work, school, family stories, and friends—all under the guidance of my father, who held court as a disciplining god who demanded respect, with my mother as god's faithful servant and my sister and I as his loyal disciples … at least for the most part. For larger family parties … my mother was the eldest of nine children in a tightly knit family … it was an opened-up playing field, where all the family milestones were celebrated and sometimes hotly contested. At those expanded times it was a lively, contentious, and occasionally very sad place.

For my mother, inanimate objects were often an equal member of the family, and she imbued these objects with a life of their own. Philosophical and scientific papers have been written on this subject, but she just took it for granted as the truth it was: the physical world was alive. My mother would always say, "If that table could talk …" In other words, it had heard and seen everything. And then she'd raise her eyebrows in a knowing way, and you'd know the import of what she meant. Or she would say, "Look at that stove! It's stayed in that same place all these years. You'd think it would want to walk away!" I would wonder years later if she were talking about herself.

We lived behind our neighborhood grocery store in the Mount Pleasant area of Cleveland, Ohio, a city that was such a perfect blend of different nationalities that no one accent dominated. Our street was an equally proud microcosm of the melting-pot philosophy popular in those days, a philosophy that, as a young, first-generation Italian American, whose father spoke with an accent, I held dear. Jews, Italians, Poles, Czechs—we were our own small and wonderfully hopeful and striving United Nations, itself a newly initiated concept I also held dear. And later, as the blacks moved out and up from the more depressed downtown area, they too found a safe harbor on our modest street, a street that believed (or was it a young and hopeful boy who invested it with this belief?) in the basic sameness and goodness of all human beings no matter their differences.

The street was lined on both sides with the popular home of the time: a two-family house, wooden shingled, with one porch up and one down. Halfway down the street, breaking the symmetry of this block, was our very practical redbrick grocery store with its one-level home behind reached by a flight of stairs. At the top of the stairs in a little hallway there was a window that overlooked the store. The first room one entered in the house was a very large kitchen, off of which was a hallway that led to the bath and to three small bedrooms. Through the kitchen was another door that led into the living room (which in Cleveland is always called the "front room," even though ours was in the back). From there a back door led onto the glory of the house: a back porch that extended the length of the home and that looked out over a good-sized backyard through a healthy grape arbor. In the basement, directly under the back porch, there was even a cold wine cellar that had a cement table running the length of it, where wooden wine barrels were meant to sit.

While my father worked at a steel mill in the area called the flats of Cleveland, my mother ran the store, which was open from seven in the morning until seven at night. That was how my parents were able to send my sister and me—the first ones to do so in our family—to college. This meant my mother would have to spend her days running up and down the stairs all day long if she was to keep her house clean, have dinner ready by six, have her bread or some *biscotti* baked, and do the laundry and ironing. Then when Pop came home from work, he'd relieve her in the store so she could put the finishing touches on her always wonderfully tasteful meals. And through all the years we lived behind the store I never heard my mother complain once. She was her husband's helpmate in every way. The only problem she ever admitted to was going to the john. That was tricky because it had to be timed between customers and salesmen, and nature was not always so accommodating. There were many times during her day when Mom would get caught, and she'd have to call out from the bathroom when she'd hear the store bell ring, "JUST A MINUTE! I'LL BE RIGHT THERE!" The customers were never the wiser.

Years later, when my sister and I had finished college and were no longer living at home and my parents had moved into the beautiful home Pop built himself in Independence, Ohio, Mom would say, remembering her constant running up and down the stairs to the store and remembering too how when the store was closed for the day our customers thought nothing of knocking on our back door at any hour if they needed a bottle of milk or a loaf of bread, "I only learned one thing my whole life: never live behind your place of business." Of my two parents it was my mother who had a sense of humor.

We always entered our home through the store, and in order to keep Mom from making an unnecessary trip down the stairs, we'd all call out, "IT'S ME!" This was our family mantra, our announcement of the self, as we grew up. That "IT'S ME!" would reverberate down the years throughout my life. And through all those years, from Andrew Jackson Rickoff Elementary School to Alexander Hamilton Junior High School and on to John Adams High School, it was always the same warm, clean, and comforting kitchen to run up the stairs into. If Mom wasn't in the store waiting on a customer, I would always find her standing on her freshly washed linoleum floor at her stove, stirring a pot of minestrone soup or some peas and pasta or Pop's favorite, *pasta e fagioli* (pasta and beans). Mom, because we were after all hyphenated Americans, cooked hyphenated, which meant Italian for Pop (he had to have the meals of his Calabrian childhood, though he ate everything) and American for us (once every two weeks or so she would cook steaks with a baked potato or a roast with some potatoes and carrots), though we ate everything too. Well, almost everything. I would never go near the yearly rabbit Pop would bring home after a hunting expedition with his friends. I mean, that was eating Bambi's best friend, Thumper. I couldn't do that! Nor would I eat the rare tomato sauce with octopus; I couldn't get past the suckers on the tentacles! And I drew a definite line at the very infrequent tripe. I could see no benefit in eating some animal's stomach lining, which looked like a sponge. Once, my father brought home a live pheasant he'd nicked in the wing. I wouldn't let him kill it. It was too beautiful a bird. So I fed it as it sat in a wooden crate … till it died, I guess, of buckshot poisoning. And then, of course, it was no longer edible.

But I ate everything else with great gusto. And I would only later come to appreciate and be thankful to my mother and father for introducing me to the glorious and rich palette of healthy and simple foods, wonderfully and freshly prepared, that was the Italian peasant diet. This was a golden legacy. And it was doubly appreciated when I saw what my non-Italian school friends' mothers prepared for them—that constant diet of glutinous macaroni and cheese, tuna casseroles, salads thick with mayonnaise, the ever-present peanut-butter-and-jelly sandwiches and bologna sandwiches, and maybe an occasional hamburger. None of that for my mother. Everything was always prepared from scratch and with as fresh ingredients as possible. So if I was hyphenated, it was happily so, for I had the best of both worlds … at least as far as food was concerned.

Because I was tall—I had shot up to six feet in height seemingly overnight in my early teen years, towering over my father who had the classic short, bantam build of the men from Calabria—and because I was always skinny, the family would look at me with amazement when I was eating. "Where does he put it?" someone would ask. Immediately after, someone else would say, "That kid must have a wooden leg!" And then would come the topper, the favorite litany of first-generation immigrant children: "Aren't you glad your father didn't miss the boat?" That always got the biggest laugh at our table. And even though I wasn't quite sure of the conditions my father had left behind in the "old country," I would join in the laughter, secretly knowing enough to be glad indeed.

So I always rushed home from school and entered my mother's kitchen with great anticipation. The first wonderful aromas to tease my nostrils— usually garlic and olive oil and tomatoes—would waft over me on the landing outside the kitchen. ("Everything good begins with garlic and oil," Mom always said.) And with the gastric juices in my stomach gurgling, I would eagerly enter the kitchen and immediately run to the hearth of our kitchen— the stove—an appliance my mother always treated with great care. Here, the dazzling attack on my olfactory senses increased. Greatly excited, I'd peer into the pots and ask the major question of the day: "What are we having for dinner?" And as long as I can remember, my mother's answer was always the same: *"Straccinata a casa casa."*

"What's that mean?" I'd ask. I knew very well what it meant, for she often made a soup called *stracciatella*, which had a whole fresh egg dropped in it that you tore apart by whipping it wildly with a fork until it became shredded and formed strands. But the fun was in hearing my mother say the Italian words. And she'd always oblige. *"Straccinata* means something tossed around the whole house from wall to wall!" She was, as I said, the comedian in the family.

Secretly delighted with this chaotic vision of life, I always replied, "That's going to be messy, isn't it?" Of course I always knew deep down that the evening meal would not be messy, for it never was. Then eager for dinner, I would ask, "When do we eat?!"

"As soon as your father and sister get home."

The store bell would ring. Mom would say, "Go see who it is." And I'd run off to the window that overlooked our store. If it was someone who only wanted a quart of milk or a loaf of bread, I'd run down the stairs and wait on them. If it was something more difficult like a large order from one of Mom's regular customers, I'd have to call her and she'd run down. Later when I could remember the prices better, I could take care of the larger orders too.

My mother was born in Bradley, Ohio, and her native language was English, of course. But she had learned Italian as a child to communicate with her parents, both of whom were born in Italy and both of whom spoke little English at first. And for some reason, she had developed her own idiosyncratic way of speaking Italian. Her teeth slightly bared and, purposely overstressing each syllable equally, she would emphasize in a funny way the different sounds of the language so that the *ci* in *straccinata* would be very pronounced and elongated and would come out as *strassshhhinata*. And in this way, the sounds of the words would somehow make physical their meaning: the *shhh* in this case telling me that something was flying around the room like the wind and careening from wall to wall. Somehow Mom, again all on her own, had figured out one of the more interesting aspects of language: onomatopoeia— words that often sound like what they mean. She loved the Italian word for a strainer: a *scuola pasta*, literally a "school for pasta." And she would delight in asking me to get it for her, wrinkling her nose as she pronounced it. I loved playing this language game with her.

I did not enjoy the Italian lessons my father tried to give me, for they always happened at the dinner table and invariably ruined my enjoyment of Mom's food. I easily picked up the Italian words Mom spoke to me because they were laced with humor. But the sessions with Pop were deadly serious. He would try to impress upon me, in his unlikely professorial mode, the beauty of the Italian language, that it was "music itself." But there were problems with his lectures. First of all, I knew the Italian language was suspect. My sister had been studying it at our local cultural center. But when the war broke out, the Italian language classes were abruptly ended. Italy was, after all, the enemy. Government posters of Hitler, Hiroshima, and the pompous Mussolini warned us: "DON'T SPEAK THE ENEMY'S LANGUAGE." I took note. I was an American. And, too, my father, who spoke the Calabrese dialect with his friends, which is what I heard, would insist on teaching me the finest Italian, *Alte Italiano*—the pure Italian he'd learned as a young man in Genoa and Rome. It confused me.

But more than anything, I think it was Pop's accent that stood in our way. As idiotic as it now sounds, I was convinced that if I learned Italian from Pop, I'd wind up speaking with an accent like him. And I didn't want that. But I was an occasionally mouthy, lacking-in-respect American boy, sometimes full of myself, even if, and perhaps because, our household was run by a tyrant; and when I told him one night at the dinner table, when another disastrous Italian lesson was about to ruin our meal, that I didn't want to talk with an accent like him, he backhanded me across my face in a flash. How frustrated he must have been by my refusal to learn from him. I'm sure he took it as a rejection of him by his only son. I can understand that now. He was a proud man. And he was proud, too, of his native language and country.

Once, when he was trying to impress me with the many great accomplishments of the Italian people, he told me that an Italian, one Antonio Meucci, had invented the telephone. I, well trained in the American school system, scoffed at this idea. "You can claim the radio, Pop! Marconi invented that but not the telephone! That was Alexander Graham Bell!"

"NO!" he insisted adamantly. "THEY STOLE THE INVENTION FROM HIM! THE CASE WAS WON IN THE COURTS MANY YEARS LATER, BUT IT WAS TOO LATE. HE WAS ALREADY DEAD!"

"And it's a good thing," I responded. "Just imagine, instead of *Ma Bell* (the familiar name of everyone's phone company in those days), we'd have *Mama Meucci!*"

That was the final straw. "NEVER MIND! I WON'T TRY TO TEACH YOU ANYTHING ANYMORE!"

There were no more Italian lessons at the dinner table. And my father saw that his beautiful language was to be a casualty of America, of this new promised land. And he said, "Mannaggia l'America!" I could tell from the way Pop said it that it meant "Goddamn America!" But I didn't want to learn Italian from him. Nor much else.

My sister Angela—her given name was really Mariangela, the same as my father's mother, a beautiful name that was arrogantly shortened by her first school teachers who didn't want to deal with such a long foreign name—was four years older than I and was in every extracurricular activity you could possibly be in at school, so she usually got home around six o'clock. Soon after Pop would pull his '39 Buick Special up the drive. Mom could actually hear his car long before he drove it up our driveway. I don't know how she knew—she sometimes had a mother's frightening clairvoyance—but she would announce to me, "There's your father!" and she would throw the pasta into the pot of boiling water. And right on schedule, in a minute or so, Pop would pull into the driveway.

Incredulous, I would ask her, "How did you know that?"

And she'd say, "I can hear that old Buick when it turns the corner at Kinsman."

It was true that Pop's old Buick did have a rattle that was unique, and mysterious too, for Pop could never find it. But Kinsman Road, the main thoroughfare, was a good half-city block away. The sounds of the traffic coursing along it could just never penetrate our street as far as our house. How did she do it? (Mom's intuition was always at work. She knew who was calling when the phone rang, and she also knew when my sister or anyone else for that matter was pregnant before they'd even announced it. She even knew what the sex of the baby was. Once, she told me that she'd lived another life on earth, for she had a memory of walking over hills and valleys in a strange land. I believed her too.) At the side door, I'd help Daddy unload the fruits and vegetables he'd bought at the wholesale market downtown before work in the morning. But until my sister and father came home and we sat down to dinner, I needed something for my famous wooden leg.

Sometimes there'd be freshly baked chocolate chip cookies or oatmeal raisin ones or some of Mom's biscotti, the simple Italian cookie Daddy had for breakfast every morning with a cup of coffee before he drove off to work. But my favorite late-afternoon snack of all was a very simple concoction, which I assume my mother had learned herself as a child. (*Concoction* was another of Mom's favorite words. It had lots of nice *k* sounds in it, funny sounds you could make a point of vocally.) Mom made her own bread twice a week, usually three loaves; and on those days I would run up the stairs, pulled along by the glorious smell of freshly baked bread that permeated the whole kitchen—that clean, biblical smell, that warm yeasty smell that portends of the continuity of life and its goodness, that has pleased little boys back to the beginnings of time—and I would stop at the counter next to the sink, where those shining loaves were lined up and cooling. And I knew it was a day for the best after-school treat of all.

My mother knew immediately what I was thinking as I stared at the still-hot loaves of bread. "Do you want a slice of bread the way I make it?"

"Uh-huh." I could barely speak, dazzled as I was by those golden loaves and what was to come.

Like all the best things in life, this concoction was simplicity itself, the virtue of which was one's recognition of the ingredients for what they really were. First you must have freshly baked bread just out of the oven. On two good thick slices of the still-hot and steaming bread, you dribble some olive oil and then shake some grated Romano/Pecorino or Parmigiano cheese and then top that with some freshly ground black pepper. Then you smashed the two slices together gently so that all those glorious flavors blend. And then you eat. But slowly! You must be careful not to burn the roof of your mouth. This was ambrosia!

I'd finish the first two slices in a flash and immediately yearn for another two. This always prompted the same outburst from my mother. "Don't eat anymore! Too much hot bread isn't good for you! It makes a hard lump in your stomach, and you can't digest it! You'll get sick!"

But I could never resist. "Just one more slice, Mom! Please!"

"It'll ruin your dinner!"

But of course she couldn't refuse me. And it never made me sick nor ever ruined my dinner.

One day while I was still in elementary school, I came home to find my father in the store, waiting on a customer. He sometimes worked the night shift at the steel mill, so he was home in the daytime. I greeted him and then ran up the stairs into the kitchen, expecting to find my mother where she had always been as long as I could remember—in her immaculate kitchen standing at the stove or the kitchen sink. But this day she was nowhere in sight. There were three loaves of her golden bread cooling on the sideboard, warmth emanating from them; and there were pots of food slowly simmering on the stove—a pasta sauce in one, a vegetable mixture in another, Mom's version of ratatouille—but no Mom. I went to look for her. She wasn't in the front room or the bathroom or in her bedroom.

I walked to the window that overlooked the store and called down to my father, "Where's Momma, Daddy!"

Busy with a customer, my father yelled up at me, "DON'T BOTHER ME! I'M BUSY!"

"But I can't find her!"

"I SAID, DON'T BOTHER ME!"

Pop was not, to put it mildly, a patient man. He had a very short fuse. And we all knew when to tread lightly and leave him alone. At those times, usually indicated by Mom with a look behind his back, we would silently tiptoe around him so as not to get him going. We knew how torrential his anger could be if let loose, so we were constantly on our guard. I'd noticed that many of the Italian men of his generation were also controlling in the same way. But none I knew—though of course I was never privy to their home life—seemed to have the fierceness my father had when he was angry, the ability to nail you with just a piercing look from his cold white-blue eyes. It made me recoil from him.

Mom, ever eager to make things go well, to pacify the roiling waters (wasn't this the reason for her sense of humor, the classical facing down of adversity?), would always tell us to ignore his behavior. Or she'd find an amusing reason for it: "He was an orphan, you know. His mother died when he was a little boy. That's what's wrong with him. He had no mother." It was a funny take on Pop, but I didn't buy it.

Not finding her anywhere, I went back to my bedroom, the last room in the house. When I opened my closet door to change out of my school clothes, there, in my closet, sitting in the dark on one of my tiny childhood chairs, was my mother, tears pouring down her cheeks. She dabbed at her swollen red eyes with a soggy handkerchief pulled from the pocket of her daily wardrobe—the sleeveless, wraparound cotton housedress that she made herself. This unusual sight—my mother sitting in my closet, the door closed tightly against the cruel world, hiding in her own home—alarmed me. I had never seen her like this before.

"Momma! What are you doing in there!"

"Where's your father?" she whispered, too frightened to speak normally.

"What's wrong?"

"Shhh! Where's your father?" she repeated.

"He's in the store. What happened?"

"I did something wrong in the store. He hollered at me. Close the door! I don't want him to know where I am! Come on! Close the door!"

This was awful. How could I close the door on my mother, leaving her in the dark, sitting so sadly on one of my little chairs, sobbing her heart out?

"I can't leave you in there, Momma! Come out! Please!"

"No! I can't come out yet, not till he calms down. Go on! I'll be all right!"

"But Momma ..."

"I'll be all right! Go on! Don't say anything to him! Just do what he says! And don't tell him where I am!"

Realizing I couldn't convince her to come out, I quietly removed the clothes I needed from my closet, closed the door on my distressed mother, and silently changed into my at-home clothes.

As I started to leave the room, my mother, still crying, opened the closet door a crack and said to me, "Stir the sauce on the stove! Don't let it burn!"

I promised her I would, and she quickly pulled the closet door shut.

I went out into the kitchen and did as she asked. I picked up her old, wonderfully worn wooden spoon and circled it through the sauce, making sure nothing was sticking to the bottom of the pot. And I stayed away from my father, never once venturing near the store, for I knew his anger well. But I could not keep from recalling the awful picture of my mother sitting in my closet on my little chair, silently crying and hiding in the dark, in great fear of my father. She was frightened of my father too.

I sat down at the kitchen table to do my homework. I could hear Pop waiting on customers in the store. I prayed that he'd be kept busy so I wouldn't have to face him. And I wondered what offense Mom could have committed to warrant such a response from my father? She'd been the butt of his anger before—we all had—but I'd never seen her like this. He must have been awful to her. I knew that Pop was demanding in his expectations of Mom. And judgmental too. But she never sloughed off. She was, like many Italian women, a workhorse. She never stopped. It was in the genes. You kept the hours the farm people kept. You worked from morning to night, nonstop. There were no late-afternoon naps. What could she have done that was so awful?

An hour passed. Happily, Pop was kept busy in the store. Then he called me to get him something from the storeroom in the basement.

"VINCENZ! VINCENZ! WHERE ARE YOU?"

I quickly ran to the window and looked down into the store. There were two customers. "WHAT IS IT, DADDY?"

"I NEED A BIG BOX OF SPAGHETTI! GET ME ONE! COME ON! I NEED IT NOW! A BIG BOX!"

I started quickly down the stairs to the basement door, where he caught sight of me. "AND DO IT RIGHT! NOT LIKE YOU DO EVERYTHING ELSE!"

I found the big long thirty-pound box of loose spaghetti that we sold by weight and cautiously carried it up the stairs and into the store. He took it quickly, and I immediately turned around and ran back up the stairs, telling him, before he could give me another order, "I'M DOING MY HOMEWORK!"

When I returned to the kitchen, my mother was standing at the stove in her usual place, checking her dinner. She was no longer crying though her eyes were still swollen and red. I said nothing and returned to my homework, casting, as I did, a longing eye on the freshly baked loaves of bread.

There was, for a while, an uncommon quiet in our kitchen, while we both thought our separate thoughts about Pop. Then Mom, to dispel the sadness hanging in the air, said to me quietly so that Daddy wouldn't hear us (I was learning to be a conspirator, us against Pop…), "Would you like a slice of bread with olive oil and cheese? It's still warm."

"Yes," I said, happy she'd read my mind.

She quickly prepared it and brought it to the table. I greedily wolfed it down.

"Don't eat it so fast!"

I was comforted by the bread and also by the repetition of our routine. Later in life I would realize that food was balm for my mother; it was the only way she had of healing her family and, in the process of the meditative preparation, healing herself. She usually ate very little.

When my sister arrived home, my mother put the pasta into the boiling water. I cleared my books from the table and set the plates and silver around it. My sister could sense that something had happened, but she was also well trained and knew better than to ask.

"Tell your father dinner is almost ready," Mom said to me.

Taking my courage into my hands, I went to the store window and called down to Pop, delivering the message. He was busy with a customer and didn't respond. I immediately returned to the kitchen. After a short while, we heard the ring of the cash register and then the ring of the doorbell. That meant the customer had left and that Pop was coming up the stairs into the kitchen. We were quiet. You could cut the suspense in the air with a knife. I watched the door. Mom busied herself at the stove, her back to the room. Pop came through the door. What would he do? What would he say? Was he still angry? I watched him intently. There was a quick glance at Mom—a glance filled with anger—and then he moved on to the kitchen sink to wash his hands. Mom turned around. So far so good, I thought. Pop came to the table and quietly sat in his place at the head of the table. My sister and I were already in our assigned places.

It was now one of Mom's favorite moments of the day: the ritual of checking the pasta to see if it was cooked properly, or *al dente*, as everyone now knows to say. Though in those days one didn't need to give a fancy name to a moment that every Italian housewife knew from all the past generations, knew in her bones, knew just the correct bite, that center of slight hardness to the teeth. Mom, wanting the atmosphere to be a pleasant one for dinner, took the chance and broke the silence. "Who wants to test the pasta to see if it's done?"

Now this was always my father's job. Mom always bowed to his expertise, for he was considered to be the connoisseur of properly cooked pasta. But he didn't make a move or speak. Not this night. So I jumped up.

"I'll test it!"

"Do you know how?" Mom asked.

This was another dialogue I knew by heart. My part now was to look perplexed so she could continue her lesson. Which is exactly what I did.

"Well," she said, "they say if you throw a piece of the pasta at the ceiling and it sticks, then it's done. Shall we try it?"

This method of testing the pasta usually elicited the same response from my father: "Are you people crazy! You're going to mess up the ceiling!" And we'd all laugh at him because, of course, Mom was never going to really throw a piece of the pasta at the ceiling. She was just trying to make the home we all shared a happy one.

But this night there was no response. Pop was not amused. So Mom and I each quietly ate a piece of the pasta and decided it was done. The game, after all, was no fun unless everyone was going to play his or her customary family role. Mom brought the food to the table. We all served ourselves. And we ate in silence.

There was never a repeat of this incident or even a mention of it. It seems that my mother forgot all about it. Perhaps in the total scheme of things it meant little to her. She was always good at forgiving and going on. And maybe in the heat of the moment, it had gotten blown up out of all proportion. And perhaps, too, there was more to it than she'd told me. Maybe she had done something really wrong. But there was never any discussion in our home about how things had gone wrong and what could be done to better them. There was no idea in those pre–self-help days about "talking things over." We just put the problem behind us and went on. That was how we dealt with crises. And that's what we did. It was over and done with. And in a day or two, things were pretty much back to normal. Maybe that was a healthy response. And maybe, too, in the privacy of their bedroom at night—their door always slightly ajar so they could hear any unusual sounds when they talked about the day's events, which they always did, their voices floating on the air to my bedroom, their words indistinguishable, a blanket of comforting music that I loved to hear, a music that said all's well with the world—perhaps then they dealt with it.

So even though we went on and my parents seemed to have forgotten all about it, I couldn't forget it. I was stuck with it. I would remember forever the picture of my mother hiding from my father in the dark of my closet in terror and fear. It was a picture permanently filed in the fresh, easily imprinted album of my young mind. And later in life I would wonder if her fear and pain had not influenced my fear of my father. Had her hiding in my closet made me align myself with her against my father?

But I wasn't conscious of any of that then; and besides, there was school to keep up with, shelves in the store to be stocked, the store windows to be decorated, and good food to be eaten; so there wasn't a great deal of time to look back. Pop was talking to Mom again, their soothing voices floating out from their bedroom, and there was hot bread with olive oil and cheese readily available when I came home from school. But I still wished with all my heart that I could understand my father better and know what made him the way he was. And I wished I were not so frightened of him, for I wanted so very much to love him … and for him to love me.

Mom's Bread

(This recipe makes four or five loaves.)

Mom never measured her ingredients; she just knew them and felt them. So I followed her through this recipe one day and wrote it down. It's a basic white, golden-crusted Italian bread. In the early years of her marriage she used only white flour, but in the later years, ever health conscious, she added whole wheat flour.

In a mixing bowl or pan (Mom often used a plastic dishwashing pan, which worked very well), mix 8 cups unbleached white flour (do not use all-purpose flour; substitute 1 cup of whole-wheat flour if you want)

Make a well in the middle of the flour and add:
- 1 cup of warm water
- 3 ¾ oz. packs of active dry yeast
- 1 tbs. sugar (it helps the yeast do its work)
- 1 tsp. salt (add this to the flour on the sides of the well)

Let the liquid rise. The yeast should bubble and foam. It's called a proof. Should take about 5 minutes.

Then add another 1½ cups of warm water to the well.

Mix with your hands to combine all ingredients. Wet your hands and scrape the bowl. This should be a rough mix.

Now knead the dough with your fists, turning it over in half every now and then, wetting your hands as you go. You're working toward a moist, elastic dough. It should take about 6 turns of the dough with kneading and pushing into it with your fists.

Dribble a little olive oil around the edge of the pan to clean and scrape it. Knead it once more, and shape it into an oval or a round peasant bread shape. Cover it with a linen cloth.

(On TV one day, Sophia Loren said that this first cloth must always be linen. And I believe her. I've always believed everything she's said.) On top of the linen cloth, place a clean warm blanket. Mom kept a blanket just for this purpose. For years it was an old no-longer-used, favorite Indian blanket of mine. You can also use a wool shirt. The old wisdom was that if you used a person's garment, the dough will rise faster. (I love all those old sayings! Not only are they expressive of a people, but they also all had a basis in truth, and, more and more, we now find the reasoning made great sense.)

Watching this chemical reaction was always a treat for me. And a great mystery. It was magic! The dough would double in size in about one hour. How did that happen? I wondered. I would keep sneaking peeks at it with my mother warning me that I would ruin the dough if I kept lifting the blanket. But surely, for matter to double in size was magic!

(This is the time, after the first rising, if you have a child nearby, to fry a little dough. All mothers in Italy did this, I'm sure, and so the tradition came to America. It's an easy treat. You take a handful of the dough and make a hamburger-sized patty of it and place it into a hot frying pan that has Wesson or Mazola oil in it. Do not use olive oil, as it will smoke too much. Fry the dough, turning it when brown on one side. When it's done, remove it and place it on a paper towel and then dust with some powdered sugar. Wonderful!)

After the second rising, take a chunk of the dough and roll it out in a length twice the size of your bread pan, which should have a little Crisco wiped on it. Bend this sausage-shaped roll—but fatter than sausage, of course—in half and then twist the two halves like a braid. Place into your loaf pan and tuck the ends under.

Or you can make a plain loaf, not twisted. Or you can roll small bun-shaped pieces and place them side-by-side in the pan.

Now place the linen and blanket over the bread in the pans. It needs to rise once more before baking.

Your oven should be at 375°. Bake for 45 minutes total. At about 40 minutes, take the loaves out of their pans and return them to the oven for 5 minutes so the bottom and sides can brown.

The bread is done when it sounds hollow when tapped.

Then wipe the tops with a little butter and let cool, standing up on the small side.

And this is, of course, the time to break off a chunk, douse it with olive oil, cheese, and freshly ground black pepper. Delicious!

CHAPTER 2
Mom and I Make Italian Sausage

::

With our magical kitchen table opened up and our manually operated meat grinder screwed tightly to one corner of it, Mom and I were ready to make the weekly supply of our own Italian sausage. We would make about a hundred pounds of sausage, both hot and sweet, and we'd put it out in the refrigerator case the next morning, and by noon it would be gone. I would sometimes, the day before, drop off fliers around our neighborhood announcing the homemade sausage.

I always looked forward to making the sausage because I was fascinated by how the meat grinder worked. First you had to grind the meat, which meant selecting the disk with the right cutting edges. That done, you turned the handle, and out came strands of meat like necklaces, which fell into a bowl. Mom would take the bowl when it was full and add some hot pepper and paprika if it was the hot sausage and some fennel if it was the sweet sausage. Next you had to place a different disk on the machine, attach the funnel, and slip the casings onto the funnel. These casings really intrigued me. They looked like pieces of dried, wrinkled skin preserved in salt. The first time I saw them I couldn't figure out what they were. Then Mom soaked them in water over and over to wash away all the salt and to be sure they were totally clean inside and out. After doing that, they were transformed into what they were originally—the intestines of a pig. Wow! I couldn't believe that was what sausage meat was stuffed in. It was more of that virtue of the people: saving and using every bit of a butchered animal. Later I learned that some people, particularly the blacks who later moved onto our street, ate them. They called them chitterlings. It seemed there was no end to the inventiveness of people using whatever was at hand.

After you had pushed the casing all the way into the funnel, you tied a knot at the end of it. Then you could start turning the handle of the grinder. This was the fun part. Out came the meat, filling and pushing the casing right off the funnel all by itself. It was a magical transformation. You only had to be sure you weren't leaving any spaces in the sausage. And there it was—Italian sausage. It was so simple and easy. And it was so good. We all loved it broiled and stuffed between two slices of Mom's homemade bread.

It was Pop's dream—and a difficult one since we weren't on Kinsman Road, the main thoroughfare—that our small one-street-block-only neighborhood store be known for its homemade Italian products like pepperoni and *soppressata* and for imported Italian cheese like provolone. Looking back now, I realize what I was too unaware to notice then: how amazing my father was, for it seemed he knew how to do everything. He knew all the methods of preserving food. He knew how to can and pickle. He and Mom put up a big crock of pickled eggplant every year that was always a big hit as an appetizer or added to sandwiches. He knew how to use the drying method, as he did making pepperoni and *soppressata*. He could even butcher a hindquarter of beef into its useable parts. And like most of the Italian-born men, he knew how to build, how to use stone, brick, and cement (a cement-block garage would rise in our backyard one summer). And he pleased me to no end by replacing our dirty coal furnace with an automatic gas one. Now I no longer had to add new coals to the fire after shaking the dead ones down and shoveling them out. He even knew how to overhaul an automobile engine, as he did our '39 Buick Special when it was twelve years old, giving it another ten years of life. There were a million little pieces of the engine laid out on old bedsheets all over our backyard. I looked at them with fear. How could he possibly remember how they all fit back together? But he did.

And in accordance with his plans for enlarging the customer base of our store, he turned our basement into a drying and curing room for all kinds of food. Large globes of ripening provolone hung from the beams of the ceiling, developing an alarmingly alive-looking greenish mold. Pop told me once of a cheese in Italy that was cured in caves and, when ripe and cut open, was filled with worms! Worms that you ate when you ate the cheese! I couldn't believe that. And when I protested, he said the worms hadn't eaten anything but the cheese for all their short lives, so they were just made of cheese and therefore all right to eat. I was glad that particular cheese was not being imported into America.

My father never threw anything out. I came to believe that this conserving of everything was a major tenet of Pop's that had probably been handed down through the centuries, maybe from his father's father's father. He believed that everything could and would come in handy one day. So there were always balls of twine waiting to be used, old wooden sticks to prop up the tomato plants, nails and screws and bits of tape. He always saved old broom handles. These were prized because when they were attached by wires to the ceiling in the basement, they were the perfect place to hang and dry the double-thick lengths of sausage called *soppressata* that he was curing. There were also long lengths of our sausage, hot and sweet, hanging in loops over these same poles, in the process of becoming pepperoni. These broom handles also served another special purpose. After Pop cut them into six-inch lengths, they were the perfect circumferences for Mom to use when she made cannoli—those wonderful log-shaped ricotta-filled, holiday-time pastries.

Way in the back of the basement, on shelves Pop built, were the quart-glass bell jars of canned tomatoes that he and Mom put up every autumn, when they harvested the tomato crop from our backyard. This was so Mom could have her own canned tomatoes all year long. One year, some of those jars exploded. Maybe the rubber seal hadn't been tight enough or perhaps something had gone wrong in the heating process. Mom said you could smell them all up and down our street for days. I was secretly delighted when they exploded, for it was another example of the mysterious physical world at work. I inspected the disaster site, hoping to solve the mystery, while Pop, mildly cursing under his breath in Italian, cleaned up the mess.

Whenever I had to go down into the cellar to get something from the storeroom that was needed for a customer or a jar of Mom's canned tomatoes, I always turned on every light in the basement so I wouldn't be frightened. And I always made sure I passed through the "room of snakes" very quickly. That was where all the sausages were hanging and drying. There was only one solitary lightbulb in each room in the cellar hanging on its electrical wire line. So when I would reach up to pull the chain on the light to turn it on, it caused the light to swing, and that movement would cast shadows against the walls, moving shadows of the hundreds of snakes that were alive and were just waiting for me to walk underneath them so they could drop down on me from the ceiling, wrap themselves around my neck, squeeze me, and bite me to death. So with one of Pop's broom handles I would hit at them, vanquishing them before I could do what I was sent to do. Our cellar was a scary and eerie obstacle course ... that I thoroughly enjoyed.

Way in the back of the cellar, there was a room I rarely ventured into. It had originally been the coal room, where every month or so in the winter, a truck would arrive and slide a load of coal into our basement. But now since we had a gas furnace, it was used as a storeroom for the house, for furniture Mom and Dad were not using, or perhaps a rug or linoleum that might someday come in handy. But this room also contained an intriguing treasure that often drew me in. Sitting on wooden slats to keep it dry in case of a flood was an old steamer trunk, the very trunk that had accompanied my father on his journey from Cirò, Italy, where he'd been born, to America at the end of the First World War.

It sat empty and forgotten now. No one ever mentioned it. But I was drawn to it whenever I was in the cellar. I would push up the top, remove the shallow top shelf that was divided into two compartments, and, after placing it aside, I would search the deep inside of the trunk for any clues I might find about my father's life and his journey to America when he was a young man. I hoped and hoped that it would reveal a secret or two about my father, something that would allow me to know him better.

The inside of the trunk was covered with a blue floral-patterned paper. About six inches from the bottom of the trunk there was a watermark that ran around the whole trunk. Had that happened, I wondered, when my father crossed the Atlantic Ocean? Had there been a major storm during which the ship had taken on water? I wondered where Pop was on the ship. Was he in steerage? Was it a terrible crossing? Was he sick? Was the ship overly crowded? What was the name of the ship? I looked for a sticker on the trunk that might tell me something, but there was none. And Pop never talked about it. Much later while searching the Internet I would learn that the ship was the *Giulio Cesare*, and it had sailed out of Naples, arriving in the New York harbor on October 1, 1922. He had fifty dollars with him. His destination was Fort Wayne, Indiana, where he had a cousin named Leto Salvatore, who was to look after him for a year. On the train to Indiana he was given a box lunch. Inside it was a banana, a fruit he had never seen. A nearby passenger laughed when my father tried to eat the skin and then showed him how to peel it.

I would sit there for a long time, just staring into the trunk's unyielding emptiness, breathing in its damp, musty smell. I imagined the little town my father had grown up in was in that smell, that it was still clinging to the inside of the trunk. I tried to imagine what my father had experienced when he was growing up. It was all there in that trunk if I could just pull it out. These thoughts would, in turn, lead me to wonder why my father had left Italy. Did he have to? And why? What was it like to leave home for an unfamiliar country, to become a person without a past that could be shared? Did he miss his family, the older brother who inherited all the farmlands, as was the custom then, and who stayed in Italy. My father had been lucky, and because he had fought in the First World War—Italy then was our ally—he was granted immediate entry into the United States. His two younger brothers, Fortunato and Francesco, weren't so lucky. They were not allowed entry into the United States and so immigrated to Buenos Aires. He would never see them or hear from them again. Did that sadden him? He never said so if it did. If only his trunk could tell me his story. But my father's trunk, like my father himself, yielded no secrets. And saddened, I would close the lid and walk back up the stairs into our kitchen, reentering my own so-far-pastless present.

Listening hard over the years, I did learn a few more things about my father. I learned that his father, my grandfather, besides running his own farm and vineyard, was also the town assayer; and every year at harvest time he was hired by all the local landowners to add up all the quantities of olives, olive oil, figs, grapes, and wine their land had produced and to help with the pricing. My father must have inherited that mathematical gift from his father, for he was always good at figures. From my mother I learned—and this really shocked me—that my father had only had three years of schooling as a child! That was all the Italian government deemed necessary at that time, the early years of the twentieth century—just three years! And after those three years, the children would have to go to work, usually on the family farm or for a landowner. But the town in the southern part of Italy where my father was born, Cirò Marina, a town that dated back to 800 BC—the area was once part of the greater civilization of Greece and was called Magna Graecia—is near Crotone, a town some claim to be the birthplace of mathematics in the Western world. Pythagoras, the Greek philosopher and mathematician, is believed to have lived there for a time. Perhaps the people there have always had a pride in mathematics, even till today. Whatever the influences, my father had a wonderful, inborn, natural intelligence, which, abetted by his childhood of learning the basics necessary to take care of oneself and one's family, made him a remarkably self-sufficient man, a man who knew how to use everything around him in his world to his benefit. With only three years of schooling he was a far more well-rounded and knowledgeable person than most people in America today who are college graduates. I marvel now, as I never did as a child, at what my father knew and could do; for I know that I'll never know or be able to do as much. Sadly, a great deal of his knowledge is lost to me.

For our homemade sausage, Pop would always buy the best pork butts he could find. He'd trim away some of the fat, though not all, for you needed some to make the sausage moist and tender; and then he'd cut all the meat into cube-sized chunks. When my mother added the seasonings to the sausage meat, she always let me taste it to be sure it had enough salt. She would always do a taste test herself, just to make sure. But I was happy to help, for I had a strong love of raw food that stemmed, I think, from my mother's tender meatballs, which I loved eating raw. Into the ground beef she added grated cheese, an egg, fresh parsley, some chopped garlic, her own bread crumbs made from bread not used and left to dry (nothing ever wasted, you see), and salt and pepper. On the days I was lucky enough to mix that recipe or be in the kitchen when she was making it, I could taste a bit of it as I went along …

to check its seasoning, of course. (No wonder I loved steak tartare as a young adult. I'd been eating that elegant meal since I was a child. We just called it meatballs.) And, of course, there was also raw cookie dough and, when Mom remembered, the end of the cake batter from the mixing bowl and the beaters that she would let me lick. In their raw state, most of these foods tasted richer somehow. But raw pork was not meant to be eaten, and she always warned me to spit it out, reminding me every time that it could make me very sick. When one casing was filled, Mom would tie it off at the end and then tie it into links. Then we'd fix it on big trays in coiled mounds and place it in the refrigerator. On Saturday mornings people came from blocks around to buy it. And everyone said it was the best Italian sausage they'd ever tasted. And, as I said, it flew out of our store. Pop had success on his hands and saw the possibility of his dream of owning a chain of Italian stores coming true.

I liked watching my mother prepare food. She always touched whatever she was preparing with great respect and gratitude. It was, I think, her form of prayer, her way of being thankful for the blessings of life. Food, to her, was holy; it was the means through which her family would be healthy and survive. The other part I liked about helping my mother in the kitchen was that, unlike my father, who was always critical of what I did, she never was. She would calmly explain how to do things. And there was another benefit from helping her in her kitchen, for I knew that it was a good time—since we were alone—to get her to tell me stories of our family. My mother was the keeper of all the family stories and anecdotes, and she loved to retell them. My father was too busy usually for any "silliness" like that because, I think, he wanted to be perceived as a modern man of the day, a man of democratic America, this wonderfully classless society where everyone was equal. So he felt that there was very little to be gained by perpetuating the old superstitions and myths. I also think he meant to protect my sister and myself from that way of thinking. So if he were around at these times, he usually kept silent, unless of course he had to jump in to correct a bit of historical misinformation, something he took great pleasure in doing. But it was Mom who relished the bizarreness of the human race and our own particular ancestors and who ran a commentary on all our family and friends, a commentary that was sometimes just cleverly observant and telling but was often very funny.

One day she said to me while cleaning her kitchen sink, "I never let the menfolk spit in my sink." I laughed but then thought to myself, *Well, yes, the men were mostly physical workers, and they were all constantly spitting to clear their throats ... I know my father was ... so she was right.* Her sink was sacrosanct. It was where her life-enhancing food was cleaned.

Another time, much later in life, she proudly told me that she never had a clogged drain in her kitchen her whole life. I laughed at that too, thinking it an odd thing to be proud of, but that was Mom—proud of her house and proud of doing her job well.

And sometimes she was wicked. She was a great mimic, and she had a wonderful knack for imitating people, for catching the essence of a person's physicality in their walk or posture. If we'd been to a party or out on a Sunday visit, when we got home, we'd often egg Mom on to do her physical impersonations of the people at the party. She never needed much persuasion. She loved the spotlight … but only in her own home. She would never have done her impersonations outside of her home; she was much too shy socially. But with us pleading, she couldn't refuse and would go into her act. Her pantomimes, like those of all good satirists, were sharp and swift and to the point. With a quick flick of the cutting knife of impersonation, her physical portrayal would catch the person she was mimicking, and we would know immediately who it was and would fall about laughing at the recognition of the person's eccentricities. (Was this an early influence on me to become an actor?)

Invariably as we made the sausage, Mom would tell me the story of the yearly slaughter and butchering of a pig when she was a little girl. Every spring her father bought a piglet, which would then be fattened up for the rest of the year. My mother was often the one who fed it the corn meal mush her mother prepared for it. Then, when it was fully grown, it was slaughtered—usually on the coldest day the following February. My grandfather would invite a small group of his friends and neighbors, for many men were needed to restrain the pig. First the pig would be hung up by its hind legs, and then his throat would be quickly cut. The blood would be drained into a vessel and saved to make a pudding or stuffed into sausage casings with raisins and other ingredients. After all the blood had been drained, the pig would be covered in hot cloths and towels so that its body hair could be shaved off. Then my grandfather would cut the pig's underside open from top to bottom with a knife. And it would be left like that for a day or two. When the pig had dried a bit, the butchering began. And that was a day of celebration, for everyone who had helped would share part of the pig.

Mom hated this day, for she had, of course, become fond of the pig, having been the one who had fed it all year and watched it grow from a one-pound piglet to a five hundred pound pig. So to avoid seeing the pig she'd raised slaughtered and to avoid hearing the pig's screams as they killed it, she always ran and hid in her bedroom on the second floor, which overlooked the backyard. And through her window she would plead with her father not to kill the pig, knowing of course that he had to.

After the butchering of the pig, her father would begin to parcel out sections of it, often some of the innards, to his helpful neighbors, making sure to use every part of it, for every single part of the pig has a use. My uncle Veto told me once: "We ate every part of the pig except the tail and the squeal." Then a month or so later, my grandfather would buy another piglet, and again Mom would begin the yearlong process of feeding and caring for it. That yearly pig would provide food for the family all winter long.

I loved hearing Mom tell of her childhood, of her dreams, of what life had been like when she and my father first married. She wanted to be a schoolteacher but had to quit school after the eighth grade to help take care of her younger brothers and sisters.

When I was old enough to realize and to be amazed that she hardly ever used cookbooks, I wanted to know how she had learned to cook.

"I learned from my aunt Carmela, my father's sister. She lived with us when your father and I were first married."

That surprised me. "You had someone living with you when you were first married?"

"Yes. Aunt Carmela. She taught me everything. She was a wonderful cook. She and her husband, Luigi, and your uncle Veto, too (Aunt Carmela was lightening my grandmother's load by raising him), all lived with us."

"Five of you in one home!" I couldn't believe that.

"Yes. It was what everyone did. You took in family. You shared the expenses and the chores."

(My mother and my father had taken in more than family in their young married days. She once told me the story of an unmarried young girl they knew who had gotten pregnant. When her family found out they threw her out and Mom and Dad took her in, along with the father of her child, her husband to be, and cared for her right through her pregnancy. They gave her my just-born sister's bedroom, bringing my sister into their bedroom to sleep. My mother helped with the delivery and always remembered how the doctor told her to "HOLD HER LEGS!")

I wanted to know where they went on their honeymoon.

That made her laugh. "Honeymoon? It was the Depression! We couldn't afford a honeymoon! We spent our first night together with Aunt Carmela and her husband in the next bedroom."

Then she continued, "I learned everything from her, more than from my own mother, who mostly cooked beans or made chicken soup, along with a lot of fried potatoes, because we had very little money. But Aunt Carmela cooked differently. She would always use fresh ingredients and make simple meals. I remember when the tomatoes were in season, she would remove the skins and seeds, and with a little olive oil and garlic she would cook them for about twenty minutes, adding a good handful of fresh basil at the end. And in those days everyone cooked their tomato sauce for hours and hours. But not Aunt Carmela. She taught me how to make eggplant parmigiana, how to make braciole." Braciole was a rolled and stuffed meat with a whole egg in it that I loved. "And she taught me how to stuff artichokes." I loved stuffed artichokes too and enjoyed the fun of putting one of the leaves in my mouth and scraping off the tender part with my teeth. "She knew so many things. I guess she'd been taught by the women in her family. And she was smart. But she died much too young. It was sad. She was very overweight, and her heart and lungs just couldn't manage all that weight and gave out."

One day as we were making our sausage, Mom told me a story about her childhood in Bradley, Ohio, and how she was always the one appointed to clean the outhouse every Saturday morning with a broom and a bucket of water. It was a job she hated and always wondered why it wasn't assigned to her brothers. But no, it was her weekly job, and she did as she was told, scrubbing the seats with the broom and dumping the water and then quicklime down the hole.

This was more surprising stuff to me. I couldn't believe she had grown up without the indoor plumbing we all took for granted.

"There were two seats," she continued. And then her sly humor kicked in. "You could have a friend join you."

I laughed at that idea. How preposterous, I thought.

"Those were different times," Mom said. "They were friendlier than now." And then she laughed. "Guess what we used for toilet paper?"

I hadn't a clue. The thought of not having toilet paper had never occurred to me.

"The Sears catalogue! That's what everyone used! I don't think we ever bought anything from it, but it's what the whole country wiped their …" She blushed, searched for the most polite word she could think of, and then continued, "Wiped their behinds with. The Sears catalogue! Can you imagine? Didn't Sears do a great service for America?"

Now we were both laughing. But the outhouse duty she had to perform jogged her memory further. "Even though I had to clean the outhouse, I got to bathe in clean water every Saturday night because I was the oldest. My brothers had to wait their turn for the tub."

I couldn't believe this. "Why couldn't they use clean water?"

She looked at me with disbelief. "Don't you understand? There was only enough hot water for one tubful. That was it!"

It was always fun to cook with my mother. We laughed a lot and I learned a lot. I learned that there were things in life one had to do no matter if one liked them or not. I learned never to take God's gifts to us for granted, that it's a good human quality to be grateful for the miraculous creature God created in us and how important it is that we acknowledge that. And I learned that one could invest the work in life with humor. It was the most important seasoning of all in life.

Italian Sausage

This recipe calls for 10 lbs. of pork butt meat, so adjust your seasonings accordingly if you expand it.

Grind the pork in a rough grind. Use a bigger grind than hamburger.

For the sweet:
Add 2 oz. salt
2 tbs. fennel

For the hot:
- Add 2 oz. salt
- 2 tbs. red pepper flakes
- 2 tbs. cayenne pepper
- 2 tbs. paprika (this is what makes the hot sausage red)

Mix. If it's too dry, and it usually is, add ½ glass of red wine.

Taste to see if you have enough salt. (Often at this point, Mom and Dad would take a handful of the mix and sauté it so they could taste the seasonings. Then when they'd finished making the sausage, they would add some eggs beaten up to that and make a sausage omelet for lunch.)

Clean your hog casings. They come dried in salt, which has to be thoroughly washed away. Soak them in water, washing them over and over, inside and out. Change the water as you need. Do this until they're totally clean. Then slide one over the machine's nozzle, and tie the end with a short length of kitchen string. Crank to fill your casings and tie into links.

That's all there is to it. Nowadays there are all sorts of wonderful sausages: veal sausages and chicken sausages, all with interesting added ingredients, but I still like the original pork sausage the best. Broiled (be sure to prick the sausage links with a fork or they'll burst) and sandwiched between two slices of homemade Italian bread as we did for all our parties, it can't be beat.

Add cooked red peppers and onions to the sandwich if you want.

My mother always had a hidden container of her treasured roasted red peppers somewhere in the fridge. They are perfect with broiled sausage or, for that matter, on any meat sandwich.

CHAPTER 3
Five Steaks for Four, with Oregano

::

For some reason unknown to me, our seat assignments at the kitchen table for dinner were set in stone. But who had set them? No one had ever asked me where I would like to sit. It was, I assumed, just one of those unilateral parental decisions that couldn't be changed. It was the way it was and always had been.

My father sat at the head of the table, closest to the door leading into the store. My mother sat across from him at the other head of the table that was close to the center of her activity, her stove. My sister sat with her back to the kitchen window. And I always sat on my father's right, my back to the open room. And that was the problem. My father being right-handed, that put me directly in the line of fire. Pop could backhand me in a split second, his arm striking out so quickly—it seemed to work on some kind of mysterious quick-spring mechanism—that I could never see it coming. Soon I learned to eat all my meals with my right eye on my food and my left eye keeping watch on Pop's right arm. The slightest jerk or movement from that arm, even if he was just innocently reaching for a slice of bread, was enough to make me jump away quickly. Like Pavlov's famous dog we learned about in school, I had been conditioned. And not only that, I was shell-shocked just like the crafts' teacher we had at school, who'd been in the war and that the boys tormented by throwing small bits of wood or metal up toward the front of the room. He always ducked too. But I'd never been in a war.

If the Italian meal was, at its best, a form of convivial daily communion, a time when our family gathered joyfully to enjoy my mother's wonderfully tasty meals and to share our thoughts and feelings of the day, it was also a place fraught with tension; for presiding over it all was our in-house god, my father, served by his obedient subjects—my mother, my sister, and myself.

29

That setup made this daily coming together a time when you could catch holy hell from that presiding Old Testament deity. Ours wasn't, make no mistake about it, your typical American household with a quiet, rational, generic TV father, but an Italian household with an in-charge, rigid Italian father, whose word was law and who demanded and usually received absolute obedience from his family—no ifs, ands, or buts. If his cold white-blue staring eyes weren't enough to frighten you into line, he would resort to his arm. He never hit anyone else in the family, certainly not my sister, because, I guess, she was a girl; and he never hit my mother as far as I know, unless it was to give her a light warning pat on her backside. No, it was only me that he hit. And it always happened at the dinner table, where his mechanical arm could strike out with a flash. But why was it only me he hit? Was it because I was a boy and therefore needed stronger discipline? I didn't feel I was a troublemaker. Yet night after night, our dinner table served as the place of a daily education, reminding me constantly of how dangerously unpredictable the world is, of how treacherous and painful a place it could be.

Resenting this lack of democracy in our home, I remember trying one day—I must have been in junior high school at the time—to bring justice to our dinner table. I decided I would change the family seating plan at our kitchen table. Before anyone else had been called to dinner, I sat myself down in my sister's seat, in front of the kitchen window, staking my claim and praying that, as I'd just learned in school, possession was indeed nine-tenths of the law. In this position, on Pop's left, it would be much harder for his quick-spring mechanical arm to swing out and clobber me. I sat there, quietly working on my homework, doing my best to pretend that nothing was amiss.

My mother was the first to spot me. Leaving a customer waiting in the store, she had made a quick dash up the stairs to check on her dinner, fearful as always that it was burning. Ever eagle-eyed and never missing a trick, she said as she ran past me on her way to the stove, "What are you doing in your sister's seat!" You couldn't get away with anything with my mother.

"Geez!" I replied in my best Jack Benny imitation. "We're all so stuck in our ways here! We need to break out of our chains!" Mom had little time during her day for philosophical discussions, and she immediately ran back down the stairs into the store to finish waiting on her customer. But she also hadn't told me to move. So far so good.

Within minutes, my father and then my sister arrived home. My sister walked into the kitchen first on her way to drop off her homework books in her bedroom. She took one look at me and knew immediately what I was up to. God! Was I so transparent?

"Oh no, you don't," she muttered, not wanting anyone to hear her. "Get back to your own seat. That's where I sit." And she left the room.

"Geez!" I called after her with an exasperation laced now with a bit of Fred Allen sarcasm (my Jack Benny imitation hadn't worked, so I thought I'd give Fred a try). "How stodgy we all are! I thought it would be fun to see a different point of view. I mean, if you don't change your point of view at least once in your life, you're nothing more than an animal!" I was kind of proud of this new idea, so I topped it with "Variety is the spice of life, isn't it?"

But my brilliance was not winning any points with my sister. From her bedroom she called out, "YOU BETTER GET OUT OF MY SEAT!" The higher law of the firstborn seemed to be taking precedent over my far more interesting philosophical ideas.

Now Pop came running up the stairs and went straight to the sink to wash his hands. This was the big test. If I could sneak this past him I was home free. But sadly, he didn't miss a beat either. "What are you doing in your sister's seat?"

"God!" I said to him. "Are these seats assigned in stone!" He continued washing his hands, his back to me, so I tried another tactic. "I'm just trying it out over here, just to see what the air's like."

My sister came back into the kitchen. She said nothing. She knew her father would be on her side. He always was. She was his pet and I was Mom's. This was another of those unilaterally legislated family decrees that I'd had no say in. I had never chosen a favorite parent. That had been done to me, to my sister and me. She was his favorite and I was Mom's. I deeply resented being pigeonholed like that.

Pop came to the table and sat down. "Stop being funny," he said to me. "Get back to your own seat!"

"Boy!" I said. "You can't have any fun in this family!"

"Come on! That's your sister's seat! Move!"

The jig was up. I'd lost the battle and I knew it. Sheepishly I slid out of my sister's chair and returned to my chair of destiny, my hot seat on Pop's right side, while my sister, who was, I suspected, inwardly savoring her victory, slid into her chair.

I tried many other ways to counter the fear of my father that was growing in me. One night when we had company and he knew it wouldn't look good to hit me, he dragged me from the table, pulled me into my bedroom, and tied me to my bed. That would teach me a lesson, he said. I can't remember what I'd done that was so wrong. I'd probably mouthed off in some way or hadn't immediately done something he wanted me to do, thereby disrespecting him. But I wasn't a member of the "Captain Marvel Fan Club" for naught. With my atomic ring on my finger—in the dark you could see the atoms exploding—I bit the knots of the rope loose with my teeth, and with my arms raised high like a winning boxer, I triumphantly jumped out into the kitchen, defying my father with my shouts of "SHAZAM!" Everyone, except my father, laughed. But he did back down; there was company after all.

But there were few of these victorious moments of defiance in my childhood. I now cheer that young man I was for his courage and his spunk, for not wanting to be a victim, for having the heart to go up against the goliath who was trying to break his spirit; and I long to keep him and his audacity a part of me always.

There was one night, however, that would remain the worst dinner in my memory. It was the night my mother broiled five steaks for the four of us. She often made more food in case someone was particularly hungry. We didn't eat steaks often. But once a month or so Mom would decide to broil some for our dinner, having Daddy butcher them from the hindquarter of beef in our walk-in meat locker. Mom would always sprinkle the steaks with oregano and serve them with the usual baked potato and a salad with an oil and lemon dressing. (How lucky we were to have the grocery store, for there was always a plentiful amount of food on our table even during the rationing days of World War II.) My mother brought the platter of steaks to the table, and we passed it around, each taking one. Then we passed around the side dishes, after which everyone dug in.

My sister, in our early years, ate much faster than I did, though I would eventually overtake her in sheer quantity in my teen years. She finished her steak before anyone else and immediately reached out and speared the fifth steak with her fork, the steak that I, of course, had my eye on too—my right eye that is, for my left eye was always glued on Pop's arm. I was becoming ambi-ocular. With no hesitation at all, she slid that fifth steak—the whole thing—toward her plate with all the arrogance and noblesse oblige of the firstborn child.

This was more than I was going to take. At least, I thought, share it or ask if anyone else wants some. But no, that steak was now halfway off the serving platter, sliding right onto her plate! And no one, neither Pop nor Mom, was making any objection. I had to do something and fast! Without any conscious thought on my part, I reacted. I reached across that kitchen table, that porcelain battlefield at the center of our lives, and I jabbed my fork into the offending arm that was carrying off that fifth steak. It wasn't a very hard stab. It was just a kind of cautionary defensive movement meant only as a warning gesture. I don't think I even drew any blood. But I did do it. I don't deny that. And that's when the pandemonium broke loose, and we all descended down, down, down into the lowest circle of Dante's hell.

My father, seeing his darling daughter's arm pricked, drew back his hand

and backhanded me across the face so hard, harder than he had ever hit me before, that I flew backwards in my chair and started to topple over. In order to keep myself from hitting the back of my head on the floor, I quickly grabbed the edge of the table and managed to yank myself forward. But I did it with such force that I hit my forehead really hard on the edge of the porcelain. That stunned me and catapulted me backward away from the table again. All of this back-and-forth movement was dislodging my brains and making me feel like a yo-yo. I thought I might even be going into clinical shock. Finally I managed to stabilize myself. And that was when I felt a knot pushing through my forehead, where it had hit the edge of the table. It was weird. I could actually feel the knot growing as it moved out from my forehead! That was when I really became freaked out, convinced now that I was going to be disfigured.

I don't remember any of the ensuing conversation at the table during the next frantic moments. I was crying too hard to hear what anyone was saying. All I was aware of was the golf-ball-sized knot that was continuing to push out of my forehead. Was it ever going to stop?

My mother, who had said nothing during all of this—she knew better— got up from the table, walked over to her utensil drawer by the sink, and pulled out her largest knife, the one with the widest blade; and with that knife in her hands, she came walking toward me. My eyes were riveted on that enormous knife. What was she going to do with it! She came closer and closer to me, and when she leaned into my forehead, I started to scream bloody murder. She was going to cut the knot off my forehead with the knife! I was beyond reason now and screaming hysterically, fearful for my life, fearful my mother was going to permanently maim me. My father still sat in his seat, saying nothing, while my sister—was it possible?—was digging into that fifth steak!

Finally my mother, realizing my concern, explained that she wasn't going to cut the knot off; she was just going to press down on it with the cold blade, which would stop the bump from growing. Well, that calmed me down a bit, and I let her apply the cool blade to my huge bump, reasoning to myself that as long as she was standing between me and Pop, he couldn't hit me again.

But Pop wasn't just watching all this like a bystander; he was thinking hard the whole time. He had to find a way to impress upon me the seriousness of what I'd done, as if I wasn't already aware of that. And he had to be clever about it. He had to try a new tactic. So he ordered my mother, who was still firmly pressing the blade of the knife against the no-longer-growing golf ball on my forehead, to broil a half-dozen steaks for me. "If he's so hungry, we'll feed him!"

(Every now and then, Pop tried the psychological approach. This was the New World, after all. But generally he never achieved any success with this method, for I could always see what he was up to and could counter him. When Pop purchased one of the new deep freezers for the store, enabling us to sell ice-cream cones, I would fill up a bowl with ice cream every night after dinner—it must have been a pint of ice cream—and, after topping it with hot fudge and nuts, have it for dessert. Pop would watch this and say as I passed, bowl in hand, "There go the profits of the ice cream for today!" And Mom would say, "Leave him alone. Let him enjoy it." And Pop would go along, hoping that one day I would get so sick of ice cream that I would stop. But new-world psychology let Pop down. I never got sick of ice cream, and I never stopped going down for my bowl of it after dinner. And Pop could only curse the New World—*"Mannaggia l'America!"*—for having too much and spoiling its children.)

My mother protested the idea of broiling more steaks immediately. She knew that even I, with my hollow wooden leg, wouldn't be able to eat them. And so it would be a terrible waste of good steaks, a sinful waste. Besides, she reminded him, it would wipe out all the profits of that beef hindquarter. But Pop was adamant. He was determined to teach me a lesson. And, being our in-house tyrant, he got his way. So Mom had no recourse but to go down into the store and pull six steaks from the refrigerator. When she returned to the kitchen, she made one more attempt to reason with Pop. He gave her the silent treatment, his index finger to his lips, warning her to be quiet. She knew she'd better do as she'd been told. Cleverly, she only put two of the steaks on the grill of her new electric broiler.

We all sat very still at the table while the steaks were cooking, even my sister. This was serious now, serious enough to make me stop sobbing, though I was still catching my breath. How, I began to wonder, was I ever going to eat all those steaks! But I knew I dared not open my mouth and question anything. No one spoke. The only sound we could hear was that of the steaks loudly sizzling under the rounded chrome top of Mom's new electric broiler. It sounded like a thunderstorm to me. Finally they were done, and Mom silently plated them and placed them on the table. I stared at them.

"Go ahead," my father said in his rational voice, knowing exactly what was going to happen. "Eat!"

The jig was up and I started to sob again. "I can't."

Victorious now, my father said, "Oh. I thought you were hungry."

"Not anymore," I managed to utter feebly.

And somehow, blessedly, that hellish dinner came to an end. My sister drifted away to do her homework, and I spent the rest of the night in my bedroom. I don't know what happened to those two steaks. But I knew my mother well enough to know that she wasn't about to waste them, so they probably wound up in a stew or maybe she ground them up for meatballs.

And as usual in our house, not another word was ever said about the events that had happened around our kitchen table that night. I'm sure my father felt he'd made his point. And I guess he had, for I never stuck my sister with my fork at the dinner table again. Nor anyone else since then. But I also thought that before one takes the last piece of food on the table, one should ask the others if it's all right. But that lesson was not taught.

But the real lesson I had learned was more fear of my father. And that led to our tug-of-war relationship. I would never go to him after that evening when he called me, fearful that I would be hit. And he, of course, hated that I wouldn't go to him when called. And that only made him angrier.

One night, when he called me, wanting to tell me something, and I refused to go to him, he lunged at me, grabbing me by my arm. I immediately jerked back away from him. And I felt something pull in my arm.

"You've broken my arm!" I yelled at him hysterically.

"No! I haven't! Come here when I call you!"

"No! You'll just hurt me!"

And so it went … over and over.

My arm wasn't broken, but it was sore and hurt for a week. For a few days after our out-in-the-open tug-of-war, I wore a sling on that arm. That really infuriated him.

Why couldn't he see that I was afraid of him? And that he himself had set up that relationship? That he had the power? That I only reacted to him? I mean, I wasn't stupid. Why go to someone who is going to hit you?

But Pop never saw it that way. Perhaps it was his upbringing. Perhaps it was the way he'd been treated as a child. Or it was the way things were done then. Still I was sure that my father saw himself as a reasonable man, one who only wanted to teach his son the best way to behave and one who only wanted his son to respect him. That was the big thing—respect. But I was living in the New World, and my head was full of democracy and justice and the bill of rights. So I only saw the danger, and I always remained frightened of my father, of the fierce look in his eyes, of how his whole face could turn to stone; and it sadly colored all my feelings for him.

This fear of my father kept building in me. I didn't even think of how to deal with it. I could only react to my environment. I was a child and thought as a child. Once, in my effort to deal with my father's anger—for that was how I saw it, as anger and not as an attempt to help me—I surprised even myself. On that day—I must have been twelve years old or so—I was invited by the older boys on the street to play baseball with them. I had never been asked to join them. Not only was I a few years younger than most of them, but I was also very much aware, as I was sure they knew, that I was inept at all the games. Gym class in school was a real trauma for me. I was embarrassed not to be able to keep up with the other boys and always fearful that I might be called that most hated name of the time: a *sissy*. I wanted desperately to be able to play sports. And there was no reason why I couldn't. It wasn't that I wasn't well coordinated. I was. I was just behind the other boys. All I needed was for someone to teach me the games. My father couldn't do it because he didn't know the American games. And because there was no one my age on our street for me to play with, to learn the games with, all I did was bike and skate up and down our street by myself. But I did hold out the hope that one day the older boys on the street would ask me to play with them. And now they had! I couldn't believe it! I was so happy to be asked! My heart leapt with joy, and filled with courage, I ran right out the door, past my mother's constant fears and worries. But what happened ended any attempts of mine to join the older boys again.

The bases were set up a few doors away from our store in front of a neighbor's home, where there was more space. When I came up to bat, being overly anxious and lacking the necessary control, I hit the ball so hard it went crashing right through a front window of the house. Fear immediately took me over. I wasn't concerned about the window so much as I was fearful of the serious punishment I would receive from my father. I dropped the bat like a hot potato and ran home immediately. I banged through the store door without speaking to my mother, who was waiting on a customer; and I ran up the stairs into our house and straight back into my bedroom, where, with all my clothes on, I got right into my bed and pulled the covers over my head. I prayed and hoped that when my father got home from work, he would think me asleep and not bother me.

I hid under those covers for two hours or more, listening to every sound in the house, fearing the moment I would hear my father's footsteps coming up the stairs into the kitchen. My mother must have been very busy in the store, for she never came up the stairs the whole time. All I could hear was the quiet in our house, the quiet before the storm. I think now as I'm writing this that I was hiding just like my mother had years before in my closet, fearful too of my father finding her. The outside darkness was beginning to settle into my bedroom. Soon my father would be home. And soon after that, it would be dinnertime, and I would have no choice but to face him. Finally I heard my father's car pull into the driveway. Then I heard the store bell ring. And then I heard my father coming up the stairs into the kitchen. What was going to happen now? Instead of coming to look for me, he called me to come out into the kitchen. Still fearing the worst, I had no choice but to face him. When I stepped from the bedroom hallway into the kitchen, I found my father and my mother; she was behind him, standing near the hallway door. It was obvious to me from the look on my father's face—it was set in that stone-hard, expressionless way he had—that my mother had told him what had happened. And I knew I was in trouble.

But then the most incredible thing happened. I flipped out. I threw myself onto Mom's just-washed kitchen floor—there were still newspapers down to keep it clean—and I flailed about like a person possessed, just like the neighborhood boy I'd once seen have an epileptic attack on the floor of the beauty parlor, where I'd gone to wait for my mother. Then I had watched in fascination while the boy thrashed about, spittle coming out of his mouth, while someone said, "Put something in his mouth! Don't let him swallow his tongue!"

My thrashing about astounded me. Was I imitating that boy? I didn't think so. I mean I certainly hadn't planned this full-blown, no-holds-barred craziness that had totally taken me over and that had me in its thrall. But what was even more remarkable was that I was totally aware of what was happening to me. Another me was actually hovering above me, right up under the kitchen ceiling, and staring down at me. And that other me up there was calmly watching the me on the kitchen floor flail about like a crazy person. I wasn't faking it. I had truly flipped out. It was real. Yet at the same time I knew exactly what I was doing. I was somehow in control. I didn't understand the dichotomy of what was happening to me. But my performance—for it was a kind of performance—had achieved its goal, for it scared the hell out of my parents, and they immediately backed off. Pop didn't yell at me or hit me. He just became silent. This was amazing. Because I was watching myself from the ceiling I came to understand that I hadn't really flipped out. And that calmed me. I also knew that the reason I had gone crazy was that I was at my wit's end. I couldn't take any more physical punishment from my father, so I had thrown caution to the wind and went for it in a big way. I had to for my own sanity. And it had worked. My father had backed off. And soon we were all sitting at the dinner table, calmly eating our supper. By chance, my grandfather had been visiting that day, helping my mother in the store, and he repaired the window. The moment was never spoken of again, and the older boys on the street never asked me to play with them again. Thinking back on it now, I wonder if this successful manipulation of my parents wasn't the beginning of my desire to become an actor? In my attempt to survive, I had created a performance—a very successful performance—that had overwhelmed my audience in exactly the way I had wanted. I had manipulated my parents as an actor manipulates an audience.

I would be forever puzzled by my father's behavior and by his monumental temper. But I was sure that I could bear and rise above the occasional slap or two to the face, even though it would leave me permanently scarred and fearful well into my adult years, making me flinch and back away if anyone's hands or a person came too close to my face or body. I realized then how permanently denigrating a slap to the face can be. I did wonder though about my reactions. Wasn't the fit I'd thrown on the kitchen floor a kind of striking out at him, a kind of rage directed inward but something really meant for him, because I couldn't hit him? And then, too, did it mean I had his rage in me? I had felt anger in myself when working on a shared garden with the older boy next door. I had hit him for coming into my space. Was it possible I had my father's anger in me? That did frighten me. I didn't want that. And I promised myself that I would never again unleash that father's anger. Whether it was immediately of the moment or a genetic centuries-old territorial anger of mankind, I would not continue it. (Though I did realize later in life that in the safe precincts of the theater, anger can be a very useful and valuable emotion.)

But it wasn't only my father's explosive anger that alarmed me as a child. His rock-solid 100-percent certainty was equally alarming and frightening to me. Pop was always right. And determinedly so. There was no free air for me to breath around him, no air of complexity. Pop dealt in absolutes; the world was black and white for him. There were no in-between shades, no ambivalences or ambiguities. And this led, on his part, to a kind of fanaticism, for if someone was bad for society, his usual response was, "THEY SHOULD HANG HIM! HE'S NO GOOD FOR SOCIETY! LIKE A WEED IN THE GARDEN, HE SHOULD BE PULLED OUT!" I sensed that this attitude was most likely the law of the land he had grown up in. And perhaps it was the way his father had raised him. Or was it, I wondered, just his nature, just who he was finally, that unsolvable mystery of character? Wherever it came from, I was only aware of his overpowering certainty. And the fierceness of his certainty was overwhelming. So I grew up at the effect of him. Always trying to justify his behavior, I often thought that his anger and impatience were because he had so many worries, primary among them being my sister's and my schooling and the money for our college. That was the most important thing in his life, that we get the education he never had, that we make something of ourselves.

Now with my more complex view of life, I wonder if his certainty hadn't also been a cover-up for all of his own insecurities and frustrations. Had he developed his rocklike beliefs as a means of survival, as blinders he had to wear to do what he needed to do. He lived, after all, in a country—America—in which he knew he'd never have the kind of authenticity as a man he felt he should have. He knew that he would never accomplish what he had in him to accomplish. He would forever be an immigrant who spoke with an accent and who had no choice but to work his butt off and give up his own dreams. And the home, his home, was the only place in this New World, this Promised Land, where he had any power or control. But if he was overwhelmed in

America, he never ever admitted that or even showed the slightest possibility that it might be true. He had, after all, his famous willpower. And he would do what he had to do. And he did just that, without ever complaining or ever expressing any self-pity.

But he was my one-and-only father. And over the years, because I knew that he had many good qualities, I kept adjusting my thoughts and feelings about him, trying always to give him the benefit of the doubt. I began to learn about his childhood. He had been born in a hard place and time. In 1900, there was corruption, terror, and persecution in his homeland. There had even been political executions that he must have been aware of. There had also been deep poverty and diseases like malaria and typhoid fever that killed many people. And there was the sadness of only three years of schooling, which must have been very painful for someone so bright and so eager to learn. I'm sure he was aware of all these things, just as I was sure they must have shaped and molded him. I tried to keep those things in mind, tried not to see him as an ogre, and tried hard to see his good qualities; for I wanted so much to love him. But he didn't want my love; he wanted my respect. Oh fathers, oh sons. We were two parallel lines that rarely met.

Slowly I began to shape my role in life as someone to be his balance, a person who would question everything and everyone, especially those people who were adamantly self-righteous. I would equate certainty with authoritarianism, and I would become a person of doubt, a person for whom nothing in life would ever have a rock-solid foundation of belief, a person for whom everything in life would be ambiguous and complex and forever shifting. I would become like Hamlet, a person who, though he appeared to be of an existential indecisiveness, was really trying to figure it all out so that he could be the best he could be. And though I would sometimes long for the ease and comfort of certainty to squash all the troubling doubts and questions of life, to reduce it to a wonderfully accessible and simplistic black and white, it was not meant, happily, to be my role. I would be objective; I would see all sides to everything. Life would be an ongoing exploration, a judgment-free exploration filled with many questions and few answers. And I would revel in this role of very human uncertainty. Someone who would know that all information and knowledge is finally suspect, as is willpower itself. And I would become a person who knew that my power would reside in the imagination.

A Calabrian Orange Salad

This is a salad my sister liked and that my mother made often. When I was young, I found the surprising mix of the sweet orange and the oil and garlic an odd taste. Recently though, I've found it in restaurants in New York City, served as a pre-dinner condiment; and I've come to appreciate its mixture of wonderfully balanced oppositional tastes. I always think of my sister when I have it and how much she liked it.

Peal an orange, pull it apart into slices, and cut in half.
Add a small amount of olive oil.
Add some chopped garlic.
And a sprinkle of black pepper.
Mix.

Options

Add some thinly shaved fennel to the salad.
Add a bit of lemon juice.
Add some long shards of Pecorino cheese on the top when served.
Add some sliced red or sweet onions.
Add a small amount of crumbled Gorgonzola cheese.

CHAPTER 4
Creamed Beef or SOS

::

My boy's heart longed for a playmate. And that longing transcended most other needs in the opening chapters of my life. I had no idea then of the importance of a playmate for a boy, of the universal need I wanted fulfilled. Nor did I know then that it was with boys my own age that I would learn, through their acceptance, that I wasn't alone in my insecurities and fears, and that this knowledge would make me confident and make me more trusting of all relationships. I only felt the need for a friend desperately, the need for someone my own age who would stand by my side, looking out at and discovering the world together—someone who would share adventures with me in a nonjudgmental way. Nothing else would assuage my loneliness.

I'd had a friend when I was five years old. He lived a few houses away from us. And for one whole glorious year, Dickie and I worked side by side in his basement, making model airplanes out of balsa wood. It was a perfect boys' time: there was no parental criticism, no one looking over our shoulders. We lived bodiless in a world of pure spirit, all our energies focused cooperatively on our joint project. We discovered the world and our role in it by doing. But sadly, Dickie and his parents moved away from our street, and I never saw him again.

Unable to express this powerful need to anyone, I often pleaded with my parents to have another child, thinking that in this way I would achieve a built-in brother to play with. I didn't realize that if that did happen, the age difference would probably have rendered that brother useless to me. No matter, it wasn't going to happen anyway. My father had always been adamant on the subject of the number of children parents should have. His constant refrain when I brought up the subject was always the same: "NO! TWO CHILDREN! THAT'S ALL!" And then one of my father's favorite rants, which

I knew by heart, would always follow: "THERE ARE TOO MANY PEOPLE IN THIS WORLD! THAT'S THE WORLD'S BIGGEST PROBLEM! BUT THE CHURCH SAYS 'GO AHEAD! HAVE CHILDREN! HAVE AS MANY AS YOU WANT! THEY ARE GOD'S GIFT!' BUT WHO'S GOING TO PAY FOR THESE CHILDREN, HUH! WHO'S GOING TO CLOTHE AND FEED THEM! AND SEND THEM TO COLLEGE! THE CHURCH? HA! DON'T MAKE ME LAUGH!" And then came the lesson part with Pop in his professorial mode: "In the old days we needed many people to work on the farms, so parents had a lot of children. But we don't need so many children anymore. It's a whole new ball game!" Every now and then, Pop did like to throw in those American catchphrases just to show he was keeping up. So no amount of pleading for a brother ever changed his mind. My father, the American man, the modern man, would only have two children.

The Espositos, who lived two doors away from us, had two sons, Frankie and Jimmy. Jimmy was four years older than I, but Frankie was just one year older. He was a short cap-wearing, street-smart kid with a wide chipped-tooth grin, who was a lot of fun to be with. And I desperately wanted him to be my friend.

Frankie's parents, Sara and Nick, were good friends of ours. Pop and Nick met accidentally one day in the New World on a train station platform and recognized each other immediately as *paesani*: they had both grown up in Cirò. They became new old friends. Nick was a shoemaker; his wife, Sara, a homemaker. I liked her a lot. She was a constantly smiling, warmhearted, and easygoing woman who liked to laugh. When she and my mother got together, she'd usually have my mother, the suspicious-of-the-whole-world type, laughing about some crazy goings-on in no time at all until they were both crying with joy. I loved seeing my mother laugh. And I adored Sara for her part in that and for her openhearted, easygoing spirit. And I felt love in return from her.

Mom always remembered how Sara had come to her rescue during the Depression. We were living, at the time, next door to the store on the second floor of a two-family house above Sara and her family. It was wintertime, and my sister, just a little girl at the time—I wasn't born yet—had a bad cold, a cold Mom was trying to keep from developing into something worse. It was the height of the Depression, the time before Pop had started to work at the steel mill, a time when he was going from job to job. For a while, he had repaired shoes with another neighbor of ours, Frank Skisano, who ran the local shoe repair shop. And with Frank, he had even started what surely must have been and what must still remain the only pick-up-and-deliver shoe repair business in Cleveland and nearby Shaker Heights. Frank stayed in the shop repairing shoes while my father drove around our area, trying to drum up business. It was a good idea, but not too many people during the Depression could afford new soles and heels on their shoes, so it folded. My father then bought a used truck, thinking to start his own one-man construction company. He'd been a plasterer and concrete pourer for the WPA, and he knew how to lay brick. But again he found few customers and finally had to sell the truck. He even peddled imported cheeses around our neighborhood. In later years, my father would always brag, "I ALWAYS WORKED, YOU KNOW, RIGHT THROUGH THE DEPRESSION!" This was often a subtle reminder to others who didn't work that they were lazy, which was one of my father's major condemnations of some of his fellow men. "IF YOU DON'T WORK, YOU'RE NO GOOD!" Pop wasn't lazy. That was for sure.

But what work there was didn't pay much. And even as adaptable and creative as he was, it was still a hard time. He soon had two young children at home, and the bills were piling up. He still hadn't paid the doctor who had delivered my sister at home four years earlier. The bill was forty-five dollars, no interest charged. (Mom was in labor for twelve hours without any anesthesia.) It would take him twelve years to pay the doctor. When it was time for me to come into the world, Pop took Mom to St. Luke's Hospital, where they had to take anyone giving birth, whether they could pay or not. I guess that means that I came into the world as a charity case, all nine ugly pounds of me. (I was so ugly at birth that they nicknamed me Primo Carnera, after the well-known boxer of the time who was not exactly known for his looks.) But the gas and electric bill had not been paid for three months, and it was winter, and my sister was sick.

One day while Pop was out looking for work, the energy company's man came out to our home and turned off the gas and electricity. My mother begged him not to, telling him that she had a sick child. The company man said he was sorry, but they'd already let the bill slide too long, and there was nothing he could do. After plunging our home into the dark and cold, he left. Mom, not knowing what to do, sat down on the back stairs of the house and started to cry. Sara, who was downstairs in her kitchen, heard Mom crying and went out into the stairwell to see what was wrong. After Mom explained, Sara immediately thought of a solution. She would run a long extension cord from her house up to ours so that Mom could at least attach a small electrical heater to it in my sister's room. And that's what they did. When Pop got home, he scurried around and borrowed enough money from his friends so that he could reopen the account.

Mom fretted and worried all through her life. She had fears about everything. Her younger brothers and sisters always kidded her about her worrying. They even sent her a "worry-bird doll" they'd found one day in a store. It came in the mail, with no sender's name. Mom was hurt by it, so their joke backfired, and they never ever admitted they were the ones who had sent it. But Mom, of course, knew they had. And because of her constant fears, she was overprotective of me, and that restricted my life. I felt her fears strangling me.

I remember one summer night when I was invited by Frankie and some of his friends to join them in one of the boys' backyards for a potato roast. I had dutifully brought, as I was told to, my own potato and had placed it alongside everyone else's on the old rusty grill above the fire. Then while we crouched in the dark around the fire, waiting with excitement for our potatoes to cook, we slipped into our own faraway and secretive world. We were American Indians conspiring around the campfire or wicked mean pirates planning their next wild adventure. It was what I had longed for, to be accepted by the other boys on the street. Then after ten or fifteen minutes or so of being a part of this wonderful conspiracy, my mother's voice pierced the air as she called out to me from our back porch four backyards away. For a relatively shy person, she sure could speak up when she wanted to be heard. "SOOONNY! SOOONNY!" she called out. "COME HOME!" I was embarrassed. No one else's mother was calling them home, only mine. And to make it even more embarrassing, she was using my hated family name, *Sonny*, a name no one outside of my family used or even knew, which was how I wanted it to remain. I think the name had come from my parents' early love, before I was born, of Jolson singing "Sonny Boy." And it had stuck to me. I tried to dissuade my aunts and uncles from using the name. I even posted a warning sign on my bedroom door: DO NOT CALL ME SONNY! But it was all to no avail. No one ever paid attention to what I wanted. Interestingly, the only one who called me by my given name was my father, who understood the importance and the respect implied by using someone's proper name in addressing them. Also, my first name, Vincent, was his first name too. I was actually the third, for I had been named after his father as he had been. He, by the way, had been nicknamed early on by his New World friends as Jim, and that American name had always stuck to him. It's what everyone called him. And I don't ever remember him objecting to that name. Maybe he liked it, for it kind of made him an American, his real first name being Vincenzo. I do remember, however, that he objected very angrily to my name change when I became an actor. But that happened later.

My mother was still calling me. And now my coconspirators around the fire were pointing it out to me, calling me *Sonny* as they did. I had no choice but to pull my potato from the fire and leave my new friends. It was the only way I could get my mother to stop yelling my hated nickname all over our neighborhood. As I walked across the backyards of our neighbors to where my mother stood on our back porch still yelling for me, I pulled off the aluminum wrap of my potato and bit into it. It was still hard and cold in the center. I remember the incompletion of that potato to this day. It was just like my childhood—not completely well-done. For some reason, my father never intervened in my search for a boyfriend. Whenever I expressed a desire to learn to play baseball or any other of the American games or expressed an interest in playing cards and board games, he would lump all those activities together and call them silly. They were, of course, games he didn't know how to play. So maybe it was his way of protecting himself. Being hyphenated had its disadvantages.

But I was being taught in school to be fearless, to reach out and go beyond what you think you can do. Yet here was my mother, always pulling me back, and my father, not noticing or caring. And in the rare times he tried to teach me something, his method was of the critical kind; there was never a compliment ... never. In my whole childhood, I never received one compliment from my father. So I became overly sensitive to all his teachings and refused to learn anything from him. I needed someone to take me aside calmly on a one-to-one basis and patiently explain to me how to play the games, the way my teachers in school did. I learned from them quickly and easily. And then I needed the constant repetition of it with others. I needed a friend my own age, who lived on my street. And the only possibility was Frankie.

Frankie was learning to play the saxophone, and I was studying the clarinet. I had begged my father to buy me a piano. I could already pick out some melodies by ear whenever I was in a house that had a piano, and I would spend hours doing it. But my father forced the clarinet on me. It was the instrument he had played, so he knew it well. (When he first came to America, he had played the clarinet in an orchestra in Fort Wayne, Indiana.) And I think he saw it as his opportunity to help me with my lessons and to show me what he knew. He couldn't help me with the American games, but here was his chance to teach me something he did know and a way for him to regain some of his father respect for himself. So I made an effort.

Frankie and I studied at the same musical school, and two nights a week, we traveled together to the school in downtown Cleveland on the streetcar. I was so happy to be with my friend. I can still remember how, in the wintertime, when it was below freezing, our recently combed wet hair would freeze solid while we waited at the streetcar stop. We laughed at that. And I remember, too, how we enjoyed our streetcar ride, sitting on the hard, woven straw seats while the conductor clanged the bell with his foot, warning the pedestrians away. But the best part of the ride was when the streetcar had to cross tracks and electrical wires with another streetcar line. What usually happened—and we always waited anxiously for the moment—was that the metal arm at the back of the streetcar that was connected to the power line above would slip off the wire at the juncture. Then the streetcar, having lost power, would come to a dead stop. And this was the part we really enjoyed. The streetcar conductor had to leave his seat, walk outside to the rear of the streetcar, grab the rope connected to the electric pole that had slipped off the electric wire, and pull it back and reattach it to the electrical line. Frankie and I would run to the back of the car and watch him do this because we knew it wasn't an easy job to accomplish. It took some good manual dexterity. And it could be dangerous, for when the pole hit the hot wires, there would be a fireworks display of electrical sparks. After he had the pole connected again, he would return to his seat, and we would continue our journey. After our lessons, we would make the adventurous journey home.

One night, Sara asked me if I would like to have dinner at her house and sleep over with Frankie and Jimmy. I said I'd like that a lot. I had never spent a night away from home, except for my summer vacations at my grandparent's home. But a whole night with a friend? I had never done that. So I begged my parents to let me do it. How old was I? Ten or eleven perhaps? Sara told my mother not to worry, that I would come for dinner, play some games with her sons, and then sleep over. And when my mother objected, saying it was too much trouble, Sara convinced her that it wasn't. She'd be delighted to have me, she said. Finally my mother consented to my first overnight with a friend.

I was really excited! This was a great occasion for me. Finally I was going to spend a night at my friend Frankie's home. We'd play games, talk about whatever, and have fun. I had my pajamas and toothbrush ready days ahead of time; and when the big night came, I left for Sara's home just before dinnertime, my pajamas and toothbrush in a paper bag and a tin of Mom's biscotti that she was sending to Sara. Our family never visited anyone without bringing a dish of food or some cookies.

Of that night I remember only two things—one unpleasant thing and one horrible thing. Everything else is a blank. The unpleasant thing was what we ate for supper. Sara made a dish that I had never encountered before, though I would come to know it in the army as SOS or "shit-on-a-shingle." It is chopped beef in a cream sauce that is served on a piece of toast—the shingle. In some parts of our country, it is even considered an elegant meal and is called chipped beef or creamed beef. My mother never used cream in her cooking, and so perhaps it was too rich a meal for me. But always adventurous about trying new foods and eager to show my joy at being in my friend Frankie's home, I ate my entire portion. After dinner, we three boys adjourned to the living room, played blackjack for a while, listened to the radio, and finally went to bed.

Frankie and his brother slept together in a double bed. They made room for me. It was a bit crowded but no one seemed to mind. People in those days often slept three or even more to a bed. And it was fun, at least for one night. So I brushed my teeth, got into my pajamas, and jumped into bed. I can see our positions in that bed till today. They are etched in my mind with the permanence that only a disastrous boyhood memory can create. I was given the outside of the bed, with Frankie in the middle and Jimmy against the wall. In the dark we all laughed for a while, telling jokes, and then fell asleep. It was great. At about two in the morning, I awoke abruptly. What woke me were my own convulsions. But the damage had already been done. In my sleep I had thrown up in the bed. There was creamed beef all over the sheets, all over me, and all over my friend Frankie sleeping next to me.

Frankie and Jimmy woke immediately and called their mother. Sara quickly changed the sheets while Frankie cleaned himself up. After that I don't remember much. Embarrassment blessedly blanked me out. I vaguely remember Sara walking me home in the early morning. I was a failure as a friend.

The incident was never mentioned nor did anyone ever kid me about it, but I was mortified. I had so desperately wanted Frankie's acceptance as a friend, but instead, I'd thrown up all over him and his bed. Sara never asked me to sleep over again. And I never mentioned it either, happy to have the whole incident forgotten. It was the last time I was ever invited to sleep over with a friend.

The clarinet lessons were also given up after three years, though I did get quite a lot of enjoyment out of playing it in the school band, for there I got to sit next to Adrienne Wieland, who also played the clarinet. Adrienne always wore tight Angora sweaters with a sorority pin attached, it seemed to me, right to the nipple of her left breast—the side (thank you, God) on which I sat. I couldn't take my eyes off that sorority pin. Sousa came in a very slow second to it. Why, I wondered, did all the girls wear their pins there? One of the boys in the orchestra, noticing how taken I was with Adrienne, told me that she had three breasts. But I discovered, on a date one night as we said our good-byes in the hallway of her home, that it wasn't true.

Frankie and I drew apart. Our lives were going down different paths. I was going on to college and he wasn't. Soon, school became the center of my life, and I put all my energies there. And I let go of any desire to have what I had for so long wanted: the neighborhood boyfriend, the conspirator, the comrade in adventure, that person you could say anything you wanted to. My studies and the many extracurricular activities I enjoyed so much—the school paper, the Radio Club, the Dramatics Club—were how I spent my time now, not coming home till dinnertime anymore ... just like my sister. My father couldn't criticize me there. And my friends in school were like myself—they were all children of working-class parents, who were as eager as I to excel. If I played outside on our street, it was always now an activity I could do alone: roller-skating or biking, both of which I had taught myself. I bought the bike frame myself for three dollars and constantly upgraded it with new white-walled tires, shiny chrome fenders, a soft wool seat, and, finally, foxtails hanging from the handlebar grips. On it I would race up and down the street.

My father treasured his *paesani*, those men with whom he'd grown up in his small town of Cirò Marina, a town that boasts that the wine served at the first Olympics games came from their humble town. And he knew where all his *paesani* lived in America. There was Tony Tridico in Chester, West Virginia; Charlie Russo in North Charleroi, Pennsylvania; and the Liottis in Buffalo. And it was always to these points of confluence that we usually headed.

These weekend trips, usually on a holiday when we could close the store, always began the same way. Mom would wake my sister and me at three in the morning. Always excited to go on a trip, we were up quickly and dressed in no time while Pop packed the car. He always brought to his friends some of his aged provolone and his *soppressata*, and Mom would bring a couple of tins of her biscotti and some of her pickled eggplant. And in the early morning dark, we would set off. The unusualness of this stealthy getaway always excited my sister and me, and we'd happily settle into our assigned seats in the back of Pop's '39 Buick: my sister behind my mother and me behind my father, who was, of course, at the driver's wheel. My mother, always too nervous, never learned to drive. Usually my sister and I would fall off to sleep for a while, but we always woke to watch the sun come up, which happened somewhere southeast of Cleveland in the open country.

The second milestone was the ritual stop at Isaly's ice cream parlor in East Liverpool, Ohio, for breakfast and an ice cream cone. Back in the car for the final leg of the journey, we passed the time reading the out-of-state license plates, the winner being the one who spotted the most distant state's plate the quickest, or, our favorite activity, reading the five Burma-Shave signs that appeared alongside the road. Our all-time favorite Burma-Shave slogan—it was both scary and exciting—was "Don't stick your hand … Out too far … It may go home … In another car! Burma Shave!"

Sometimes though the danger was inside our family car, for Pop was a spitter. I always wondered what caused his spitting. Was it a sinus problem? Or was it perhaps related to his work in the steel mill, with all of its attendant air pollution? Or did he have allergies? Whatever it was, Pop spit constantly all of his life. At home he'd jump up from his chair and run to the bathroom. But when he was behind the wheel of his car, he didn't have that option, and that was what made it a dangerous time, especially for me. As soon as we heard him start to clear his throat while rolling down his window—those were the warning signs—we all knew what was going to happen. Then my mother and my sister would yell for me to duck because I was, once again, as I was at the dinner table, right in the line of fire. If we were going at a good clip, the wind could be fierce, and it could blow some of Pop's spittle back into the car and into my face. Pop always did his best to spit as far out as he could, but if I didn't duck quickly, a little spray could reach me in the backseat of the car. And just as I had learned to spring back quickly when his arm sprang out and backhanded me, I also learned to duck quickly the second I heard Pop clear his throat. But when this happened, unlike at the dinner table, I rarely got hit. And everyone had a good laugh, including Pop. And odd as it sounds, it actually became one of those ritualized family moments you look forward to with eager anticipation. "DUCK!" everyone would yell, and we'd all start laughing.

There were other serendipitous adventures on the road. If Pop spotted a good area for mushrooms, he would quickly pull over onto the shoulder of the road and make a quick search in the woods. And often he'd come back with a handful of mushrooms that we'd take to the weekend festivities that could be used in a frittata, a thick Italian omelet. Mom would have her moments on these trips too. Often, as we were flying along, she would yell out for Pop to stop the car. He always obeyed immediately, thinking there was an emergency, and alarmed, he would ask my mother, "WHAT'S THE MATTER!" And Mom, as innocently as she could, would always respond, "I saw some beautiful Queen Anne's lace back there. I want to pick it." And calmly she would open the car door and slip out. And Pop would shake his head in disbelief, that disbelief of the husband for a wife's strange behavior. My sister and I thought it was funny. Mom would take the Queen Anne's lace to our hosts, where she would make a batter of flour and eggs and sauté the white flat blooms. I was amazed, of course, to discover that what I thought was just a weed was edible. Mom often prepared zucchini blossoms in this same way. Also on these trips, my father, if he saw a good patch away from the pollution of the traffic, would stop to pick dandelion. Like most Italians, he knew about the health benefits of dandelion—what they called *cicoria*—and he would always pick enough for a salad. Pop loved it with some olive oil and vinegar or even cooked with a little bit of garlic. I thought it was too bitter. That was the iron in it, of course, the very reason it was so good for you. But later I, too, would eat it.

With his *paesani*, my father was someone I hardly recognized. Usually severe, strongly opinionated, and often angry, in the company of his friends he was a changed person. With them he was outgoing and jovial and pleasant to a fault, full of laughter and smiles. And I noticed surprisingly that his friends liked him. This was a different person, a person I didn't know. With these men who shared his background and the same stories, he could finally relax. He was no longer in money-driven America but in a fair country ruled by the comforting subtext of a shared language, of friendship and community. And naturally, these times, when the *paesani* got together, were some of the best times of my childhood.

The *paesani* were all lively men, and they loved playing games on each other—innocent, guileless games. Once, I remember we left our home much earlier than usual so that we could join up with Charlie Russo and his family at an agreed-upon crossroads and then, all together, drive on to Chester, West Virginia, arriving at five o'clock in the morning where, with Charlie playing his guitar and the rest of us singing, we serenaded Tony Tridico and his wife, Margaret, under their bedroom window. It was a surprise visit. We weren't expected. But immediately everyone in the house was up and welcoming us. And amidst a great deal of laughing and joking and the women starting the coffee and breakfast, the weekend festivities began. After breakfast, there might be a visit to the amusement park across the street from where they lived. There the women, most of them on the plump side, would have a great deal of fun cavorting in front of the fat and skinny mirrors. Then we might visit some other friends and relatives of the *paesani* in the town.

But the best part of it all, and the part I'll always remember, happened before dinner in the late afternoon, when the heat of the day was over. Against the background of happy sounds coming from the women in the kitchen as they prepared the elaborate meal for the evening, the men would take their seats under Tony's grape arbor and, with their guitars and mandolins cradled in their arms—they had all learned to play either the guitar or the mandolin while growing up in Italy—and with a jug of someone's home-made red wine sitting at their feet, they would begin to play and sing the songs of their youth. I sat entranced. One of the men would say, "Do you remember this one?" And after plucking out the first few chords, the others would immediately and happily join in, nodding their heads in unison in recognition of the song. "Ah! Si! Si!" they would say as they played the song.

When the women in the kitchen heard a song they knew, they would take a break from their dinner preparations and would file out of the house onto the back porch, their kitchen aprons in place over their housedresses and, taking the form of one of the popular girl singing groups at the time, they would treat everyone to a show. While singing the lyrics of the song in their high voices, they would go into an act that consisted of teasing and coquettish gestures, all accompanied by lots of giggling. They would have great fun, laughing all the while at themselves, at the ridiculousness of overweight, housedress-and-apron-wearing women carrying on like movie stars. With a combination of shyness, charm, and outright wickedness, they were a delight to watch. Sometimes the men would entice the women out of the kitchen with a tarantella—that lively music no one could resist. You just had to dance to that exciting, slyly sexual music, that music that went right to the heart of the man-woman relationship. My father was particularly good at this dance and always outlasted everyone. Then the women, feigning exhaustion, would retreat to the kitchen and the preparation of the evening meal. In my child's eyes, I could sense in their easy laughter and banter with the men a secret life that spoke of a simple and joyous sexuality that was just a normal part of life—not a wild, overwhelming devouring passion, but a pleasurable and amusing natural joy.

Later at night, the men would tell off-color jokes. A couple of the *paesani* were expert at this, particularly one who was an Electrolux salesman. Interestingly though, my father, while he enjoyed hearing these jokes, never contributed to these sessions of off-color jokes, for he was not a keeper of them in his soul. The men always told these jokes in their regional Italian dialect so that all the children present would not be able to understand them. But we could usually figure them out just by the physicality of the joke teller and the sounds of the words. And again the pleasure and simplicity of their sexuality came through, not only in their amusement, but in the jokes themselves; for they were mostly jokes of character and of human eccentricity, jokes that often made fun of the unnaturalness of the life of a nun or a priest, jokes that were mild by American standards.

How pleasant it all was. And what a difference from how we entertain ourselves today, sitting in silent isolation in the partial dark of our homes in front of the TV. How lucky I was to be the benefactor of those wonderfully sunny, simple, and innocent days spent among these guileless men and women, who enjoyed life in its most basic and true way. Those were the golden times, the times I wish I could live over again. And perhaps, too, they were the last great time for an innocent childhood in America, a childhood not absorbed by television or of mechanical devices, but by the community of one's family. To hear my father and his friends tell the old stories of their childhoods, to hear them playing and singing the beautiful music of Italy again, and to see the women dance and laughing all the while—that was the best of it. No one ever had too much to drink. No one ever misspoke. There was never an argument nor ever a discordant moment among these wonderfully friendly and civilized men. Just great good times with friends who thoroughly enjoyed each other's company and who all shared one thing in common: a great zest for being alive. While I learned something of their shared childhood, I was also learning something about my father. I noticed that the part of my father that was lost in America, the part that propelled him as he ran with blinders on from one chore to another, always in his own thoughts, was found again among his hometown boyhood friends. With them he was no longer an immigrant with a laughable accent but an authentic, intelligent, respected, and civilized man. I have nothing like that in my adult life now, this actor's life of nervous ambition that I lead, but I still remember, and I still bask in the radiance of that good time.

My father had his friends. But I wasn't so lucky. Maybe childhood longings, just like childhood vaccinations, are meant to wear out eventually and are meant to be replaced by more immediate adult concerns; but I continued to feel deeply the lack of a male friend all through my childhood and throughout my teen years. But my father and his *paesani* never seemed to have that problem. They knew exactly how to play their relationships. Perhaps it was years and even centuries of their culture that had made them the civilized, appreciative men they were. And, too, though united by a shared childhood, perhaps they were more united and enjoyed each other's company even more so because of the difficulty of being an outsider in America. With each other they could remember who they were. I, however, was becoming more and more of an outsider.

Biscotti

This is the basic dough for the simple Italian cookie and not the "twice-baked" cookie popular today in coffee shops. My father's only breakfast for all of his life was a couple of these dunked in a cup of coffee.

- 5 cups of flour
- 4 eggs
- 1cup sugar
- 2 sticks of melted butter
- 1 tsp. vanilla
- ½ cup milk

First, melt your butter and set aside. Then beat the eggs well, add sugar, vanilla and milk, and then the melted butter. Add 6 tsp. of baking powder and a pinch of salt to the flour. Blend.

Add flour slowly to the egg mixture and mix by hand. Don't over mix or the cookies will be tough. (Mom always added the flour in quarters to be sure she got the right amount. This takes a bit of playing with because the dough should not be too sticky. If it is, slowly add more flour.)

Add a cup of walnuts or whatever nut you'd like.

On greased cookie sheets, place the cookies, made either in twists, like a braid, or S shaped. For the twists, roll a piece of dough in your hand till it's about six inches long, bend it in half, and braid over once or twice.

Bake at 375° for 20 mins. It should make 36 cookies.

Icing

Mom always iced half of the cookies for my sister and me. This is a quick icing:

- – 1 cup powdered sugar
- – 1 tbs. soft butter

Cream the above and add the following for flavoring:
Small amount of lemon juice or vanilla flavoring.
Add this liquid a little at a time for the right consistency. If you add too much, add some more powdered sugar.

CHAPTER 5
Romeo and Juliet

::

Behind our mysterious kitchen table, there were two double-hung windows that looked across our shared driveway and onto the porch and backyard of the home next door, the home of our neighbors, the Mascalzones. Mr. Mascalzone had himself built our redbrick store and the home behind it, along with the white-shingled, single-family house next door to it. And he had placed the driveway between the two buildings so that it would serve both properties. He had done this, thinking, of course, that the two properties would always be his. He hadn't reckoned on the Depression. We were renting the second floor of the two-family house on the other side of the store for fifteen dollars a month, when my father heard that the bank was foreclosing on the store property because Mr. Mascalzone had not been able to pay their mortgage.

Immediately interested in the property, my father expressed his desire to a friend of his. The friend quickly warned him, "Be careful! They're Sicilians, you know." That meant they could be like the Mafia—brutal and vindictive. But my father wasn't having any of that old-world nonsense. This was America, wasn't it? Where everyone was equal? This wasn't a small town in Italy where the residents were immediately suspicious of strangers, and outsiders were quickly demonized. There, it was a way of life, for that land and its people had been pillaged and raped by everyone down through the centuries— the Greeks, Romans, Phoenicians, Turks, Spanish, French—for as long as the collective memory existed. And this history made suspicion the major character trait of the people. It also made them skeptical and pessimistic and conspiratorial. My father would have none of that. As a young man he'd read and become impassioned by the writings of Giuseppe Mazzini, the egalitarian political philosopher who, along with Giuseppe Garibaldi, had freed Italy from its centuries of civil unrest and warring among the feudal factions and turned it into a free, democratic nation. Also I know that he never pushed any of the old-world enmities because he wanted to keep my sister and myself from being poisoned by old-fashioned ideas. The word *Mafia* was never spoken by Pop in our home nor was its existence ever mentioned. He was sure he'd left all that behind. But had he?

Ignoring his friend's warning and not wanting anyone else to buy the property before him, my father quickly scrambled around to raise the three hundred dollars down payment the bank wanted on the three-thousand-dollar property. That was an out-of-reach sum in those days, a time when 20 percent of the workforce in America was unemployed. And it was a sum Pop didn't have. Nor did anyone else he knew. He did have a life insurance policy that he had taken out on my sister when she was born. It was worth $150. He cashed it in. Then he asked a good friend of ours, Jen (his full name was Eugene Cerchiaro), who was doing quite well because he owned the two best shoe repair shops in Cleveland – one at the Higbee's Department Store in downtown Cleveland and the other at the upscale Shaker Square – if he could lend him the remaining amount he needed; and Jen said he would. The cash in hand, my father ran quickly up to the bank on Kinsman Avenue and immediately purchased the store and home where my family would spend the next twenty-seven years and where I would grow up.

The Nabisco Company trimmed our two huge plate-glass windows with a red border and a logo at the top that said Romeo's Grocery. And with credit from a local wholesaler, Pop stocked all the shelves. And so our store was opened. We were now in the grocery business, and my father was a property owner for the first time in his life. The year was 1940. The very first thing he did when he'd made some extra money was to pay off the debt to his friend Jen. He never liked owing anyone money. My father knew that money dealings could often bring out the worst in people and could destroy relationships. Two years later, he paid off the bank debt. The officer in the bank told him that he was the only one who had paid off what he owed the bank. And for the rest of his life, Pop paid cash for everything he bought. Certainly the Depression had put the fear of God into everyone, for being in debt meant you could lose everything you had. It was, I'm sure, also a matter of pride with him. He was determined to take care of his own responsibilities.

Not too long after we had moved into the store, my father found a new job at the Otis Steel Corporation. It was a lucky opportunity for him. At the time he was hired, the mills were only being run three or four days a week. But very soon, when the United States entered World War II, the mills would be going full blast, seven days a week with three shifts around the clock. The war would pull the United States out of the Depression. My father would stay with that mill, whether it was called the Otis Steel Corporation or the Jones and Laughlin Steel Company or Republic Steel, until he retired. When my father died, I would be amazed to see as I looked through his papers that he had made only three thousand dollars a year at the mill in those early days. And yet he had still managed to send my sister and myself through college. Of course the supplemental income from our grocery store had helped enormously. But I was still amazed, for we had never wanted for the basics in life, and we had never felt poor. And that, I think, was due to the fact that my parents never complained about money or the lack of it and just pressed on with their work.

In our new home behind the store, I had to share my bedroom with our dining room furniture, but that was all right with me. I used the drawers of the credenza for my clothing, and I turned the dining table into my desk. And in the summertime, my favorite time of the year, when time itself stood still for me, I could prop my new RCA Victor radio in my bedroom window, lie on our glider on our big back porch, and listen to music while reading my latest issue of the *Classic Comics* or one of my favorite books about animals. And often on summer evenings, after the store was closed, the four of us would enjoy our back porch together—Mom and Dad swinging gently on our secondhand but luxurious dark-green glider and my sister and I enjoying our two also used metal rocking chairs. From there we could look out into our very own beautiful backyard and feast our eyes on the hundred or more tomato plants my father planted every year.

When I was in high school, during my scene design period (Jo Mielziner's great poetic scene design for Arthur Miller's *Death Of a Salesman* had made such a strong impression on me that I made a model of the set for school), I scalloped all the bricks on our back porch with crayon one afternoon—four different colored scallops to a brick—so that I could have a painted backdrop for my fledgling thespian efforts. For some reason, my father did not punish me for doing that. I wondered if it was because I was older at the time.

When we sat down to dinner, our store was still opened and that meant that someone, usually Mom, had to eat their dinner on the run. Pop, forever irrational, would always get angry: "WHY THE HELL DO THEY BOTHER US WHEN WE'RE EATING!" And no matter how many times I'd say "Daddy! They don't know when we're eating! All they know is the store is open!" he was never mollified. He just couldn't or wouldn't understand it. On occasion he would run down to wait on the customer, letting Mom enjoy her meal, but it was usually Mom's job. Still, the store was heaven sent for us. It had improved our lives immeasurably. And if we just broke even, we would always have food enough to eat.

But Mr. Mascalzone, no matter how much we ignored him and his family, kept his vendetta against us alive. He told a friend, who then repeated it to my father, that "a Calabrese (meaning my father) had made a fool out of a Sicilian (meaning himself)." In all the years we lived next door to the Mascalzones, not one of them—well, with the exception of one member—ever spoke to us or ever came into the store to buy a single item. Again my father did his best to ignore the old-world, generation-to-generation memory of wrongs committed, and he paid no attention to Mr. Mascalzone. (Pop had his own list of the Ten Commandments. The first one was "MIND YOUR OWN BUSINESS!" and the second was "WORK HARD!") But Mr. Mascalzone was not going to forget. And it would be our shared driveway that would become the battlefield one day, a day my father almost lost his life.

Though the driveway Mr. Mascalzone had built was wider than a normal one, it was not wide enough for two cars to pass. And that was the problem. My father—and I when I started to drive—always pulled our '39 Buick all the way up into our space at the far back of our property, next to the Mascalzone's garage. We never left our car in the driveway, blocking it for our neighbor's two son's cars. But our neighbors, vindictive and spiteful, always did just that; they were not ever going to acknowledge that we had a right to use the driveway. So instead of pulling their cars up into their garage or the space in front of it, they always left their cars in the middle of the driveway near the entrance to their back door. That meant, of course, that whenever we wanted to drive our car out, we always had to ask them to move their cars, which meant that someone in our family had to knock on their back door and ask them to move their cars. And for some reason, that was a job that always fell on me.

On Sunday, when we usually visited my grandmother, we would all cluster at our back door, dressed and ready to go. And my father would say, "Vincenz! Go tell them to move their cars!" And off I'd dutifully go to the back door of the enemy to relay the message. I'd climb the stairs of our neighbor's porch, politely knock on their screen door, and ask whoever came to it to please move their cars because we had to go out. One would have thought that they would have tired of this constant interruption in their lives, but their stubbornness was great. So every Sunday, for all the many years we lived behind the store, I had to climb their back porch stairs, knock on their door, and ask them to please move their cars.

I never questioned why I was always the one to ask them to move their cars. For one thing, I always did as I was told. And, too, I knew it wouldn't be right for my mother or sister to do it, and Pop was usually locking the store or starting the engine of our car. So it seemed logical for me to do it. And I always ran over innocently when told to do so, never thinking I was in any danger. We knew Mr. Mascalzone kept guns in his house. We also knew that he was often drunk, for he could regularly be seen sitting on his back porch playing cards with friends of his and drinking. And we had witnessed occasions when his own family had to call the cops because they couldn't handle him. But despite all that, there was a very good reason I never minded being the one designated to knock on the Mascalzone's back door. And her name was Cecilia. She was the youngest daughter of the family, was the same age as I and she was slowly blossoming into a knockout. Well, maybe her face wasn't that of a movie star's—she had a bit of a hooked nose and kinky black hair—but her packed, silky-smooth young body was beginning to burst with life and was radiating a golden glow from within its slightly burnished amber color. It was the body of a young goddess, and it had an aura of compelling differentness for me, the privileged bystander watching it mature. And I think she liked me.

Cecilia attended Catholic school, and I went to the public schools, so I didn't know her from school. My father would never have sent my sister and myself to the Catholic school. Because he wanted to keep his children away from the prejudices and the antidemocratic institutions of the Roman Catholic Church, he figured that the best education we could get was in the public schools. That was fine with me, for the public schools were excellent in those days. And they would be where I—miracle of miracles—would excel because it was in school that I got the uncritical approval and acceptance I didn't get at home and needed so badly. So I came to love my public school and my teachers, who were all wonderfully committed and supportive of their racially and ethnically mixed students and saw to it that we got the very best education possible. They would be my gods and goddesses … my magic portal to a new and better world of understanding and enjoyment.

Not only did I love my teachers for themselves, but I also loved their strange and odd names, names that reverberate with me still. There was Ms. Posekenny, my strict kindergarten teacher; my first-grade teacher, Ms. Prune; my second-grade teacher, Ms. War; and my third grade teacher, Ms. Dressler. Her blonde hair was cut short in the back like a man's and combed straight back in rows of waves. She seemed to wear the same dress all the time: a greenish-yellow one that cascaded in spiraled rows of fringe from the top to the bottom. I'd never seen anything like it.

In the fourth grade we moved to the "big side" of the school, and there I had a homeroom teacher named Ms. O'Brien. A top-heavy woman, very large bosomed, with skinny toothpick legs, she was often absent from school. And when she returned, she would always have bandages around her ankles. We boys figured that her breasts were so heavy that the weight of them sprained her ankles, and that was the reason she was out of school so often. Ms. O'Brien caught me running down the hallway one day—we were not supposed to run, of course—and asked me what I thought I was doing. I said, cleverly I thought, "I'm trotting!" Not impressed by my quickness, she immediately responded, "Horses trot!" She had me there.

For gym and music, we had Bertha M. Marx. Oh, she was tough. She also ran the school choir, of which my classmates had voted me president. One day during the lunchtime half of our choir-practice period, I blew up the brown paper bag my mother packed my lunch in and popped it. It made a terrific bomblike sound, which greatly amused my fellow choir members. Ms. Marx, who was standing outside the door in the hallway talking to another teacher, came storming into the room, demanding to know who had made that noise. I was always honest. I stood up right away and admitted that I'd done it. She immediately kicked me out of the choir. I was devastated. I loved to sing. I even had solos. And I was president of the choir! No matter. I was out. No due process of the law for children. And not one of my fellow choir members came to my defense. Though I was always one of the bright kids, one of the "good kids," I was also part clown and devilish and would get into trouble in school again down the line.

Alexander Hamilton Junior High School brought new beginnings. There I had the caring Ms. Gaffney; a new wonderful homeroom teacher, Ms. Sugarman, who was also my joyous French teacher. In high school there was the sympathetic and attractive Ms. Lee, the supportive Ms. Follin, the sexy Ms. Do—our own Jane Russell whose Spanish classes were always popular with the boys. I continued my French lessons with the wonderfully funny and fey Mlle Jarrett, and then there was the elegant Ms. Lodwick, who touched my hands one day in a private session and told me that I had "artist's hands." There was the pristinely blonde and glowing Grace Kelly–like Ms. Welch. I always sat in the seat right in front of her desk just so I could bathe in her overwhelming blonde beauty up close. I had never seen anyone as beautiful as her. One day we bumped into each other outside the principal's office. I turned crimson and didn't know where to look. She, cooler than I, commented on my attractive belt. Oh boy! On the distaff side there was our laid-back biology teacher, Mr. Bopp—he was the birds-and-bees guy—and Mr. Mills, our music appreciation teacher. What memorable names and what memorable, giving people.

I was lucky for my high school, John Adams, at the corner of East 116th Street and Corlett Avenue was one of the very best in the city. It was an oasis of innovation and excellence in a working-class neighborhood. And its student body was an eclectic mix of first-generation students, all being prepped by our remarkably caring teachers for a wonderful future in America. Everyone, it seemed, whether you were one of the smart section-one kids or in a lower section, got along with each other. I don't remember any problems among the students at all. We were all good kids and we all got along. Maybe we were, compared to today's students, a little numb; it was the fifties, but there were very few incidents of bullying or of nastiness in any form. Even the leather-jacketed, motorcycle-type kids in high school with their Duck's Ass haircuts—the "fast kids"—were good kids. And they were all friends of mine. Not close friends, not friends I would hang out with, but not separate either. We were all one.

And thanks to our teachers who wanted us to be right up there with the best, many of us would be the first in our families to go on to college. (When Mlle Jarrett found out that I was going to Carnegie Tech in Pittsburgh to become an actor, she invited me for a late, splendidly set out afternoon tea at her beautiful antique-filled apartment near the Art Museum. There, while pouring me a cup of tea from her silver teapot, she shared with me that she herself had wanted to go to Carnegie Tech to become an actress, but her parents wouldn't let her do that. She would have made a wonderfully batty, adorable character actress.) Oh I loved my teachers and so looked up to them, for I felt they knew the secret to living a good life, a secret they were willing to share with me. I revere and bless them all to this day.

But Cecilia (was it the strict Catholic regimen?) didn't like school at all. She was just doing her time there till she could get out. Nevertheless, I was smitten with her. And this infatuation, which started at the age of six or seven and lasted into our teen years, led invariably to an exploration of each other's physical difference. These explorations always happened in our secret place, a narrow enclosure behind her family's garage and the fence of the home on the block behind us—a space that was about two feet wide by maybe twelve feet long—a place no one could see into. And it was there, where we'd run to when no one from her family or mine was looking, that we taught each other the simple facts of life. I already knew the basics, but I needed some hands-on knowledge. Cecilia, who had older brother and sisters, was more knowledgeable than I; so she was the leader. And so we were, as were most children in those days, sexually self-taught.

The only birds-and-bees lecture I ever had from my father happened on a night when, because of a streetcar strike that took effect at midnight, I had to walk home from my date's house in Garfield Heights. That was quite a distance from our house. And I didn't arrive home till two or so in the morning, way past midnight, my high school curfew time. I undressed quickly, getting into bed as fast as I could, hoping to put off any prolonged discussion or reprimand by pretending to be asleep. But Pop fooled me. He came into my bedroom, sat on the edge of my bed, and said to me in his professorial mode, "Some women are bad." And then he walked out of my room. That was it! "Some women are bad." I was in shock. What did he mean? Did he think I'd been out with

Lucrezia Borgia? I'd been on a date with a girl named Carole. She was in my freshman class in high school. And she was adorable. She always dressed in long skirts, bobby sox with her loafers, and those ubiquitous angora sweaters that were so temptingly soft to the touch. She knew more about kissing than I did. And I was eager to learn. But was she "bad?" I didn't think so. I fell asleep puzzled. And that was my only birds-and-bees lecture from my father, his only attempt to introduce me into manhood. I promptly decided, as I did with many of my father's pronouncements, to pay little attention to it.

Cecilia's and my explorations were innocent, equally desired by both parties without any force or persuasion on either side, and based on the powerful human instinct of curiosity about our innate truth and ourselves. And since we were both prepuberty when it began, there was no danger. This physical intimacy led to a wonderfully intimate friendship. We told each other everything about our lives, about our families, and about school—none of which I ever repeated nor did she. We never talked about the problem between our two families. We were just for each other.

My mother, father, sister, and I often walked up to the Imperial Theater on Kinsman Road to take in a double feature. One movie that made a big impression on me was a lurid Technicolor jungle fantasy called *The Cobra Woman*. It starred the exotic Maria Montez and the handsome Jon Hall. The scene that remained with me the most took place between two children by the side of a pool. They pledged their eternal faith to each other by making cuts on their fingers and by pressing those cuts together, mixing their blood. I was wide-eyed at this scene. The two children, of course, true to the inevitability of coincidence in the plots of all Hollywood movies, grew up to be Maria Montez and Jon Hall, who had been lost to each other and are, of course, finally reunited.

I saw Cecilia and me up on that screen, and the next day when we met in our secret hiding place behind the garage, I asked her if she would reenact the scene from the movie with me. I had brought one of my mother's small paring knives with me. I explained to her that it meant we were pledging our eternal faith to each other just as the two children in the movie, who grew into Maria Montez and Jon Hall, had done. She promptly agreed. I made a light cut in both our fingers, and we pressed them together, sealing our eternal faith and love to each other. The children in the film pledged their love beside a beautiful pool; we, in our secret place, behind a garage. I was not unaware, even at that young age, of the irony of my family name: Romeo. I'd been kidded a lot in school already and would constantly be asked, "Where's Juliet?" or "Wherefore art thou Romeo?" And yet, here was my eternal love, the daughter of a family that was our enemy.

Cecilia and I continued our secret relationship all through our growing

-up years. We never met anywhere else but behind the garage. Nor did we ever see each other except in those secret stolen moments. If anybody was aware of our relationship, I never knew of it. My mother, who watched and knew everything, never said a word. Sometimes, but very rarely, when I was working in the store, Cecilia would sneak away from her family and come in to see me under the pretext of buying something—a cookie maybe or a bottle of pop—but she would leave quickly. So it was only in our secret rendezvous behind the garage that I could take great pleasure in watching her beautiful young body grow into its adolescent fullness and ripeness.

(My curiosity about all things sexual did lead to one of, if not the, most embarrassing moments of my childhood. As I was searching in my parents' bedroom one day for clues to them, I found my father's rubbers in his chest of drawers. I took one, and when I was alone I played with it, blowing it up, of course, and then, to see how perfect the latex itself was, I experimented by pouring water into it and making water bombs in the privacy of our bathroom. One day—I must have been twelve or thirteen years old or so and in the thrall of the craziness of puberty—I decided I would take one to school. And I wouldn't just take it to school, hidden somewhere on my person or in my wallet; I would wear it to school! Having a secret like that made me feel very grown-up. So with a rubber band I secured the rubber onto my penis and left for school. And there it stayed all day long, attached to my not-as-yet-fully-grown penis. It's a wonder I didn't wind up with gangrene of the penis. But what a secret I had! I told no one. When the day was over and I headed home, I found my sister and her girlfriends jumping rope in front of our store. Always the cutup, I jumped right into the middle of the rope and leapt off the ground as it came around and around. What also leapt off was the rubber band that was not very securely holding the rubber onto my still-small penis. With all the jumping about, it had become loose, causing it to fall down and out of my pants' leg and right onto the cement sidewalk. And there it lay ... for all to see. I had a moment of panic. Then instead of grabbing it and running, I left it there and ran into the store. To this day I don't know what happened next. No one ever talked about it to me—not even my father. Did my sister and her girlfriends have a laugh about it? Did they know what it was? Most of all, I wondered for years and still wonder about who picked it up. My sister? Or one of her girlfriends? And who was it that brought it to my parents' attention? Someone did, for I could never find my father's rubbers again. I searched and searched my parents' bedroom for weeks, but I never found them. My father hid them really well. Needless to say, I never tried wearing one to school ever again nor did I try jumping rope with one attached to my penis, though I did buy one a couple of years later to keep in my wallet ... just in case, you know.)

From our kitchen window, I often watched the activities of our mysterious neighbors. And the one activity that really fascinated me was watching Mrs. Mascalzone make tomato paste. None of those little store-bought cans for her; she made her own. At the end of every summer, on two big sheets of plywood placed on top of wooden horses, she would spread out to the edges of the plywood the tomato purée she'd made. As this coating on the plywood sat in the hot sun, it would lose its water content, making it thick and concentrated. I would be glued to our kitchen window every year, watching this unusual process. My mother didn't make tomato paste. In fact she rarely used tomato paste in her sauce, preferring a lighter sauce. It was usually the Sicilian people who liked what was called a gravy or *sugo,* those heavy sauces that were cooked for hours and hours, which used the tomato paste. What alarmed me the most about this process was what it attracted: flies! Hundreds of them! All swarming and settling onto the surface of the tomatoes!

"Look at all the flies!" I'd tell my mother. "Think of all the eggs they must be laying in that paste!" I knew what flies did from my science class in school.

"Come away from that window!" my mother would say. "Don't let her see you!"

"Yuck!" I would say as I stopped peeking out our window.

One Sunday after we'd closed the store at the usual hour of one o'clock and were getting ready to visit my grandmother, my father left the house through the back door to warm up his '39 Buick. (It was the model with the stick shift on the steering wheel shaft that moved up and down like the letter *H,* with reverse at the upper-left top of the *H* and third gear at the lower-right side of the *H,* the bar of the *H* being neutral, and the car I would learn to drive on.) As usual there were two cars in the driveway blocking our path. So Pop decided to knock on Mr. Mascalzone's back door himself. It was my job, of course, but on that day, for whatever reason, Pop decided to do it. Maybe I was in my bedroom still getting dressed or maybe it was because he was already outside. Or perhaps for a moment—Pop's mind was often somewhere else—he forgot the long-standing grudge his neighbor harbored. Whatever the reason, he let his guard down, and he casually walked up the Mascalzones' back porch and knocked at their door.

I walked out into the kitchen at this point to find my mother standing to the side of the kitchen window so she couldn't be seen while looking out across the driveway. Because I sensed she was upset, I went to the window to see what she was looking at. What I saw was my father knocking on our neighbor's back door, no doubt wanting to ask them to move their cars. Of course I knew that my mother worried about everything, about all the possible dangers that lay outside the home, so I was not immediately concerned.

"What's the matter?" I asked her.

"Your father is knocking on Mr. Mascalzone's door to ask him to move the cars."

I couldn't see why Mom was so upset. I mean, I did that all the time. But Mom's instinct was better than mine. Though her fears were often imagined, she was also, on many occasions, right, as she turned out to be on this occasion.

We watched together. Pop's hand was now on the screen-door handle when all of a sudden the door flew open and Mr. Mascalzone himself came charging out of the house, yelling furiously at my father and gesturing wildly. And then we saw the gun in his hand! Mom no longer cared now if she was seen, and she threw up the window and started screaming, "JIM! JIM! HE'S GOT A GUN!" But Pop was already backing quickly down the porch stairs. And as he turned to run, Mr. Mascalzone shot at him!

Mom was hysterical. "JIM! JIM! GET OUT OF THERE! COME HOME! OH MY GOD! MY GOD!" Then she said to me, "GO OPEN THE SIDE DOOR! QUICK! LET YOUR FATHER IN!"

Knowing this was serious now, I raced down the stairs to the side door as fast as I could and unlocked it. Pop came crashing through it at the same moment. I quickly locked the door behind him and followed him up the stairs into the kitchen, where he collapsed into the first chair he came to. He didn't look as though the bullet had hit him, at least I couldn't see any indication of that.

Mom was still looking out the window, and hearing loud voices, I went to her side to see what was going on. Mr. Mascalzone's sons were trying to subdue their father and quickly pull him back into the house, hoping that no one had seen what he'd done.

Mom said, "He's drunk! Look at him! That crazy old man!" Then she turned to Pop. "And look at you! You're crazy too! Why did you go over there! Why didn't you send your son, the way you always do!"

Gee, thanks Mom, I thought.

Pop muttered a quiet "Leave me alone ... " And there was something in his voice, a sound I'd never heard, that made me turn around and look at him again. He was speaking in a higher register than usual, not in his normally strong and confident voice. Mom, still involved with the drama going on outside our window, quickly turned back to my father and said, "You could have gotten yourself killed!"

Mom could switch emotions in a flash. I'd seen this in her before. From fear she had turned to attack. Instead of comforting someone, she would often push them. Part of it, in this instance, was her own fright, of course; but a large part of it was an attempt on her part to get you doing something and to keep you from wallowing in self-pity, something you couldn't have too much of around my mother. "Are you going to sit there all day and mope! Come on, do something!" was her usual admonition to me if she found me daydreaming. It was her outlook on life. The worst could happen, but you mustn't let it get you. You had to get up and get on with it.

But my father was no longer responding. And now I noticed something else I'd never seen before: Pop was white as a sheet. That frightened me. There wasn't a bit of color in his usually ruddy face. He looked like a ghost. And he continued to mutter to himself. I wondered if he was in some kind of shock. My father was a short man, but he was like a bantam rooster. I had never seen him afraid of anything. Straight backed and feisty, he always spoke his mind, whether anyone wanted to hear it or not. I always wondered at his total fearlessness and confidence. But I'd never seen him like this. He was a different person. The certainty and total confidence were gone. I was surprised to discover that he, too, could be frightened, as frightened of another person as I was frightened of him. I was going to have to rethink my understanding of him.

I could now understand what he was muttering: "You see what kind of crazy people there are in this world? You work hard all your life, like a jackass, for your family, and that's what they do. They try to kill you! Crazy people!" He went on for a while in this same vein, slowly bringing himself around, I guessed, while I, and now Mom, watched him. I heard fear in his voice and something else I'd never heard from him before. Was it a bit of fatalism? Or self-pity? Then I thought that in a close call as he'd just had, maybe he was allowed to slip back into such emotions. He must have seen his life pass before his eyes, seen all his hard work go for naught, all his dreams ended. And he'd been frightened to the bone.

"You work all your life …"

Now Mom sensed that this was serious too, and she calmed down. "All right. That's enough now. You're okay. It's over …"

"… and then some crazy person like this could ruin everything …"

Mom tried another tack to bring the color back into his face. "Yeah, well, who's the crazy one? You know what he's like! What a hardhead he is!" And then she attempted a little humor: "It's a good thing he'd been drinking that terrible wine he makes, or you wouldn't be here now."

Her efforts at humor were of no avail. Pop wasn't moving. He'd been shaken to his soul.

I looked out the window. One of the Mascalzone sons quickly and quietly came out the back door, got into his car, and moved it up into their garage. Then he came back and moved the other car that was blocking the driveway up in front of the garage. And without so much as a glance in our direction, he quickly retreated into their home.

"They've moved the cars," I said.

"Now they move them!" Mom said.

And Pop, with a bit more of his own voice now, said, "How do you like that! That son of a bitch could have killed me!" My father rarely swore. His most used outburst was an occasional "son of a gun," hardly a swear word. He might call someone a *carogna*, which meant, I figured, a kind of swine or bastard. But he never used serious swear words. So I knew he was shaken. And he *was* lucky; he could have been killed.

My mother and I were quiet now. We watched the color slowly return to my father's face. When he looked his old self once more, Mom said, "Come on, let's get in the car and get out of here." And Pop raised himself slowly out of the chair he'd collapsed into and, with all of us following him, he walked out the back door, pulled the car down for us all to get in, and, once we were all in our assigned seats, backed the car out of the driveway and off we went in a more subdued manner than usual down the familiar roads that led to my grandmother's house on that almost-tragic Sunday afternoon.

The Mascalzones never inquired to see if my father was okay nor did they ever apologize for the old man's behavior. They were not the kind of people to admit their guilt. There was even a word for them, a word one often heard about this kind of person from the southern part of Italy: *capotosto*—a person with a hard head. My father could have reported the incident to the police but chose not to. He didn't want to make matters worse for our two households, not alike in dignity. And I'm sure the Mascalzones were delighted to let it go and pretend it had never happened. And that was how it was treated. But they still parked their cars in the driveway, obstructing our passage, and I was still sent into the enemy's territory to ask them to please move their cars.

Sadly, it would be my "Juliet" who would be the only one to comment on the incident. She came into the store one day when I was waiting on a customer, and she said to me in a nasty, spiteful tone when the customer left, "That was all your father's fault!" (Did our blood pact of eternal love mean nothing?) What did she mean? Had my father done or said something at their door to her father he shouldn't have? Had he perhaps, after so many years of asking them to move their cars, finally lost his temper? I didn't see any evidence of that while Mom and I were watching the scene unfold, and I found it hard to believe that he would have since he knew with whom he was dealing. But Pop did have a temper. And maybe he had expressed some exasperation over the situation. But she didn't comment further, and I didn't ask, for her anger seemed to be the defensive self-righteous anger of guilt.

Soon high school started to consume all of my time. I now arrived home usually just in time to sit down to dinner. And after that there was homework to do. So Cecilia's and my visits to our secret place were coming to an end. I also knew now in my heart that we were not alike enough to be true eternal lovers like Maria Montez and Jon Hall. Nor were we destined to end tragically like the doomed lovers of Shakespeare. I was going on to college, which didn't interest her at all. I figured she'd marry young, right out of high school, as her brothers and sisters had. And there was that other important consideration: we were both physically adults now, and any further explorations could be dangerous. Soon thereafter, my fickle Juliet began to date older boys, and I never saw much of her anymore.

There were no more incidents with her father. I went on to college. And one day, when I was home on vacation and helping out in the store, she came in. She'd probably seen me backing the car out of the driveway or in the yard, so she knew I was home, and I guess she wanted to talk to me. I think she wanted to brag a bit, for she had jumped, as I knew she would, into full-grown womanhood quickly. She was married, no longer living at home, and she already had two children, with an obvious third one on the way. She had wasted no time in becoming a mother, as I knew she wouldn't, and she looked happy with her new life.

There was still a residue of affection between us. I could feel it. We had, after all, been each other's teachers in the most basic lesson of life. And I was much beholden to her for that, though I wasn't able to consciously articulate that at the time. It would be an understanding that would come to me later in life. And so, though we had not been meant for each other, we had nevertheless been a very important and good part of each other's lives.

A customer came into the store, ending our unexpected last meeting. And we parted, not tragically, but hopefully, and with a finality that tolled the ending of childhood and the beginning of adulthood. I never saw her again, but I will always remember her. I hope that she fulfilled her destiny and that she occasionally remembers the boy next door, the boy named Romeo, with whom she made a blood pact one day and pledged her eternal love.

Mom's Spaghetti Sauce

(When I went off to NYC to begin my own life, Mom sent me, in one of her first letters, this recipe written in long-hand on yellow-lined paper. I have it still.)

Ingredients:

- sausage
- onions
- garlic
- tomatoes
- tomato sauce
- parsley
- basil

Sauté sausage or any kind of pork meat (it makes the sauce sweet) or you can use beef or lamb. Add a little oil, add ½ chopped onion, one clove of garlic. Add one can of tomatoes (2 ½ cans) and one small can of tomato paste. Add salt and pepper. Add ½ tsp. of sugar. Let cook for 2 hrs. Add parsley and basil.

Boil 4 qts. of water, add salt. When water boils, add spaghetti. Cook until tender. Drain.

Note: Mom varied her basic recipe for sauce over the years. She stopped using the sugar and, as I said, the tomato paste, saying it made the sauce too thick. In later years she put the tomatoes into a blender before cooking for an even lighter sauce. And she lessened the cooking time too, just until the meat was done. If it was a meatless sauce she would only cook it for 20 mins. or so.

Mom's Tender Meatballs

(Everyone said they were the best meatballs they'd ever tasted. The secret, of course, was the soaked bread. Used originally by women in Italy to extend the little amount of meat they had, it wound up being the way to make tender meatballs.)

Place three slices of bread (you can use stale bread, but fresh will work too) in cold water and soak. Squeeze the water out of the bread, and add one pound of ground beef, a quarter cup of grated cheese, salt and pepper, finely chopped garlic, fresh chopped parsley, and basil. Add one large egg (if small, use two). Add 2 tbs. of olive oil and ½ cup dried breadcrumbs.

Originally, Mom made her meatballs with beef, of course, but in later years, her eye always on the health factor, she switched to a half-and-half mix of ground turkey and ground beef. And sometimes if she were being luxurious she would use equal parts of ground veal, ground pork, and ground beef.

Mom always used the same recipe for meat patties and would always keep some in the freezer for emergencies. And I use the same recipe for hamburgers. It makes delicious hamburgers … much more tender and tasty.

Before you add your meatballs to your sauce, they have to be sautéed and browned in a small amount of olive oil in a frying pan. This is a good time to ward off the hunger pangs of a child and let them eat one of the meatballs out of the sauté pan. I would always hang around the kitchen at this point in the process, hoping that one of those meatballs had my name on it, and it usually did.

The patties, placed between two slices of Italian bread and spread with some of Mom's red peppers in olive oil, were another favorite meal.

CHAPTER 6
Pasta e Fagioli: The Simple Pleasures of Life

::

Everyone was welcome at our dinner table. My father was a gracious, generous, and expansive host to all; and if you happened to arrive unannounced at our home at dinnertime, you would be entreated to join us. And Pop could be persuasive: "COME ON! COME ON! YOU WON'T FIND FOOD LIKE THIS IN A RESTAURANT!"—a compliment to Mom actually, though an indirect one of course.

My mother made *pasta e fagioli*—pasta and beans—once a week for my father. He insisted on his weekly fix of this hearty, rustic soup. I couldn't understand his craving for it. As a boy it seemed to me to be a very mundane dish, lacking any real excitement. I always ate a small bowl of it while keeping my eyes on the main course, usually meat and potatoes. Yet, even I, the American boy, sensed something almost legendary about this modest dish. Everyone always knew of it. It was called, a dialect no doubt, *pasta fazul*.

Mom and Dad even owned a very early tan-colored, 78-rpm record in their collection named for it. Imagine! A song that praised a dish of food! It was a novelty song, of course, a popular form in those days; and I can still remember its jaunty beat and the first line of its lyrics: "Pasta fazul, makes you big and makes you fat!" The name alone always evoked laughter from everyone; there was that funny *fazul* that rhymed with *fool*, and then, too, the humble lowly bean itself evoked laughter for its own humorous side effects. But there was the added embarrassment the dish brought of reminding one of one's poor beginnings and poor ancestors in the "old country," who had very little meat and so had to cleverly use whatever protein was available. But for my father, and for me too later on, it was a dish that expressed, in its simplicity and healthiness, our whole identity as a people and our strong connection with our ancestors. Our table became timeless, graced as it was with the same food

71

of our forefathers, and it became their table, too, and we were all sitting at it together across the centuries of time.

One of my father's friends who often joined us was Frank Skisano, our local shoe repair man. He lived on our street and often dropped in to say hello on his way home at the end of the day. Frank—he was called *Ciccio* (Cheech) by his male friends—had a unique way of saying hello. He'd open our store door, and if there were no customers, he'd hit a ringing stentorian high C and hold it dramatically. I knew immediately who it was, of course, and would jump up and run to greet him.

Frank was our small Italian American community's very own *tenore straordinario*, our very own extraordinary Italian tenor. He sang at all our community functions, the parties, the occasional funeral, but mostly the weddings, which were my favorite function. At the end of the evening, after the grand march with everyone joining the long line that snaked across the hall's floor and then split and circled back on itself, dividing again and again till finally winding up in a four-across triumphant move down the floor, Frank would sing, "I love you truly" as the newly married couple danced alone on the floor. He was, like Caruso, a Neapolitan and had been blessed, also like Caruso, with a God-given natural voice that, though he had never had a voice lesson, poured out of him in effortless golden perfection. Frank knew this voice had been a gift, an accident of nature that had blessed his vocal cords, and he matched that gift by his equally generous use of it, donating it freely whenever and wherever it was needed and wanted. He even sang in his shoe repair shop on his lunch breaks, accompanying himself on the guitar and serenading any passerby or customer.

I was totally enamored of Frank's vocal prowess. I had grown up listening to my father's records, those ubiquitous early Victor recordings of Caruso and Ponselle, of Louise Homer and Giovanni Martinelli. On Sunday afternoons, when our store was closed and we'd finished dinner, my father would wind up the RCA Victrola, carefully place the steel needle of the arm on the record, and we'd listen to "Ai Nostri Monti" from *Il Trovatore* with Louise Homer and Caruso; the quartet from *Rigoletto* with Caruso and Galli-Curci, Perini and deLuca, and of course the favorite audience pleasers of Caruso—"Vesti la Giubba" from *I Pagliacci*, and my father's favorite, "Una Furtive Lagrima" from *L'Elisir d'Amore*, though Pop always gave Beniamino Gigli the edge over Caruso on this aria. Gigli had the more lyric voice, my father said, and it was more appropriate for the aria.

It was my father who took me to my first live opera when I was in high school. The Metropolitan Opera in those days always spent a luxurious week in Cleveland on their grand tour across the country, a tour that, alas, no longer happens. On one occasion we heard Risë Stevens in *Carmen* and, on another,

Jussi Bjoerling in *Aida*. Pop thought Bjoerling not as good as Caruso. How could he be? He wasn't Italian. He didn't have "the sun in his voice" that Caruso had, that big open sound.

My father and I got all dressed up for these evenings, for they were the peak cultural events of our lives. Pop always wore his good Sunday suit, his fine pair of dress shoes, a beautiful silk tie held in place by a jeweled stick pin, a white silk scarf on the inside of his jacket that he always affected—just a bit of it showing along the edge of his lapels—the chain of his gold pocket watch looping across his vest, his gold ruby ring on his pinkie finger that he wore only on special occasions, and, over it all, his velvet collared top coat and gray dove-skin gloves. I was amazed at this transformation in my father. Gone were the dirty work clothes and the simple pants and shirts he wore at home. He was elegant and dapper and really knew how to dress! And his obvious enjoyment on these occasions was palpable and rubbed off on me. And since I liked opera, too, I loved going with him. And it was always just the two of us. Mom was not crazy about the opera and usually pleaded exhaustion or a headache from her day's work. These outings with my father down to the public auditorium were the high points of my growing-up years, indelible memories of my father's love for music, a love he wanted to, and did, impart to his son.

When our windup Victrola that my father had later electrified was made obsolescent after the war by the new TV/radio/phono consoles, he immediately bought one of them. It was a beautiful cherry wood Magnavox, the phonograph of which had the famous "cobra" arm that was shaped like a snake's head and had two white dots for eyes! When the phonograph changer was turned on and a record was dropped, that snake head moved over into its proper place on the record's edge and slowly dropped down. I could hardly wait till the store was closed on Sunday and I could place on the spindle our new LP recording of Toscanini conducting *La Traviata*. Then while we ate our early Sunday afternoon dinner, we would listen to the sad strains of Violetta's music as she passionately and inexorably moved to her tragic ending. Or we'd listen to my second long-playing opera album purchase: the sweetly humorous delights of the new recording of *The Barber of Seville* with Victoria de Los Angeles. Pop had taken me to see an Italian film of this opera with the great Italo Tajo.

My father always sang along with the recordings, but sadly, for someone who loved opera as much as he did, he had no voice for singing. He knew music well, and though he wished with all his heart that he could sing, he had not been blessed with the proper musculature of the vocal chords and diaphragm that make it possible. But that never stopped him from showing his enjoyment of the music by humming along, sometimes annoyingly, with the greats.

But Frank was someone in our own world, someone we knew who could do what Caruso could do, and so he and his voice enthralled me. Where did a voice like that come from, I wondered. Why did some have it and not others? It seemed to be a miracle that came from another world, from someplace outside the body. I noticed, too, that in many of the families we knew, there always seemed to be one person who could sing. I loved going to Chester, West Virginia, on our Sunday drives because one of Daddy's friends there had a daughter named Antoinette who was also one of the vocally blessed. Again a person who had never studied singing but who always sang at everyone's weddings, usually at the moment in the Mass when the bride presented a bouquet at the altar of the Virgin Mary. Then, and I waited with great anticipation for this moment in the ceremony, Antoinette's glorious voice would float out from the choir loft: "Mother, at your feet is kneeling, one who loves you, 'tis your child …" She, like Frank, only sang for her own community.

After announcing his presence by hitting that glorious high C, Frank would bound up the stairs into our kitchen, and I would always beg him to do it again, to hit that note again. Pop would tell me to leave Frank alone, but Frank, his singer's energy up, was always delighted to oblige a young boy. He'd strike a pose, raise his chest, throw back his head, and begin a dazzling run up the scale to that unbelievably high note. Oh how I wished I could do that! And when I'd express this desire, my father would always say, "You have to be born with a voice like that! You don't have it!" How did he know that? I had sung in the school choir and had even had solos. Did he think because he had no vocal abilities I didn't either? Then Pop, always delighted to see his friend, would immediately invite Frank to sit down with us: "Rosina! Get a plate for *Ciccio*!" And to me: "Get a chair! Come on! Go get a chair!" And because it was for Frank, I would scramble off happily for a dining room chair from my bedroom.

Frank and his wife lived on the second floor of a two-story home on the opposite side of our street, seven houses down, with their son, Stanley. On many evenings, after we'd closed the store, Mom, eager for a bit of fresh air, would say, "Let's go visit Josie and Frank!" and I'd be the first out the door, for Josie was another very pleasant and lovely woman that I liked enormously.

Josie's father was a stonemason. He had been one of the first property owners on our street, buying not only the land for the two-family home he built but also the two empty lots on the right side of his future home, which he would turn into his private folly and which would become my secret hiding place. He bisected the two extra lots with a large crushed stone driveway that he covered with a trellis to support his grape vines and climbing roses. This driveway extended all the way to the back of the property, where his garage and workspace defined the perimeter of his property. In his triple-car garage, he stored and cut the large slabs of slate and marble that he used in his work.

Each side of the driveway was then divided into two equal areas so that the whole was a garden of four parts. And each of these quadrants was a special and different magical world. As you walked into the garden you passed on the left a formal garden, French in its design, with a small Versailles-looking pool and a draped statue of a beautiful woman in the middle of it. On the right side of the driveway was a most unusual star-shaped pool made of rough rock, stone, bits of mosaic, glass, seashells, and even children's playing marbles. In the middle of this pool was a lighthouse, made of the same eccentric materials, that did indeed light up at night. This pool was a work of art, Gaudi-like in its rough patchwork design. In the upper-left quadrant was a heart-shaped pool made of slate with, for a bridge, two enormous gold fish kissing. How could anyone have ever thought of such a wonderful idea! I never tired of walking across those fish. And in the upper-right quadrant there was a log cabin, big enough to sleep two, with a porch and a bench on one side. Of course, all of these different worlds were filled with hundreds of flowers of many different varieties that I'd never seen before: peonies, tall Easter lilies, small lilies of the valley, many different kinds of roses, and, my very favorite, white and pink bleeding hearts. I marveled at this flower. It looked like a human heart. And as I was always looking for the evidence of a divine being, I wondered if this flower wasn't it.

This beautiful separate world, this hidden and quiet secret place, for there was rarely anyone in the garden, was my sanctuary, my sacred grove, my refuge from the tensions of my home and my overcritical father. It was where I went to hide and to read in peace and where I could dream away a summer's afternoon. Though, even here, my mother would often intrude. Once, not knowing where I was, she left the store unattended and came running along the street yelling out my name. I couldn't bear her distress, and so I left my sanctuary and went home with her.

My only company in the garden were the many dogs that lived there— Josie's and her father's dogs that ran loose. I loved dogs and would play with them for hours ... until one of the males would get too intimate and would grab hold of one of my legs and would not let go. I was amazed at how strongly they could grasp and hold onto my leg! Still, I wanted my own dog desperately and begged my father to let me have one.

"Will you take care of it! No! I'll have to take care of it and I don't have the time!"

"I'll take care of it. I promise."

But it was no use. Dogs were, to my father, a practical animal. You kept them for hunting or working a farm. They were not meant to be idle no more than people were. Nor were they meant to be pets, a way of thinking that must have come from his childhood in Italy where one kept animals for useful purposes only. He'd once told me that his grandmother kept a snake under her bed for good luck and to keep the rodent population down. Even a snake had to be useful. I wondered about that snake often. Was it loose or in a basket? Was it let out at night to hunt? The thought of it slithering around freely worried me constantly, and I would often check under my bed at night to be sure it wasn't there. So I never had the dog I wanted.

Our home was simplicity itself, for Mom had little time to be bothered by a lot of decorative and ornamental bric-a-brac or artwork that required extra hours of cleaning or plants that required constant watering and attention. We had the basics and that was it. Always clean, cleanliness was major to Mom, and always freshly painted and well maintained, our home was serviceable for our minimal needs.

But Josie and Frank's home was amazing. It was the exact opposite of ours and was, for me, like entering a fantasy world. And that delightful world began as soon as you approached Josie's main door, for there, waiting to greet you, was a very raucous green parrot that squawked loudly, announcing you as you came up the stairs. "JOSIE! JOSIE!" it screeched over and over. I was warned to keep my fingers out of the parrot's cage, so I would just stare at him, and on occasion, with Josie present, I would get to scratch his feathered head if he'd present it to me between the bars of his cage. When Josie came to her door, alerted by the bird's squawking, she'd grab me—I always looked forward to this moment with excitement, for I knew what was coming—and she'd squeeze both my cheeks really hard, giving me what she called a "pizzicato" kiss, a pinch kiss. Then we'd enter her museum-like home.

Josie's living room was filled with enchantment for a young person's eyes. There were glass-fronted curio cabinets filled with beautiful objects: glass paperweights with brightly colored floral designs embedded deep within them (how did they get in there?); glass balls with scenes inside that, if you shook them, created a snowstorm; delicate china cups and saucers; glass vases of beautiful and intriguing color and design; souvenirs from all over the world; big conch seashells that when placed up against your ear roared like the ocean; and everywhere little ceramic animals and marble statues of mythical figures. The walls were covered with paintings and scenes from foreign and exotic lands. There was an ornately carved cuckoo clock that thrilled me on the hour when its little door popped open and revealed its secret dweller for whom it was named. And in every nook and cranny there were plants, many huge-leafed rubber plants that touched the ceiling, and flowerpots. It was all very heady for a young boy used to the simple basics.

There was though one item in this museum-like room that I loved the most. It was a bronze, life-size statue of a nude boy that greeted you as soon as you entered the room. I knew that when I walked through the doorway into that room and looked to my right that the boy would be looking right at me. I figured later on that he must have been a likeness of Bacchus, for he had a very mischievous gleam in his eyes and a sly, somewhat lascivious, knowing smile on his face. And he held, forever raised above him in his right hand, a bunch of deep-purple glass grapes that he dangled teasingly over the opened mouth of his slightly upturned head. I was intoxicated by him. And I would spend hours staring at him, thinking if I looked at him long enough he would come alive and be the friend I so wanted to play with. Sometimes I was convinced that he had actually winked at me. And then, fearful that he *was* alive, I would back away quickly. Here was the other side of the duality of life as it was showing itself to me: in church I had looked longingly at the crucifix with the stabbed and bleeding Christ on the cross, identifying with his pain, hoping he were alive and that I could talk to him. And here in Josie's house was his opposite, the Dionysian statue of Bacchus, wickedly dangling the pleasures of wine and of the sensuality of an exotic world. What I didn't know then was that they were both alive in me.

When my father offered Frank a glass of wine at our table, from a jug that one of Pop's friends had made, Frank always accepted: "It'll clear the shoe leather dust from my throat!" But he always refused any food for, of course, dinner was waiting for him at home. And my mother was not the type to force her food on anyone. Not for her the clichéd Italian American mother telling everyone to "Mangia! Mangia!" Eat! Eat! She was delighted if you liked her food, but humbly, she never pushed it on anyone. But if Frank saw that Mom had made her *pasta e fagioli* that evening, he, too, like my father, could not resist its welcoming nostalgic simplicity; and to assuage his guilt, he'd always say that since his wife never made it because she didn't like it, it would be okay for him to have some. And after his first spoonful, he'd always exclaim, "Rosina! It is so wonderful! How do you make it!" And my mother, secretly delighted to have her food praised, would deflect the compliment with her usual answer: "That old mish-mosh!" Lots of nice "shhh" sounds she could play with there. "Well, I comb my hair, wash my hands, put on my apron, and I make it." We'd all laugh, having heard this before. And then we'd dig in.

And now the heated discussions would begin, for in truth the main course at our table was always the conversation led by my father. And there were two topics that Pop was wildly passionate about: politicians and priests. And of the two it was the priests he disliked the most. "THEY'RE NOTHING BUT

CROOKS! AND CAFONE (fools)!" he would say, exploding in anger. "THEY HAVE THEIR HANDS IN MY POCKET! AND THEY WANT TO TELL ME HOW TO LIVE!" Pop wasn't about to have anyone tell him what he should do with his life or, for that matter, what he should do in his bedroom.

One evening when Josie and Frank were both visiting us and the topic had turned to religion, my father as usual called the priests and the church "CROOKS!" That prompted Josie to ask my father the major question: "Don't you believe in Jesus Christ, Jim?"

"What does it matter what I believe? Whether he exists or not, I still have to do my work!"

To this, Josie, warmly smiling as always, calmly replied, "But he does exist, Jim. I saw him."

Now Pop was engaged, as I was too. He said, unbelieving, "You saw God?"

"Yes," Josie smilingly replied, "I saw him."

"Where did you see him, Josepina?" my father asked sarcastically.

"I saw him on that big Oxydol billboard at the corner of Ninth Avenue and Superior."

My eyes grew wide. I had learned just recently that Josie was not a Catholic. Up to this point in my life I thought all Italians were Catholic. But Josie was a Jehovah's Witness. I wasn't quite sure what that was, but I thought if it made people as warm and loving as Josie—you could feel the love as a force radiating out from her—then it must be a good religion. And I always imagined her standing on street corners in downtown Cleveland, smiling warmly at people as they passed, handing out her religious information. I'd seen the Jehovah's Witness people doing that. So despite her strange religion I still loved her. And I think she loved me. She told my mother once in a letter to her in Florida, "I think of Sonny—I always thot [*sic*] he was a little bit of mine." And I had always felt that. She made me realize that there were other choices you could make; you didn't have to follow your givens.

But this new information of hers was fascinating, and my father couldn't believe his ears. "You saw God on a billboard at Ninth and Superior!?"

We all knew that billboard and were picturing it in our minds. It was right across from where you waited for the streetcar to come home.

"Yes," Josie calmly replied, "it was one late afternoon, and I looked up and there he was, stretched out across that whole billboard, our Lord Jesus Christ. His arms were open wide, and he was looking right at me and smiling."

I couldn't believe what I was hearing. Nor could Pop. He was struck dumb. His jaw had dropped. But he soon recovered. "Josepina! You were tired! You saw something you wanted to see! That's all!"

But Josie was firm. "No, Jim, I know what I saw."

Pop was stuttering and about to explode. Mom gave him a look, telling him to be quiet. She said, "If she saw Jesus Christ on an Oxydol billboard at the corner of Ninth and Superior, who are you to say she didn't!"

Pop tried to continue the conversation but Mom wouldn't have it. "That's enough now! No more politics or religion! You're like a broken record! Change your tune once in a while!" Here was Mom again, leading the way philosophically. She'd hit on a major theory of human behavior that said that everyone who claims to be an adult must change his point of view at least once in his life. Mom was right up there with the latest thinkers, only she expressed it in simpler and more direct language: "CHANGE YOUR TUNE!" And Pop, sensing he was going too far in front of company, would laugh at himself and pull back. He did have the saving grace to know when to laugh at himself ... at least when we had company.

Then Mom would try some humor: "You know everything! They broke the mold after they made you! When you die, I'm going to give your body to a museum so they can study you!" Pop's rebuttal to this mention of his future death was always the same: "I DON'T CARE WHAT YOU DO WITH ME WHEN I DIE! DIG A HOLE IN THE BACKYARD AND DUMP ME IN! WHEN YOU'RE DEAD, YOU'RE DEAD!" That was Pop's whole philosophy of life, and it was based on the natural cycles of the earth. One could call it a remnant of a pagan society. He would call it a realistic view of the world, a recognition of things for what they really are. And that to him was a virtue.

My father and mother were not, as I've said, churchgoers. Keeping our store open on Sunday mornings, as a convenience to our customers, was just a part of it. The real reason was that my father had little use for the church itself. His belief that priests didn't do an honest day's work, I later realized, was a holdover from his childhood in Italy, where the church functioned differently than in America. There you often went into the church not because you were called to God's work, but because it was one of the only ways to pull oneself out of the poverty one had been born into. It was a financial arrangement for the most part and not a spiritual one. Once in the church, you and your family would be taken care of, and that was why parents were delighted to send their sons and daughters into the church. It also bothered my father that the church's money was mostly coming from the poor people. Pop resented that. So he had little use for any of it. And he held that view strongly.

"JIM!" family members would always say, "IF YOU EVER WALKED INTO A CHURCH IT WOULD FALL DOWN!" It was an often-repeated one-liner that always got a big laugh and a rueful "mmm" from my father. One time my father said to his brothers and sisters-in-law, "I have use of the church on only three occasions in life: at birth, at marriage, and at death." Consequently we never went to Mass on Sunday morning, though we had been baptized as Catholics.

One Sunday afternoon we had a surprise visitor. A priest from our local St. Cecilia's RC Church came into our store. He'd been to visit a sick parishioner on our street, and seeing our store and our name, he must have thought he would stop in and introduce himself to fellow Catholics. Pop and I, already dressed for our afternoon trip to Grandma's, which we would start out on as soon as we closed the store, were in the living room reading the Sunday *Plain Dealer* and listening to some music, when Mom called out from the store. "JIM!" My father and I, both hearing something different in her voice, jumped up immediately and ran to the window that overlooked the store.

"What is it!" my father wanted to know.

I saw what it was immediately, for there was a priest standing in our store. I recognized him because I had been to an occasional Mass at our local RC Church. His name was Father Gallagher, and he was a very mesmerizing priest who usually delivered a wonderful sermon.

Nervous with this unusual visitor, my mother asked my father to come down into the store; and I, full of curiosity, followed him.

The priest extended his hand warmly to my father. "I'm Father Gallagher from St. Cecilia's, and I just wanted to introduce myself to you, Mr. Romeo." Father Gallagher pronounced our name the Anglo-Saxon way, the way everyone in America did, the way it's pronounced in *Romeo and Juliet,* the accent on the first syllable.

My father immediately corrected him. "Our name is 'Romayo,' the accent on the second syllable. Please! Respect the accent!" This didn't bode well.

But Father Gallagher accepted the criticism and went right on. "You are Catholic, aren't you, Mr. Romeo?" He pronounced our name correctly.

"Yes," my father said, "we are Catholic."

Father Gallagher went on, "Do you and your family attend Mass on Sunday, Mr. Romeo?"

"We don't have time," my father said. "We have to keep the store open."

"It's a sin to miss Mass, Mr. Romeo. You know that, don't you?"

I could tell my father was starting to get angry ... but he was still speaking calmly. "Who said it was a sin? God? No. It was some people in the church who wanted more people to come and put some money in the basket. You're not talking to a fool, you know."

Mom tried to interrupt and suggested that we had to leave soon. Pop said to her, "You go finish dressing. I'm talking to the priest."

Then Father Gallagher asked about me. "I take it this is your son. He looks like a fine young man. Do you have any other children?"

That was a tactical error on the priest's part. I think my father had been waiting for years to have this discussion. And now he wasn't going to let it go. I was now riveted on my father, and he didn't disappoint.

"A-HA!" he said victoriously. "WE GET RIGHT TO IT!"

"Right to what, Mr. Romeo?"

"TO THE CHURCH AND CHILDREN!"

I knew what was coming next, for I'd heard this speech often.

"THE CHURCH SAYS, 'GO AHEAD! HAVE KIDS! HAVE AS MANY AS YOU WANT!' BUT WHO'S GOING TO PAY FOR THESE CHILDREN! HUH! WHO'S GOING TO FEED THEM! CLOTHE THEM! EDUCATE THEM! THE CHURCH? HA! DON'T MAKE ME LAUGH!"

My mother, hoping to calm my father, interrupted him, telling him not to yell.

"I'M NOT YELLING!" he said. "I'M SPEAKING IN MY NATURAL VOICE!" Then more calmly he said, "Years ago we needed a lot of people to farm the land, so the church said, 'Be fruitful and multiply! Have as many children as you want!' It was necessary. And it also made the church more powerful and rich. But now we don't need so many people anymore. The world has too many people. They live miserable poor lives. They're hungry. Little babies die. It's terrible! Yet the church says, 'Go ahead! Have more babies!' Why! Because it's all politics and greed! That's all it is! Power and greed! And that's why my wife and I have only two children. Because I am responsible here...not the church, not the government, not God ... just me!"

His major speech about religion and politicians and power and greed now given, Pop said, "Now please, we have to close the store."

But Father Gallagher was game and continued, "Do you practice birth control, Mr. Romeo?"

My father was offended. "Please! You want to peek into my bedroom and see the intimate details of my life?"

Now Mom was getting fearful. "Jim! Go get the car! I'll lock the store!"

But Father Gallagher pressed the issue. "The church allows only one method of birth control, Mr. Romeo, the rhythm method."

My father picked up on this musical term immediately. "Rhythm?"

"Yes," Father Gallagher said. "Do you know what that is?"

"Of course!" my father quickly shot back. "I am a musician! I played the clarinet in an orchestra. I know what rhythm is. That means keeping the beat. Don't worry! I keep the beat!"

Mom's face started to turn red, and she tried to stop this line of thought: "That's not what he means, Jim."

My father continued, "You know, you people are obsessed with sex. That isn't healthy. Sex is a normal, everyday thing. No big deal. Everybody does it. If it interests you so much, go out and get your own. But what I do in my bedroom is none of your business. Now, please, we have to go." And my father came around the counter and headed for the door to lock it.

I had never heard Pop hold forth on sex before. I was taken aback, but at the same time, I was fascinated by what he felt.

At the door Father Gallagher said to my father, "I didn't come here to argue with you, Mr. Romeo."

"I'm not arguing! I'm talking man-to-man! Because that's what we are! Two men! You want to feed people fantasies about life! But I tell the truth! The truth is beautiful! The truth is sacred! Look around you! What is, is! And that's beautiful! It is a beauty that goes on forever! But people don't want to hear that! They want fantasies! They want somebody else to save them, to do their work! I only believe what I can see! Now please, we have to go!" And at that, Pop opened the door and pointed the way out.

In the opened doorway now, Father Gallagher turned and said, "We need to believe, Mr. Romeo, we need to have faith in life, that miracles can happen. Sometimes it's the fantasy, the dream, that keeps us going. A certain mind is a closed mind, Mr. Romeo. Only a primitive mind can be so certain."

My father was a bit stung now. "Please! We have to go!" And with that he started to close the door on Father Gallagher.

But Father Gallagher was determined to have the last word. "You have some interesting ideas, Mr. Romeo, that come, no doubt, from your childhood in Italy. I would like to continue our discussion. I can always be found at the church. Come to see me." And Father Gallagher walked away from our store.

Pop was a bit flabbergasted as he locked the door. "He wants me to come and see him? How do you like that? Is he crazy?"

"No! You're the crazy one for talking to him like that!"

"Listen! I told him! Okay! He won't come around here anymore! They should take all those people who don't want to work and hang them! In my town in the old country they castrated a priest who made one of the young girls pregnant. They cut off his balls and kept them in a jar in their house!"

This was too much for my mother to absorb, and she quickly disappeared up the stairs and into her bedroom. I, however, couldn't stop thinking about that priest who'd had his balls cut off. My father and I walked up the stairs into the kitchen and toward the back door, where my mother met us, and we walked out the back door and got into our car and drove off down the driveway—fortunately there were no neighbor's cars parked there—and to my grandmother's house. All I could think of for the whole trip was that jar with the priest's balls. I wondered where it was now.

Mom couldn't resist telling the family of this incident. It was too good a story on Pop. But my father's reaction was only one of surprise. With total disbelief, he said, "Can you imagine! He came right into my house to tell me what to do!"

Then someone kidded Pop, "YOU'RE A CHARACTER, JIM!"

And another of my uncles said, "DAMN! I WISH I'D BEEN THERE!"

And the family had another good story to tell about my father.

Because of my father's volcanic certainty in his own beliefs, I never brought friends home for fear of what Pop would say to them. Would he say something racist about colored people, how they were "lazy" at the steel mill? Would he make his usual disparaging remarks about priests and politicians and launch into a vehement attack about the church or the government? One could never know with Pop. A sad side effect of my distrust of what Pop would do or say was that I also never brought any of my problems to him, for I felt he, irrational as he was, obviously wouldn't be able to handle any problems I had. This wasn't a conscious decision on my part; it just evolved that way. Finally I felt I had to protect him from any ideas that might upset him. So there was, sadly, not much communication between us.

But I would always love to visit Jo and Frank, to be announced by their parrot the second I appeared on their steps—"JOSIE! JOSIE!"—and to hear Frank sing. In later years I did wonder why Frank had not done anything with his glorious voice besides singing for our community. And when I asked my father why Frank had never considered a professional career, his response surprised me: "Because he didn't want it!"

I couldn't believe that. "Didn't want it! Why not!" The joy and fun of all those gorgeously Technicolor and vibrant movie musicals of the time made me believe there could be no better life than one that garnered so much love from people while, at the same time, also giving so much joy to people, not to mention that it was also an entrée into a larger and more exciting world.

What my father told me then really surprised me. "He was offered the chance but he turned it down." Then he related the rest of the story. And except for the ending, it could have indeed been the plot of one of those glorious MGM movie musicals my father and I loved so much.

It seemed that one day during his lunch break in his shoe repair shop, Frank, as he often did, was playing his guitar and singing. It happened that a professor from the Cleveland Institute of Music was passing by and heard Frank's beautiful voice floating out of his shop. Intrigued, he followed the beautiful sounds into the shop and, asking for an encore, which Frank gladly obliged, was very impressed. He told Frank right then that if he wanted, he would set up an audition for him when the Metropolitan Opera was next in town. He felt strongly that they should hear Frank. There was even an article in the evening paper quoting the professor as saying, "I've found a supreme voice of greater volume and power than Caruso's."

Frank agreed to the audition and to being coached in his choice of audition arias. When the big day arrived, Frank, our local shoe repairman whose voice was the pride of our small Italian American community, traveled downtown on the streetcar to the public auditorium where the Metropolitan Opera was performing. He bravely walked out onto that huge stage and sang for the greatest opera company in America. How I wish I could have been there! There was, according to my father, an immediate positive reaction. They would be delighted to have him join the company, but—and it was a major *but*—Frank would have to spend the next five years or so in New York City, learning the repertoire and learning new languages. And that meant it would be a while before he could make his debut. Frank went home to mull over their offer, promising his decision by the end of the week, when they were to leave town. On their last day in town, Frank turned down the Metropolitan Opera's offer.

I was astonished. "How could he do that!"

"He didn't want to leave his family and go away to study for all that time. He was happy repairing shoes and singing for everyone here." My father didn't seem surprised by that decision.

I, filled with the simplistic and hopeful exuberance of youth, found that hard to believe. How could anyone so gifted turn down such a wonderful opportunity? I was sure I wouldn't have.

But Frank, a simple man, a man who didn't need the larger recognition, a man happy and content with his life, with his wife and son, would stay close to what his heart dictated and could turn down the offer. And in so doing, he reaffirmed his joy in the simple pleasures of life. He would continue to bless us all with his magnificent voice, our very own Caruso, and he would continue to enjoy a simple but deeply rewarding bowl of my mother's *pasta e fagioli*. And I had learned something more about the complexity and mystery of the human soul.

And my father—though of a pricklier, more political mind, a mind I would always search for clues to the reasons for his beliefs—would always come back to the basics too. For the truth was that praying and gratefulness to God takes many forms. My mother prayed when she prepared her food. You could see that in the reverence with which she touched food. It was her way of connecting to a higher power. You could palpably feel her gratitude to God. And Pop prayed with his humble enjoyment of the basic goodness and simplicity in what the earth produced. He saw the divine in the ordinary. He had faith that God would provide as long, that is, as he did his work. I also realized that he didn't believe in original sin. He felt that was a myth perpetrated by the church to control the people. Man was just who he was, born neither good nor bad. And it was up to man himself to do the right thing, to do his work well, to keep his agreements, and to take care of his family. Wasn't that faith? Wasn't that prayer? And yes, wasn't that God?

The phone rang late one night. We were all in bed asleep. But we all knew immediately that something was wrong, for the phone never rang at this time of the morning. By the second ring, my father, my mother, my sister, and myself were all gathered around the phone in the living room. My father answered it. He listened quietly. Then a *Dio mio* (my God) escaped his lips. Slowly he hung up the phone.

"What's happened!" my mother asked, fearing the worst.

"Ciccio is dead."

"What!" my mother said.

"He had a heart attack."

"My God."

Without any discussion we were all dressed in minutes and walked down the street to Frank and Josie's home to pay our respects.

As we walked the dark, empty, sad sidewalks of our street, Mom, always the one to remember the telling moment, said to my father, "Do you remember when he came and, without us knowing, sprinkled perfume all over our honeymoon bed?" My father looked away. It was a surprising image of a Frank I didn't know. But it spoke beautifully of his and my parent's long and close friendship and of his warm heart.

When we got back home, all my father could say was, "He was a good man and a good friend. But too young to die, too young."

My sister and I went back to bed. Mom told me a few weeks later that my father, a man whom I feared, a man I never understood, had locked himself in our bathroom that night and had cried for more than an hour over the loss of his good friend.

Our lives went on, of course. Josie would continue her work with Jehovah's Witness and would stop in often for a visit. She was still her wonderful sweet self. A few years later my mother wrote me, telling me that our much loved local doctor, Dr. Menzalore, who was the warmest, most pleasant, and even-tempered man I knew and who spoke the Italian language—and the English language too for that matter—in the most mellifluous low basso key that was indeed music itself (I loved going to his office just to listen to him talk), had asked Josie, after his wife died, to marry him. It turned out that he too had always been under the spell of her lovely persona. But Josie had turned him down, saying, "I'm a widow!" And for the rest of her life, even after my parents had moved away, as had so many others, she continued to live on our old street, still a widow, still silently proselytizing for her religion, and still believing in the basic goodness of people.

Dr. Menzalore would die from a heart attack in his car at the side of a road. At least that was what his obituary in the evening paper said. But my mother told me one day that there was a rumor he'd been killed by the mafia. When I asked why, she said he had once been asked to perform an operation on one of their members and that he had refused, saying he didn't know how to do that operation. They let him off but warned him never to operate. And that's why he was a general practitioner.

All in all it was a wonderful community, and I was the lucky recipient of its humanity. Frank who shared freely his golden vocal gift with us all; and his wife, Josie, who was just pure love. Dr. Menzalore who opened up possibilities in my life by the beauty of his caring and learned being. And farther down the street there was Mrs. Nuby, who, with her husband, was one of the first black families on the street and who, when her husband couldn't go, took me to see the Cleveland Indians play. They were all good and kind people. And they taught me so much about life … about enjoying the simplicity of it … and about the joy of doing for others. I bless them all.

Mom's Pasta e Fagioli

Ingredients:

- 1 can kidney or cannelloni beans
- ½ onion, chopped
- 2 cloves chopped garlic
- 1 stalk celery with leaves, chopped
- ½ carrot, chopped
- 2 tbs. olive oil
- 1 can diced tomatoes (14 oz.) or ¾ can of tomato sauce. Or you can use four fresh chopped tomatoes. You don't want, however, a lot of tomatoes in this dish.
- 1 tbs. fresh basil
- 1 tbs. fresh parsley
- a *pizzico* (a pinch) of salt
- a couple twists of pepper
- 1 tbs. of lemon juice (It's not necessary but it helps to lighten the strength of the beans.)
- 2 cups of water (or more to achieve the right consistency)

Drain the beans and wash. Set aside. (Some people use the liquid in the beans in the sauce. Mom always used water. Using the bean liquid makes a thicker soup.)

Sauté the onions in the oil. When they appear translucent, add the garlic. Cook a short time and then add the amount of tomato sauce you need (about an inch and a half in a two-quart sauce pan) and then add the celery, the basil, the carrots, the parsley, the salt and pepper, and let simmer for 10 mins. Add the water and the beans. Bring to a boil and cook for about 10 mins. (The celery, Mom always said, helps you digest.)

Cook the shape pasta you want: shells, elbows, *tubetti* (little tubes), *pennine*, or break up spaghetti into inch-long pieces. Mix the two together and serve with cheese and hot pepper flakes, if desired.

This same recipe can be used for Pasta and Peas and Pasta and Chick Peas, both of which impart a different and wonderful flavor.

CHAPTER 7
Dice Niente: Say Nothing!

::

"Sonny!" It was my grandmother calling me into the walk-in pantry off her kitchen.

"Sonny!" she called again in a hushed voice so no one could hear. "*Vene ca*! Come here!"

I always ran to my grandmother when she called me, for I knew what was in store.

And there, in the privacy of her pantry, my adored grandmother, who was, as I later realized, the typical-looking Italian grandmother, as wide as she was short, her hair pulled straight back into a bun, with even a wart on her forehead, would pull out from a hiding place something I had never seen in our store and that I was sure was forbidden: a giant Hershey's chocolate bar! Then as she surreptitiously slipped it to me, her finger to her lips, she would always say to me, "Shhh! *Dice Niente*!" Say nothing! And I would happily hide the giant candy bar on my body and later slip it in among my clothes in my suitcase. I was enthralled as a boy to share with my grandmother the delightful power of secrecy.

Those two words, *Dice Niente,* could sum up many an Italian-immigrant philosophy. Regularly invaded and enslaved over the centuries by every new powerful country that wanted its southern farm lands—excellent for growing wheat, for its olive groves and for its wine-producing vineyards—ancient Italy was a land where the truth was hard to find. And its philosophy, a centuries-old pagan religion that was cunning, mysterious, and skeptical of others, was based not on faith but on the survival of its people. All of which led to the Italian family's overly developed genetic marking for secrecy and for minding one's own business. You protected yourself by keeping everything secret. And the Italians' distrust of the stranger was palpable. I could even feel it in my mother, who, though born in America, had evidently absorbed that fear from her parents; for she was always looking out the window of our house to see if there was anyone unusual around.

But I knew little of that then. What I did know was that I loved my grandmother in a very uncomplicated way, and I knew she loved me unconditionally. Though she would often raise her voice to her children, she never yelled at me nor said an unkind word to me. So I was delighted to be included in that ancient world of power, of how to "say nothing." We shared a conspiracy, something no one else knew and that brought us closer to each other. There would be more lessons in secrecy as I grew older, lessons learned from observing the adults in my family and hard lessons learned from my own experience.

My grandparents lived in a big house on Cedar Avenue, close to downtown Cleveland. Compared to our very simple home, to me it was a mansion. The main door of the house led into a hallway, off of which to the right was the living room which you entered through two huge mahogany sliding doors. Here was another mystery of the physical world. I always wondered in amazement where those doors went when they were opened and disappeared into the wall. I pulled them back and forth as often as I could, looking for the secret but without much luck. The living room had a carved wooden fireplace and three large, tall windows up-front, overlooking the street. There was another sitting room next to it, also with sliding doors, which functioned, when needed, as an extra bedroom. Then there was the large dining room with its great wooden table and huge breakfront. And then, continuing toward the back of the house, a back stairs that separated the main rooms from my grandmother's constant place of activity, the kitchen, where she spent most of her days, off of which was the walk-in pantry. A door from the kitchen led onto a small back porch and then downstairs into the backyard.

On the left side of the front hallway there was a wooden staircase that led to the second floor and all the bedrooms. That staircase had the widest and smoothest cherry wood banister that I loved to slide down, to be caught at the bottom by an aunt or uncle of mine. There might have been five bedrooms on the second floor though I was only ever in two of them: the big one up-front with four double beds where my uncles slept and where I, too, would sleep when I visited. Lying next to one of my uncles, in my very early days on a mattress of straw, I could never fall asleep right away, entranced as I was by my strange surroundings, the unfamiliar sounds coming from the busy street below, and the constant movie of reflected lights from the passing traffic on Cedar Avenue that played across the top of the walls of the bedroom. Next to that main big bedroom was a smaller one, where my three aunts slept on one big bed and a cot. Then situated at the top of the stairs was the only bathroom in the house. It had a door with two clear panes of glass. I'd never seen a bathroom door with windows. Happily, someone had covered the windows with fake stained-glass sticky paper, which allowed for privacy. Next to it was a very small room in which my grandmother slept. Oddly enough, I was never quite sure where my grandfather slept, for he was always up and doing things when I arrived at the house. On occasion I would stand in the doorway of my grandmother's room, watching her brush her surprising, waist-length hair and then put it up into the bun at the back of her head. I believe there was another bedroom at the very rear of the second floor, but I never ventured down that part of the hall. My grandmother's brother, Uncle Tony, who had a big handlebar mustache that I loved to twist when I was a little boy, slept there when he was in town. There might even have been, at different times, a boarder living there, for many people in those days took in boarders to bring in some extra money. Above that floor was a very large but empty attic that I never explored, for it held no interest for me.

Entered by a door between the kitchen and the pantry was a very scary, dark basement that I never ventured into alone. Always curious about the physical world, I did, on one singular occasion, follow my grandfather down the stairs when he invited me to see him kill a chicken for our supper. At the bottom of the stairs sat a tree stump meant for just that purpose. My grandfather held the chicken's neck on the stump and, with an axe, chopped off its head. Then we watched as the chicken ran around without its head. I was amazed. I had never seen that before. I couldn't believe it was possible. My grandfather laughed at my surprise.

Upstairs in the kitchen, over the sink, my grandfather plucked the feathers of the chicken, burned off what still remained over a gas burner on the stove—that smelled badly—and then opened up the chicken at the sink to clean it. When he did, he discovered one fully developed egg about to be hatched, and many, many more—hundreds of them, in fact, in all the different stages of development. I was riveted by the number of eggs inside the chicken and how they looked. They weren't white and hard like the one about to be hatched. They were soft as flesh, light gray in color, with traces of red veins. And they were in every size imaginable, from tinier than my little fingernail all the way up to the size of a golf ball. My grandfather was immediately sorry he had killed that particular chicken. If he had known it had so many eggs, he said, he would have let it live. I was wide-eyed at the natural miracle I had been allowed to see. I felt that I had seen into a deeper mystery of the world, and it was a feeling I liked. Besides the chickens, my grandfather also raised rabbits in a hutch in the backyard, where there was even a wooden pail full of dangerous snapping turtles that also intrigued me. "Be careful!" my grandfather always warned me when I leaned in too close to the turtles. "They can bite off your fingers!" There were also numerous dogs over the years, one called Whitey that I remember, a spitz-looking bitch that seemed to have puppies every year to the aggravation of my grandfather. Not too many years later, that dark basement would become the place of another more intense childhood memory.

For all my growing up years, I only knew that home on Thirty-fifth and Cedar, and it became imbued for me with a great sense of place and anticipation. Besides the constant Sunday dinners we attended there, we always celebrated Easter Sunday and my favorite holiday, Christmas, at my grandmother's house. And every summer I got to spend the best two weeks of the year with my grandparents and my wonderful aunts and uncles, all of whom I loved and looked up to, in that big lively place full of fascinating people.

My grandfather, Joseph Pecora—*Pecora* means sheep in Italian, and his family in Italy had indeed always raised and butchered sheep—was born on March 15, 1884, in the same town in Italy, *Cirò Marina,* as my father, making him and my father *paesani,* those men who were related by their town of birth. He came to America at the age of twenty-one on the *Buenos Aires* out of Naples. And he settled first in the small towns of southern Ohio and Pennsylvania, where he found work in the coal mines. And it was there one day, in Bradley, Ohio, that he saw my grandmother digging in a garden and told her brother, Tony, that he wanted to marry her and that he didn't want her working in the garden ever again. His wishes were followed, and when he'd saved the money needed for the wedding they were married in 1909 by a justice of the peace in Bradley, Ohio. She was nineteen years old.

My beloved grandmother, my mother's mother—I never knew any of my father's family, for he was the only one of his family to come to America—was born Concetta Maria Pagliarulo on May 20, 1890, though there was always some question about the date, because of the lack of records at that time. Her town of origin was Avellino, which lies just outside of Naples and dangerously close to the slopes of Mount Vesuvius. As a child, my grandmother remembered gathering lightweight pumice stone on the slopes of that ominous mountain to make soap that was used for washing clothes. In the great Vesuvius eruption of 1904, both her parents, Veto and Maria, were killed. Was that why, I wondered, she had then journeyed to America to join her sister Florence and her brother Nick in New York City? The timing would seem to be right. Soon after her arrival, her brother Nick was crushed to death between two horse carts on the streets of the Lower East Side and my grandmother then went to live with her brother Tony, who was a barber in Bradley, Ohio, which is where she met my grandfather.

My mother, Rose Frances Pecora, my grandparents' firstborn, was named after her father's mother. Born in Bradley, Ohio, close to a crossroads called Mingo Junction, my mother would forever be kidded by her siblings: "Rose! You were so poor when you were born you couldn't even afford a town! You were born at a junction!" Then came Paul, who was named after his father's father. A new job took the family of four to Bradenville, Ohio (a town now demolished by an interstate highway), where John, Veto, Florence, Theresa (my grandfather nicknamed her Blackie because she had straight pitch-black hair when she was born), and Anthony were born. The worldwide flu epidemic, the deadliest plague in history that killed more people than World War I, hit in 1918. Six hundred seventy-five thousand would die in America; twenty million worldwide. The country ran out of coffins. Corpses were stored anywhere a suitable space could be found. My grandfather soon had a new job, digging graves in Butler, Ohio. And my mother, watching the wagons of the piled dead as they passed their home, the last one in town, worried that Florence, just born, would also die. Her mother assured her she wouldn't. And she didn't.

After the epidemic died down, Grandpa got another job in a coal mine, so they moved back to Bradley, Ohio, and into company housing, where Viola, the prettiest of my aunts and my favorite, was born. Even though she was a brunette I nicknamed her Blondie after the wife of Dagwood Bumstead, one of my favorite cartoon strips; and I would sing the hit song "Amapola" to her all the time, thinking the lyric said "my pretty little puppy" and not "my pretty little poppy." But it was the *pretty* that was the important word. When my mother was ready for high school, her father vetoed any further education for her because, he said, the school was a two-mile walk from their home. My mother thought that was an excuse; she was sure his real intention was for her to stay home so she could help with the raising of the younger children in the family. Though saddened at this turn of events because her dream was to be a schoolteacher, she did as she was told.

It was there in Bradley that my father—prompted by Carmela, my grandfather's sister who lived in Cleveland, where my father had settled after completing the one-year immigration requirement of living with a sponsor in Fort Wayne, Indiana—started wooing my mother. He made numerous trips down from Cleveland, but my mother didn't want anything to do with him. She was only sixteen years old and too young to think of marriage. He brought her gifts: a beaded forty-five-dollar hat one time that was an extravagance and, another time, a beautiful embroidered coat. Her girlfriends were jealous. They thought he was a catch. But still my mother wasn't sure. Finally he told her if she didn't want him to come anymore she had to tell him so and he wouldn't. Aunt Carmela told her she was making a big mistake. He came, she said, from a very good family; he'd make an excellent husband. So finally my mother told him he could come back. But my grandfather, after agreeing to the marriage, told my father he'd have to wait till she was eighteen. My father said he would.

Then Aunt Carmela told her brother that he needed to get out of those small towns, where there was nothing of any practical benefit for his family, and move to Cleveland where the children could go to nearby decent schools and he could find safer work. Because of a back injury in the coal mines and so that his children could have a full education (though not my mother who would still have to help at home), he made the final move and took his family to Cleveland, Ohio, where, in 1915, he and my grandmother consecrated their marriage at a ceremony in St. Anthony's Church and where the last of their children, my uncle Frank, was born. When my mother was told there was a ninth child on the way, a child she most likely would wind up taking care of, she was for the first time delighted: "I sure am glad I'm getting married and getting out of here!"

Except for the killing of the chicken I wasn't much involved with my grandfather. He often sat quietly at the kitchen table, drinking a glass of homemade red wine and smoking a stogie, a vile-smelling cheap cigar, all the while watching his wife make supper. To me he always seemed a bit removed and even more severe than my own father. Later I would hear stories about his terrible temper and how he had abused his boys by hitting them, a behavior often blamed on his drinking. And more than once I heard how he would lock the boys out of the house, making them sleep in the rabbit hutch, if they came home later than their assigned curfew hour. My mother told me she would often wait till he was asleep and would then sneak downstairs to unlock the back door and let her brothers into the house.

On one occasion when he had been drinking too much he had gone after my aunt Theresa; and she, to avoid being hit by him, jumped out of her second-floor bedroom window. Luckily she didn't break any bones; she only bruised herself on the sidewalk below. Then while my uncle Frank and my grandmother held my grandfather down, she managed to call the police. They always told these stories about "the old man," as he was most often called behind his back, and laughed. But I wondered if he hadn't been a very troubling father. I heard once that he slept with a gun under his pillow. Well, those were not the safest of times nor was the neighborhood they were living in. I do remember though that at Easter time he always made many wonderful items out of the palms given out in church. He would make the usual number of crosses, of course, but there would also be more intricately woven, accordion-pleated lengths of palm that he used to make, I remember, little animals. I would play with these palm toys for hours, amazed by the ease with which he made them.

But the one thing I remember the most about my grandfather was a favorite joke of his he liked to play on me. If I came upon him sitting alone in a room, he would extend one leg and, feigning a terrible pain in it, would beg me to pull it, telling me that was the only way the pain would go away: "*Tida! Tida!*" Pull! Pull! And though I always knew what was coming, I would eagerly play the scene out, exactly as he said, and with total innocence every time. As I pulled hard on his leg he would, as he always did, fart. And we would both laugh and laugh. This ritual, the only game we ever played, was all that brought us together happily. In a world of few toys, I guess one made do with the natural world.

However, I wasn't to know my grandfather for long, for he would die of prostate cancer when I was still a boy. When he came home from the hospital after being operated on, he lay in one of the boys' beds in the big bedroom up-front. I accompanied my father up the stairs to the second floor to pay him our respects. But when my grandfather pulled the sheet back to show my father the scar from the operation—I, doing my boy's work of understanding my world, was naturally wide-eyed to see it—my grandfather, noticing my interest, told my father to send me out of the room. And my father did, closing the door behind me. But it was too late, for I had already caught a glimpse of his scar. I was shocked by the ugliness and rawness of it but mostly by the length of it. It went from the right side of his rib cage down into his abdomen and then over to his left side. That was the last time I saw my grandfather, for he died not too long after. Not having had a deep relationship with my grandfather and too young to understand the permanence of death, I was not moved by his death. However, the coming war would soon change that, and I would have my first lesson in the pain of death.

But it was with my grandmother that I happily spent most of my time in that big house on Thirty-fifth Street. Because she was called Mary, and my grandfather was called Joseph, which were Christ's parents' names, I always thought of them as the original biblical couple—my own Adam and Eve—for hadn't they started the first family, the only family I knew, on the new continent? And wasn't there a new child born every two years like clockwork? And my grandmother was religious enough to be biblical. Up every morning at five—bathed, her hair brushed and into its bun, wearing her churchgoing black dress with a pair of sensible black oxfords on her feet—she set off immediately for St. Anthony's, her local Roman Catholic Church, where she always attended the first Mass of the morning which was usually at six. And she did this, without fail, for as long as I knew her. No one else in our family was as religious as she was. Her American-born children, though they'd all had their First Holy Communion and Confirmation, were never as religious as she was. It made me wonder if her religion was just a matter of how she'd been raised. Or was it, because she so often prayed to St. Gennaro, the patron saint who protected against Vesuvius, that she was warding off the fate of her parents who had been killed by the fury of Mount Vesuvius? Whatever it was, she remained a daily supplicant all her life.

When I spent my highly anticipated two weeks with her during the summer, I often tagged along to Mass with her in the mornings. And though I was unused to the ceremonies of the Roman Catholic Church, I was immediately taken with it all: the beautiful stained glass windows, the exotic smell of the incense that created an otherworldly atmosphere, and the dramatic robes of the priests. I was particularly fascinated by the statues, those of the Virgin Mary and Joseph, but mostly those of Christ, especially of him on the cross, with nails through his feet and his hands and with blood pouring out of the wounds on his side. Transfixed I would stare at these statues for as long as I could and occasionally they would come alive and would smile at me.

When the bell rang for Holy Communion and my grandmother walked up to kneel at the marble balustrade, I dutifully followed her and kneeled right next to her, keeping my eyes on her so I could mimic every move she made. When the priest came along with the wafer and the wine, the body and blood of Christ, I closed my eyes and opened my mouth just as my grandmother did and accepted the wafer. And like her I mumbled a few incoherent words, hoping that I sounded as if I were speaking Latin. As we walked back to our pew, I played with the wafer with my tongue, enjoying how it stuck to the roof of my mouth just like the wrapper on the Christmas candy we always had that was called *torrone*. I didn't know, since I'd never had my first Holy Communion, that I was not supposed to partake in this sacrament of the Mass. And I'm sure my grandmother never realized that either. I'm sure she, the devout Catholic she was, just took it for granted that I'd had my First Holy Communion.

My grandmother also took me to my first church funeral. Before the Mass started, we walked up to the open coffin in front of the altar to pay our respects. Grandma leaned into the coffin and kissed the cheek of one of her neighborhood lady friends. Then she advised me to do the same, saying, "If you touch a dead body, you'll never be afraid of death." (My grandmother knew a lot of sayings. She had a proverb for every occasion, as did many of the Italians I knew who were born in the "old country." Even my mother who spoke fluent Italian so she could communicate with her parents—her younger siblings never did—surprised me all of her life with proverbs and sayings I'd never heard before, ones she had obviously learned as a child. I finally realized that it was how the people who had no access to schooling had educated themselves down through the centuries. And it was quite an education, too, for the proverbs taught you how to live a good life, something our educational system doesn't do.) Somewhat fearful, I did as she suggested and leaned into the coffin and kissed the woman on her cheek. The woman's skin was cold as stone and immovable. I had expected that. But what really struck me was that the woman had a very heavy mustache. That was strange. A woman with a mustache! I followed my grandmother back to our pew and while we waited for the Mass to begin, all I could think about was that strange mustache on that woman's face.

Immediately after Mass, my grandmother and I were off to the Central Market in downtown Cleveland, where she bought the food she needed to feed her large family. Undeterred by her own short stature, she would vigorously haggle with the merchants, the arteries on her neck bulging frighteningly while they pumped her blood to, I thought, the bursting point. She would tell them in a very loud and very determined voice exactly how much she'd pay for their goods, and no more. She was a tough customer. And when I accompanied her on these early morning marketing adventures, I would again be amazed that this woman who had just moments before been a dutiful, praying supplicant of Christ, her rosary beads clicking quickly through her fingers as she mumbled the Latin, was now berating the vendors and winning her price battles. Or I'd watch in amazement as she would pretend to speak no English on the bus if she didn't have the right amount of change for the fare. (She always kept her coins tightly wrapped and tied in a handkerchief, and opening that handkerchief up and removing the coins was painstaking and could take a lot of time.) But I knew she spoke excellent English, plus a good Italian and a couple of dialects. It was another lesson for me about the complexity of human beings.

I loved to bask in my grandmother's unspoken and unconditional love during my two-week summer stay in her big house. I would happily push myself into her apron while she stood preparing a meal at her old wooden-fired stove and then later at her gas one, letting her clothing envelope me in a warm combination of flour and eggs and whatever else she was preparing, an aromatic sensory gift that wafted over me as love. I can remember the smell and the warm comfort of that moment till today. And because she never criticized me, I would happily go anywhere with her and do whatever she wanted. How I enjoyed my position as the baby of the family, a joy that lasted for a glorious ten years.

Meals at my grandparents' home were usually simple, except, of course, for the holidays. With very little money and with six of her nine children still living at home, she made a lot of fried potatoes. There was a big cast-iron pan full of them every night. And I loved them. Sometimes there'd be chicken along with the potatoes or sausage. Or sometimes just potatoes with peppers and onions. And always a salad. My mother, being more modern and healthy minded for her family, only made baked potatoes. And not understanding the circumstances, I always wondered why my mother never made fried potatoes, which I came to think of as a treat. When my aunts, who had all taken home economics courses at Jane Adams High School so they could find employment in schools and institutions, came home from work, they'd always help their mother complete the dinner; and if it was summertime, they would invariably make a big wooden bucketful of fresh lemonade. Once dinner was over and the kitchen was cleaned and the dishes put away, my grandmother, after her long day on her feet, would climb the back stairs off the kitchen to her bedroom and would be in bed and asleep by nine, exhausted by her day.

(I loved my grandmother even more in my high school years, when she intervened one day between my mother and me. My aunts and uncles always rented a cottage on Lake Erie for two weeks of the summer, where they always let me stay with them for one of those two weeks. Mesmerized by the water, I spent the whole day at the water's edge, only going up to the cottage for meals. Determined to know how to swim, I threw myself into the water one day when no one was around and forced myself to swim out to a diving raft, where the water was way over my head. Soon after I'd accomplished that, I discovered the Cumberland Pool in Cleveland Heights. It, however, was a two-bus ride from our house; and I'd have to go by myself. My mother, worrying even more about me now that I could roam farther from home, was against it. Who'd watch me in the water? What if something happened? I begged and pleaded with her but to no avail. One summer day when my grandmother was visiting us to help my mother out, I again pleaded my case, and again my mother said no. But this time I had an ally. My grandmother understood a teenaged boy's needs and yearnings, and she broke through my mother's resistance. With her usual forthrightness she told my mother to let me go. "You can't keep him in the house all the time! It's wrong! Let him go!" And her insistence won the day. My mother let me go that day and every other summer day. She was a wise grandmother. Bless her.)

Once my grandmother had gone to bed and the kitchen was cleaned up, the fun would begin. My aunts and uncles, most of whom were still unmarried and living at home, were full of life and liked to enjoy themselves. They were like the characters in a Charles Dickens novel—fascinating, interesting, and complicated. I had to watch them closely to learn everything I could about the world of the "big people." Because they were a tightly knit family bound together by their number and poverty, they didn't need anyone else to have a good time; they had each other. I envied them their fun. It was another reason I so desperately wanted a brother. After dinner they would all adjourn to the big table in the dining room, where they would play cards—seven-card poker was a favorite—or to the living room where there would often be impromptu dance evenings. I loved those evenings the most.

As soon as the new console radio/record players came on the market, my aunt Florence, always up-to-date and attuned to what was stylish in America, bought one of the first ones. With the latest swing bands' 78-rpm hit spinning on the turntable, my uncles would roll back the carpets in the living room, move the furniture out into the hallway, and the jitterbugging would begin. They were all good dancers, but my uncle Dutch—his real name was Anthony, but I think he was called Dutch because he had once gotten himself into some innocent trouble during his youth—was the best of them. He was a real zoot-suiter, and he had all the moves. He could roll his sisters over his back and pull them through his legs. He was amazing. I would stand and watch from the hallway so I wouldn't get in the way and wouldn't get hit. They had the grand fun that makes a big family so desirable. And I was part of it all.

But it was the Christmas holiday that was the high point of my year. For that holiday, my aunts and uncles went all out. There was always a beautifully decorated tree that was so tall it touched the high ceiling in the living room, causing the yearly problem of how to get the ornament—the star or the angel—on the top of the tree. But somehow they always managed it. My aunt Florence was usually in charge of decorating the tree. One year she pleased my sister and myself by developing a new technique to replace the tedious one of placing the icicles on the tree one by one: she would throw them randomly at the tree, hoping to fill all the empty spaces. I was delighted by her experimentation. We had a great time that year, throwing the icicles at the tree. But the experiment turned out to be a little too messy, and we soon went back to the old tedious way.

When my sister and I arrived at Grandma's house on Christmas Eve, we would run immediately into the living room to see the many gifts under the tree. Because the family was so big and because everyone exchanged a gift with everyone else, there would always be at least a hundred gifts under the tree with many others spilling over onto the nearby floor and behind the furniture. My sister and I would immediately check all the gift cards to find our names.

But before we could open our gifts there would be the traditional Christmas Eve fish dinner, in symbolic deference to Christ himself. When my grandfather was still alive it was his holiday contribution to buy the fish. That meant an early visit on Christmas Eve morning to the main fish market in downtown Cleveland where he would fill a basket with a variety of fish, the traditional number of fishes for the Christmas Eve dinner being seven. My mother remembers that in the basket there would be squid, octopus, some smelts, other more non-descript fish and often, at the bottom of the basket, a few eels, which she wasn't found of. The *baccala*, the dried cod, which was the most important of the fishes for the evening meal, would have been purchased a few days earlier because its preparation took at least three days. I would always stare with concern at the flat V-shaped slab of dried cod as it sat in the kitchen. It looked like a piece of wooden board to me. How was it possible that we were going to eat that thing? But after it had been soaked for three days in water that was changed daily, that flat board was miraculously transformed into a thick white fleshy fish. That transformation was a miracle to me. It was always prepared with a delicious anchovy, black olive, and caper sauce—what today we call a puttanesca sauce, named, they say, after the whores, the *puttana* in Naples who would place a bowl of it in their windows to entice the men inside. But I never heard it called that then. It was just what had been prepared for generations and generations. When dinner was over, those who wanted to go to midnight Mass left. Grandma would always say, "Leave all the food on the table." When I asked her why, she would tell me, "So the angels who are going to visit while we are gone will feel welcome and will have something to eat."

Then when everyone returned home from church at about one thirty in the morning, the best part of the holiday would happen: the opening of the gifts. We always opened our gifts on Christmas Eve night, though it was really Christmas morning by then. For that special occasion my sister and I were allowed to stay up as late as necessary, however long it took to open all the many gifts under the tree, which sometimes meant until two or three in the morning. Though I loved the Christmas Eve dinner, my mind was always concentrating on the gifts under the tree. I could hardly wait to start ripping the paper off my gifts. My aunts and uncles always knew what I wanted: any book about dogs or horses and atlases, too, for I was fascinated about this world I had been born into and all the many places I could look forward to traveling to.

After all the gifts had been passed around for everyone to see and all the wrapping paper had been bagged and brought into the backyard and placed in the trash cans, my sister and I would load our cherished pile of carefully guarded gifts into the two biggest boxes we could find and take them out to our car. And in that silent and holy night of Christ's birth, we would head off for home. On the quiet trafficless streets of the city, with perhaps a light miraculous dusting of fresh snow falling, our car making virginal tracks in it, my sister and I settled comfortingly and warmly into the womblike backseats of our car with our gifts possessively arranged in the boxes at our feet, where we could look at them and appreciate them over and over. Looking out my window at the early morning dreamscape we passed through, oohing and ahhing at the festively lighted and decorated homes we passed, we made our deeply contented quiet journey home. Oh, the comfort and warm security of that early morning ride. I felt safe and sound as we drove home. The deep satisfaction of the holiday with its good food, the many treasured gifts, and the fun of being with my aunts and uncles and my grandmother would carry over into the rest of the year and would be the bridge of expectation to the festivities of the following year.

On Christmas morning, our small family of four would be up early to make the return trip to my grandmother's house for her Christmas Day dinner. Her preparations for this dinner would have begun days before. First she would have made her braciole, a thin slice of rolled beef stuffed with hard-boiled eggs, cheese, breadcrumbs, and parsley. I loved the surprise of it when you cut through the meat and revealed the hard-boiled egg inside. When we arrived there would already be two big pots full to the top with tomato sauce simmering on the stove. In one would be her braciole and in the other her meatballs and sausage. But she would wait till the early morning of Christmas to make her ravioli. And that was a favorite part of the Christmas Day meal for me because I was allowed to help her make the ravioli.

As soon as we arrived at her house I would run into the dining room, where I'd find her at her large dining table surrounded with all she needed to make her ravioli. There were the smooth rounded mounds of her homemade pasta that were waiting to be rolled out and flattened by the nearby old broom handle she preferred to use as a rolling pin. Also at the ready was the ricotta filling in a white plastic pot. And there was some white flour at hand to throw on the wooden table to prepare the space for rolling. My grandmother's ravioli were not the small ravioli we are used to today. Half-moon shaped and about five inches long on the straight side, two of them were a meal, three or four an overindulgence you wished later you'd avoided. Most of the family only ate one or two of them; they were, after all, a first course. But one year when I was a burgeoning teenager, when I could eat anything I wanted and still stay skinny, I ate thirteen of them. If I wasn't the most athletic boy in the family, I could at least take the prize for eating. And I am proud to say that my record still stands till today and will always stand, for now, with our family scattered all over the USA, there is no longer a central home to go to for a grandmother's wonderful Christmas Day dinners.

Immediately after she saw me, my grandmother would start to roll out a sheet of the dough. Then with her round cutter she would cut the first square, place a heaping tablespoonful of the ricotta filling in the middle of it, fold one half over on the other, trim the open-sided edges with her cutter into a more round shape, and then pass it to me. That's when I got to work. My job, which I had to do very carefully and methodically, for it was a most important one, was to press and seal the edges together all the way around with the tines of a fork. If I didn't do my job well and press the edges very tightly closed, the ravioli could come apart in the boiling water and spill all their contents, thereby ruining them. After finishing that, I would poke three sets of holes on the top of the ravioli with a fork so that the steam could escape and they wouldn't explode. My grandmother and I would make about fifty or more of these monster raviolis, which would take us two hours or more.

Christmas Day dinner would usually be about one or two o'clock in the afternoon. Along with the ravioli and the second course of meat, there would always be a large green salad with a vinegar and oil dressing and platters of olives, celery, fresh carrots, and my mother's popular pickled eggplants. When the food dishes were cleared, plates of Christmas cookies that held thirty or more different kinds—all the women in the family made them—would be placed on the table. My aunt Pauline, whose background was Slovakian, would always contribute a holiday heritage of hers: poppy seed rolls and walnut rolls, both of which I loved. And my mother always made two dozen or so of her wonderful cannoli. There were always bowls of fruit and platters of freshly roasted chestnuts, a cross cut deeply into them so they wouldn't explode in the oven, though I always thought the cross symbolized Christ and the holidays. And there was always a bowl of nuts and figs. My father would slice the dried figs in half and stuff them with shelled walnuts or almonds, an old Italian tradition that I loved. Naturally there had been some red wine with dinner, usually a friend or neighbor's, which was always passed around the table with great respect, for it was that very best thing: homemade. And then, of course, coffee for the adults and a glass of anisette.

My aunts and uncles—they were always called "the girls" and "the boys" by the family no matter how old they became—were all good and decent young people. Like most of the first-generation children of immigrant parents, they all hoped to enjoy the lives and opportunities that were just beginning for them in America. As soon as they graduated from high school they all immediately set off to find jobs—the girls looking stylish in their fashionable new wardrobes, the boys handsome in their new suits and ties. There was no self-pity, no crying about being born into poverty and into difficult times. And they approached everything with a great sense of humor. My aunt Theresa always looked very chic as she set off to Higbee's Department Store on the Public Square to work at our friend Jen's shoe repair shop on the third floor, taking in and marking the customers' shoes for repairs. She stayed there for years, always dressed in style thanks to her Higbee's discount, until she married.

My aunt Florence was a gifted seamstress. In her early twenties she taught sewing at the local YWCA. When her brother John married, she designed her own gown as the maid of honor. The design was unusual: it had triangular flying panels over the bottom skirt. I wasn't born yet, but I'd seen the photos of my uncle John's wedding and the famous dress. Higbee's department store wanted to buy the design from her for a hundred dollars so they could reproduce it, but for some reason she refused their offer. One day in my teen years, my parents bought me a longed-for new bed. And soon after, my aunt Florence came out to our house on the streetcar one late afternoon, carrying two big bolts of fabric, a dark green one and a matching checkered one, to make a pleated skirt and boxed cover for my bed. Without a pattern, she finished it all by the end of the night, even adding a beautiful rolled piping around the top edge of the mattress. I bought four small-framed Van Gogh reproductions for my bedroom wall, a new lamp for my dining table desk, and I was ready for the large amounts of homework I now had in high school. My aunt Florence was, I think, looking back now, the most capable of the girls; she could accomplish anything she set her mind to.

The boys all worked whatever jobs they could find: selling newspapers, shining shoes downtown in Public Square, selling whatever they could collect to the local "paper and rags man." Once, my uncle Frank, along with a friend of his, tore down a neighbor's new wooden fence so they could sell the wood. That time they were caught and were made to return the wood and rebuild the fence. My uncle Veto, the possessor of a very likable and smiling persona, started working at a young age at a local pharmacy doing whatever had to be done. As he got older, that "whatever" meant a little numbers running. The central office of the numbers racket in Cleveland was in a house that butted right up against the pharmacy and it could be accessed through a concealed hole at the back of the prescription department. Through that hole, Uncle Veto would slip the bets of the day. Sometimes his job even meant going into a local house of prostitution to take the ladies' bets. You did whatever you could in those days to make some money to bring home to your family. When my uncle Frank was older, he, too, worked at the pharmacy and then spent many years at the downtown YMCA, handing out towels and instructing the younger boys. In the summers he was a counselor for the YMCA camp. I longed to go to that camp but we couldn't afford it. However, if you saved an agreed upon very large amount of the state sales tax stamps, you could go to the camp free for two weeks. So all year long, all my aunts and uncles saved their state sales tax stamps and brought them to our house, where I kept them in a huge department store coat box that I kept under my bed. I checked that box constantly to see how I was doing. And when it was full, my uncle Frank took it downtown to the Y, where it was counted. And that was how I got to go to summer camp two years in a row. And I loved the experience. It was great to be with all those boys my own age, even if for so short a time.

Of course all of my aunts and uncles had their chores at home—the girls helping in the kitchen and doing the weekly laundry of which there was a great deal. One year, to make the ironing of the sheets an easier chore, they bought a mangle. I'd never seen one before and was fascinated by it and how it worked. Oh, they weren't going to miss a trick in this new country America. I adored them all and always looked up to them, hanging on their every word.

And then my safe, cozy, baby-of-the-family world abruptly changed. One night my father looked up from our evening paper, *The Cleveland Press*, and said, "Well, it looks like there's going to be war. That idiot in Italy and that other crazy one in Germany are going to start it." And start it they did. I was still little aware of the outside world. But that would change a year later on a Sunday when, our store closed and our midafternoon dinner over —the date was December 7, 1941 —we gathered around our big cathedral-shaped radio in our living room and listened to the president of the United States, Franklin Delano Roosevelt, announce that the Japanese had attacked Pearl Harbor early that morning at 1:20 PM, Washington DC time. Now I could tell, from the looks on my parents' faces, that the ground under us had shifted and that no one knew when or how it would settle. Three days later Mussolini declared war on the United States. And we were in a world war.

It seemed to me, a boy who knew nothing of the deeper implications of war, that we had all slipped with amazing ease into an acceptance of World War II. I don't remember anyone questioning what had to be done. There was no talk in our household of isolationism or any anger or cursing of the powers that be. Just once I heard my father refer to Mussolini as a *buffone*, a clown, a laughing stock; but I never heard anymore talk of that or of staying out of the fight as the pacifists wanted. No, the conflict was immediately accepted in our family with the fatalism of a people long used to the struggle against adversity. It was what had to be. And this clear moral imperative of World War II created a great spirit of community across the land as everyone dug in and did their duty, all to the swinging music of the day: Glenn Miller's orchestra playing "Chattanooga Choo Choo" and Jimmy Dorsey's group swinging and singing through "Green Eyes." Pop songs told you everything you needed to know then. It promoted the philosophy of our monoculture, for there was no divide in those times among the generations in America. Everyone, the young and old, had their spirits lifted up and guided by the music of the day. The people of the country felt good about themselves, felt good about the sacrifices they were making for the war effort and for their loved ones serving and fighting across the seas. This grand pulling together made everyone proud. It was certainly a better feeling than the down-and-out one of the Depression, which the war would soon end.

One of the immediate changes would be the rationing of food and fuel, basic necessities needed for the war effort. Everyone would soon have a sticker on their car windshield—A, B, or C—indicating to the gas station attendant how much gas you were allowed weekly. We had an A sticker because my father needed to use his car to buy what we sold in our store, where we now had to collect coupons and little red penny-sized cardboard coins from our customers, keeping them within their limits of buying. These coupons and red coins we then had to turn over to the proper authorities.

In our backyard my sister started a Victory garden, a project initiated by the public school system so that families all across the country could grow their own vegetables, allowing what was produced by the farmers of the country to be shipped overseas to our fighting boys.

And my beloved grandmother—my illiterate grandmother who had spent her lifetime caring for her nine children, hoping always to avoid any outside attention so as not to tempt the fates—my modest, hardworking grandmother who had five sons, would lose four of them to the war. My uncles Paul, Veto, John, and Anthony were all the right age and were immediately drafted into the army. And in quick succession, one after the other, they received their orders to report to basic training and would leave by train from the main railroad station under the Terminal Tower in downtown Cleveland. I was very proud of our city's Terminal Tower. I knew the main facts about it by heart. It had been built in 1930, it was 708 feet tall, and had fifty-two stories and an observation deck. It was said that on a clear day from that observation deck you could see Canada across Lake Erie. But most important to me was that it was the seventh tallest building in the United States and that the first six tallest buildings were all in New York City. And that made Cleveland the second most up-to-date city in the country. So I was excited to see my uncles off in that very building.

The trip downtown to the Terminal Tower took forty-five minutes from our home in the Mount Pleasant area. The crowds on the train platforms were enormous, a powerful crush of families and young recruits with their duffel bags all joined emotionally by the same circumstances. It was just like one of those epic scenes in a Cecil B. DeMille movie. Fearful of being pushed off the platform, I stayed close to my family. Everyone in the family, except my grandmother who preferred to say her good-byes to her sons at home, made those trips.

The first to leave was my uncle Paul. He was the oldest of the boys, very tall and handsome and generally considered the smartest of the boys, for he was really adept at numbers. He was also a born speed-reader. He would come to our house, pick up one of my mother's recent novels, and read it in one sitting. I wished I could do that. He also had the knack for being able to talk to anyone, which would help him in his future work as an insurance salesman.

The second to leave was my personable uncle Veto. He would wind up in the Eighty-second Airborne Division. Next to leave was my uncle John. He was a well-known Golden Gloves champion boxer in the middleweight division. He even looked like a boxer, with the same rough, strong face and the massive hands that Joe Louis had. Under aliases, he often fought from Cleveland to Chicago and towns in between. He was famous in Cleveland for a fight at the Arena in which he and his opponent knocked each other out at the same time! But because my uncle John was the first to get up, he won the fight.

On the night before he left for the army, Uncle John took a streetcar out to our house on 144th Street for the sole purpose of bringing my sister and myself a pair of roller skates each. I was so happy to receive those skates. I had very few toys to play with when I was a boy, so the skates were like a gift of gold to me. That night before he left our house, my uncle John promised me that when he came back from the war he would teach me all the boys' games I needed desperately to know. I couldn't wait for him to return home from the war, for he was going to be my savior and keep me from being called that dreaded word: *sissy*. While I waited anxiously for that day, I quickly taught myself how to skate and went zooming up and down our street for hours and hours.

The last to depart, at least we thought he would be the last, was my uncle Dutch. Not only was he the best dancer in the family, but he was also the best storyteller and the one with the best sense of humor. Once when I told him I wanted a wristwatch, he pulled up his shirtsleeve, exposing five or six watches, and let me pick the one I wanted. Could that be why he was sometimes called Mooch?

My uncle Frank, the youngest child of the family and only six years older than I, was too young for the conflict. But he would still pay a price for the war. With all the older boys gone and no money coming in to keep the house going, Uncle Frank was told he had to quit school and get a job. He had just begun high school, and he wanted to graduate just as his brothers and sisters had. They all had their high school diplomas, except for the firstborn, of course—my mother. But his father laid down the law, and he had to do as he was told. And the unfairness of it, the injustice of it, made him resentful; and it would stick in his craw for the rest of his life. So the war, which was just beginning, had taken its first casualty in our family. Years later I would find a V-Letter from my uncle Veto, written during the war, telling his sisters to "be sure Frank finishes high school." But my grandparents needed money coming in more than they needed their last boy educated. As for serving his country he would get his chance to do that in the Korean War.

Then in 1942, Congress created the Women's Army Auxiliary Corps. Soon after, my aunt Florence—she was twenty-three years old at the time—appeared at home in her new tan WAAC outfit, an enlisted woman's cap smartly cocked over one eye. She had decided to do her duty too. The family was shocked. She had not told anyone of her plan. Why had she done it? What had made her enlist? I always sensed there was a defiance in her, a prickliness, a chip-on-her-shoulder attitude. She often repeated a favorite saying of the time that expressed exactly how she felt: "If you don't like my peaches, don't climb my tree!" In other words, don't mess with me. She'd always been competitive with her brothers too. She had an anything-they-can-do-I-can-do attitude, and she could too. She could play baseball as well as they could, she could beat them at card games, she could talk as loudly as them, and she could smoke and swear as well too, her favorite swear word being "shiiiit," the vowel of which she liked to elongate. She even beat them all by becoming the best swimmer in the family, cultivating a strong, almost robotic, competitive form in the water—one they never had. Still that didn't explain her enlisting. One family member thought she had enlisted because her strict father had refused to let her marry the man who'd asked her, because he'd been married before and had children. And that had so angered her she decided she just wanted out. I wasn't ever sure of her reason. But she was a natural. And she had … and was proud to show me … the best military salute of all her siblings; no one matched the sharpness with which she brought her arm up to her cap.

I liked her a lot because she was more curious and adventurous than her siblings and certainly more so than her sisters. In 1939 she had traveled to New York City to visit the World's Fair. I have a treasured photo of her standing with a male friend in front of the Trylon and Sphere, confronting the camera in a nifty tailored white dress that came down just above her ankles, with a matching light-colored jaunty hat that poked the air defiantly like the new buildings around her. When the Ringling Bros. and Barnum & Bailey Circus was in town, she was the one who took my sister and me to it every year. One time she bought herself an upright piano and started taking lessons. I was eager to take piano lessons too, but my father wouldn't buy me a piano. He didn't think I would stick with it. So whenever I was at my grandmother's house, I would spend hours picking out melodies by ear on Aunt Florence's piano. And I would respect her more when I heard in later years that she had been the only one of her siblings who had the nerve to stand up to her father when he hit her brother Frank. "If you hit him again," she finally told her father, "I'm going to call the cops! And they'll put you in jail!" From that day on my grandfather thought twice about ever hitting his youngest son again. She was something.

With four sons and one daughter in the conflict, my unassuming grandmother was now a five gold-star mother, a rarity in those times. Her picture, with her sitting stoically in her "good black dress," her gray hair pulled straight back into her constant bun, and posed under the five-star flag hanging in her living room window—you could see the ancestral acceptance of fate on her face—would appear in both the *Cleveland Press* and the *Cleveland Plain Dealer*. My grandmother was a celebrity, though a reluctant one to be sure.

The country was never more united. Like all children in the public schools, I believed strongly in the melting pot philosophy that was taught then. If pop songs expressed everyone's feelings, then the good, decent morality of the movies that we all went to see three times a week told us that we were all the same, no matter our skin color or our religion or our different cultural backgrounds. We all celebrated America and felt good about ourselves, about the sacrifices we were making for the benefit of mankind and for our loved ones across the seas. To a young first-generation Italian-American boy, with four uncles and one aunt in the service, it was necessary to believe. And I did with all my heart.

And our family, just like the country, became united and swung into action on the home front. My mother and her two other sisters, Theresa and Viola, and Viola, my uncle Paul's wife (we called her Big Vi, not because of her size, but to differentiate her from the younger Viola), and sometimes John's wife, Margie, and Uncle Veto's intended, Pauline, would arrive at our home, their arms filled with all kinds of goodies: cigarettes, pipe tobacco, shaving blades, candy, lots of home-baked cookies—the chocolate chip and oatmeal ones usually made by my mother—all meant for their four brothers and their one sister in the war. There was even an occasional birthday cake at the appropriate time of the year, a daredevil attempt to test the questionable military postal service, an attempt which actually worked on more than one occasion when the cake arrived at its overseas secret APO destination in more or less one piece and still edible. All this abundance would be laid out to the edges of our kitchen table, opened up, of course, to its full size to accommodate everything. And there would always be an overflow of goodies onto the chairs and the sideboard. It was unlike anything I had ever seen. It was a child's fantastical sweet dream come true, a cornucopia of treats and surprises. This family ritual took place once every month for the duration of the war.

I, of course, watched from the edge of this magnificence, eager-eyed and sorely tempted. Besides the cookies there were Baby Ruth candy bars, Clark bars, and a brand-new candy that was my favorite: M&Ms. I liked holding them in my hand for a long time, allowing the heat of my body to warm them, and melt the bright primary colors off into my palm. Then I would pop them into my mouth, holding them there and letting the outside melt away, releasing the soft, chocolaty interior—their luxurious reward.

All of this bounty spread out before me was almost better than all the wonderful gifts and goodies at Christmas time. And while my mother and her sisters separated and packed these packages—four to their brothers in the European conflict and one to their sister in Amarillo, Texas—I watched and prayed for any crumb that might come my way, and I would say, "Boy! I wish I was in the war! Look at what you get!" And my mother and my aunts would always hush me. "Don't say that!" Then when no one was looking, my aunt Viola would sneak me a tollhouse cookie or some M&M's. But that was all I ever got. Everything was for the boys fighting and for their sister doing her duty for the war effort too. During the war my father also sent an occasional package of his own to his family in Southern Italy. His packages were mostly filled with clothing and blankets, items they needed desperately.

The battle was now raging full force in Europe, and all my uncles were in the thick of it, though we didn't know exactly where that was, their whereabouts being classified information. It was only after the war that we would find out where they had been stationed. My uncle Paul, because of his quickness with numbers, saw action in France where he was a sergeant in the artillery. His job was to calculate arithmetically the angle at which the big guns had to be adjusted so they could hit their target dead-on.

Uncle Veto was with the intelligence unit of the Eighty-Second Airborne Division. Early in the war his company was forced to leave him behind in Africa, believing he had been lost on a forward intelligence mission. Determined to return to his company, he walked a great distance to a port on the Mediterranean, where he found a ship to take him to Sicily and then another one to take him to Italy, where, walking up the Italian coast, he miraculously found his way back to his own outfit. Later in the war, in the great push to invade Europe, he was released by glider into Holland, where unfortunately on September 23, 1944, when his glider crashed into a tree and was shot up by the Germans, he was captured and became a prisoner of war in a German camp near the Polish border. My uncles rarely talked of their experiences in the war when they came home, so it was only years later that I learned that while my uncle and a good friend of his were sitting in the glider's opening waiting to land, his friend had been strafed in his midsection, ripping his abdomen open, spilling his guts out into his hands and killing him instantly. My uncle could do nothing to help him. For his part in the war, he would receive two Bronze Stars.

Uncle John, the Golden Gloves champ, was a combat engineer stationed in Germany, building bridges across the Rhine River. And my uncle Dutch, the best dancer and storyteller of all the boys, was with the Eighty-Fifth Division that landed south of Naples near Anzio and Salerno, hoping to march quickly up to Rome. But the German soldiers were well entrenched, and at a soon-to-be-famous abbey founded in 529 by St. Benedict, Monte Cassino, the allied forces found themselves, at the end of 1943, in a deadly stalemate after a brutal series of battles. Finally the Allied generals ordered the abbey bombed. Uncle Dutch helped pull some of his wounded friends to safety and was awarded a Purple Heart and a Bronze Star.

And my aunt Florence, doing her duty stateside, was a telephone operator first in Amarillo, Texas, and then in Boys Town, Nebraska. The US Army had figured wisely that this sharp, snappy woman would be an excellent switchboard operator. And they were right. Loving the exactness of it, the clipped pronunciations, the way in which certain numbers and words were to be elongated, like the number *nine* which could become three or even four syllables when pronounced, she took to it immediately. Of course she found the humor in that and was only too happy to demonstrate her technique to me on her first leave home. One Christmas during the war, she sent the family a record she'd made in one of the new recording booths that were a novelty at the time. Its new technology produced a vinyl record about five inches in diameter with a recorded message on one side. But my aunt Florence's message was not the usual yuletide greeting. The whole recording was her singing just two words, *pine tree*, over and over again—she was in the Pine Tree State after all—to the tune of "God Bless America." That was it. No "Merry Christmas" message, no "Happy New Year" greeting, just the words "pine tree, pine tree-ee-ee" sung and elongated for the whole song. The family thought it weird. They didn't get it. They thought it was their sister's usual odd behavior. I thought it was funny. It was pure nonsense, gibberish, like *Alice in Wonderland*, and maybe a kind of honest response to the horror and stupidity of war. Because no one wanted the record, I kept it. It was another piece of the puzzle of adult behavior.

The war continued, but it was not going to be over as soon as our leaders had promised. The packages continued to be sent out monthly to my uncles, who, in return, wrote their many letters of thanks, telling how much everyone else in their company also enjoyed them and waited for them. (I would get my turn to be the recipient of my mother's wonderful packages in the '60s, when I was stationed with the US Army in Germany. And just as my uncles and my aunt had enjoyed and shared with their barracks mates the packages from their sisters during WWII, so did my barracks buddies enjoy my packages during the peacetime years that were sent by my mother.)

Back home we did our best to continue the family traditions. We still went on our wonderful Sunday summer picnics, sometimes to Fell Lake but more often to a beach on Lake Erie, though now it was my father and Big Aunt Vi who drove the cars. And we still celebrated the Christmas holiday at my grandmother's house though now it was a bit more muted. There was no longer the beautifully decorated tree that always touched the ceiling nor were there the hundreds of gifts spilling out all over the living room floor, though my grandmother continued to make her huge ravioli.

As soon as we had addresses where we could write to our uncles and our aunt, my sister and I began a steady correspondence with them for the duration of the war. And it was always a great event when we received a letter from them. One day I saw an opened letter from my uncle John lying on my sister's dressing table. I quickly pulled it out of its envelope, eager to read what he had to say. It was written on January 3, 1944, at "10:30 AM Monday morning." It was addressed to "My dearest niece: Angela-" After a bit of news—he'd been in the hospital for a stomach problem but was now all right and was hoping that we were all right and a promise to my sister for a pair of Ice Skates when he got home—I turned the page to read the following:

> *I don't think Sonny is a sissy. When he grew [sic] older he'll be all right. I miss you and him very much.*

I was stunned. There was that dreaded word: *sissy*. Though I had always been aware of my lack of athletic ability, I had never fully applied the word to myself. But seeing it now written and used in connection with me made it real and true. That's who I am, I thought, a sissy. Children all over America knew the response to a painful word: "Sticks and stones may break my bones, but names will never harm me." But that couplet was only an attempt to deflect the truth, for as all children really know, words *can* harm and *can* hurt even more than sticks and stones. The physical injuries can heal, but the name calling never does.

What hurt the most was that I knew that all I needed was someone to help me, to teach me the games. There was nothing wrong with me physically. I was tall and I was well coordinated. I just needed help from a person unlike my father (who didn't know the games anyway), someone who wouldn't be critical of me, who would be patient with me, and then I could learn the games quickly. But I had never found that person. So I was pinning all my hopes on my uncle John, for not only was he the best athlete in the family, he had also promised to teach me all the games I needed to know before he had left for the war, even boxing. But there was that dreaded word in black and white. I guess everyone knew that I was a sissy. That was how they thought of me. It was like being made permanent. That's who I was. At the bottom of his letter to my sister, there was a note to me:

"Jan 3 – 1944 Monday morning 10:40 a.m."
"Dearest Sonny=Nephew: -
How are you boy. I hope you are fine. How did Santa Claus
treat you.
Is there anything you want. When I come home let me know.
Good-bye and take care of yourself.
Love
Your Uncle Always
Johnny

I have that letter still. It was the only letter I had saved from the many I'd received from my uncles and my aunt during the war. And that told me of its importance to me as a boy. Though life had gone on and new territories had been achieved, that letter had hurt me deeply.

When the big Allied invasion of Germany began, it finally looked as if the ending of the war might be in sight. So far my five gold-star grandmother had been 100 percent lucky; all of her sons in the battle were still alive. But one day toward the end of the war, she told one of her daughters that she had had a vision of Christ on the second-floor landing of her home. He said to her, "You have all your children now, but soon you won't." A few days later a military letter arrived from the headquarters of the 249th Engineer Combat Battalion. It was dated July 16, 1945. It said that my uncle John—the Golden Gloves champ, the one most physically fit and probably the strongest and the one I was most counting on to teach me all the sports games I didn't know—had died on March 24, 1945. The cause of death was "by drowning." The formal letter went on to say that his boat had capsized, and in the struggle among the many prisoners and their guards, he had somehow drowned. His body was not found immediately, but when it was later recovered, he was buried in Bensheim, Germany.

The family found it hard to believe the circumstances of Uncle John's death as detailed in the army's letter. They felt sure the German prisoners of war, whom he was ferrying across the Rhine River in rubber rafts, had started an ambush in an attempt to escape and had knocked him unconscious, thrown him overboard into the water, where he had drowned. In fact, an American soldier who lived in Cleveland told my mother that he himself had seen the Germans hit John and knock him out. But there was no official word of that. And there never would be. The irony was that the war, for all intents and purposes, was over. The German defeat would be announced in three weeks. For my uncle John to have lived through all the years of battle and then drown in suspect circumstances was tragic, of course, but also senseless. Because his body had not been recovered from the water immediately, it had greatly decomposed and was difficult to identify. And when his remains were shipped home at the request of my grandmother, there was an accompanying letter informing my grandmother that it was indeed her son, for they had been able to identify him by his dental work. At the funeral home his coffin was closed. Some members of the family weren't convinced it was Uncle John's body. But the family had no choice but to take the army's word for it.

My uncle John's funeral was the first funeral of my life to hit me hard. And it took me totally unawares. While sitting with my family on wooden folding chairs at the funeral home and staring at my uncle's coffin—that closed box of such terrible certainty at the center of everyone's attention—I began to sob, quietly at first and then uncontrollably. Not one of my family members was crying; they were all dry-eyed. I was the only who was crying. Embarrassed by my open sobbing I got up and moved away from my family and sat at the far back of the funeral parlor by myself, where I continued to cry. Most of my family let me be. It was only my aunt Viola who occasionally turned around to look at me. She was concerned.

Oddly enough, I had no idea why I was crying so hard. I wouldn't have been able to explain to anyone if I'd been asked. It would be years before I would realize what I was feeling, though my body and my heart knew. My savior was dead. The uncle I had counted on to teach me all the games I needed desperately to know was not coming home. And I was devastated. I had placed all my hopes on him returning. He was going to make everything better for me. And now it wasn't going to be. I'd lost my longed-for mentor, my role model, my substitute father figure, who had cared so much for me that on his last night at home before going off to the war he had made a special trip out to our home to bring me a pair of roller skates. And though I could not articulate it, my heart realized for the first time in my life, that nothing lasts, that life is a betrayal of experience, that no one can be trusted to be there. And, all alone—I can still see myself—I sat in the back of that funeral parlor, grieving and sobbing my heart out till it was time to leave.

Soon, at the train station under the Terminal Tower, where I had watched all my uncles and my aunt depart, I now watched them all one-by-one, return from the war. Would they be changed, I wondered. Would the war, the fighting, the killing, my uncle Veto's prison camp experience, have made them different forever? Would the holidays at Grandma's house no longer be the same? From the foot of the banister in my grandmother's home, that banister I had slid down so many times, an aunt or uncle catching me at the bottom, I watched my uncle Veto see for the first time in four years his beautiful blonde-haired fiancé, my aunt-to-be, Pauline. She had not come to the train station to see him arrive, preferring to greet him alone. And when my uncle Veto and I came through the front door of the house on Cedar Avenue and he saw his sweetheart waiting at the top of the stairs, he immediately dropped his duffel bag and ran up those stairs three at a time. When he reached her, they embraced and kissed for a long time. It was like watching my own homecoming scene from *The Best Years of Our Lives*. How happy they were! How happy we all were! My uncle Veto, claustrophobic from his prisoner-of-war experience, would sometimes have to get off a streetcar quickly because he couldn't stand being closed in. And for months after, whenever he came to our house, we would immediately place a big bowl of vanilla ice cream in front of him. It was the one thing he had missed desperately in the prisoner-of-war camp where he and his friends had all existed on a diet of potato peelings.

Everyone did their best to swing back into the peacetime world with determination and energy. Because we had sacrificed and won, there came over everyone in our country a complete feeling of euphoria that once more connected all the people of the land in a joyful embrace. Everyone was lifted up, this time to the upbeat tune of the Andrew Sisters singing their somewhat salacious big hit "Rum and Coca-Cola." The war was over, as was the Depression, we were young, and there was a new country to build and lives to restart.

My uncle Paul picked up his marriage to my always easygoing Big Aunt Vi, and he became a successful insurance salesman after turning down an offer from the FBI, who had been wooing him to join their ranks. The FBI liked that he knew Cleveland well and that he went into every neighborhood with ease. But he decided to stay with the insurance business.

Uncle Dutch had hurt his back in the fighting to regain Monte Cassino, and true to form, on his first night at our home, he turned his battlefield injury and the Purple Heart he had been awarded into a funny story. He claimed his injury happened when, to avoid enemy fire, he had quickly jumped over a stone wall and right up to his neck in a huge pile of manure. I was glad to know that the best storyteller in the family had not lost his sense of humor. He would continue to live at the house on Thirty-fifth and Cedar and would slowly ease his way back into civilian life with a monthly disability check. He even received a monthly stipend for his underwear, which amused everyone. And eventually, for he was in no hurry, he found a job. And my wonderful aunt Florence, my sassy aunt Florence, returned from Texas, looking fit and sharp as always and quickly found a job too.

Soon on the weekends, the carpet in the living room would be rolled back once more, and the jitterbugging would begin again. Oddly enough, Uncle Dutch's back seemed much improved. Then the first Christmas holiday after the war returned too, with the wonderful food and the piles of gifts under the tree that once more touched the ceiling. The summer picnics were back to their robust size now and included, until she married again, my uncle John's wife, Margie. There would be a wondrous spread of plenty at the picnics: platters of the usual cold cuts, loaves of Italian bread, Mom's wonderful pickled eggplant that was fermented in a big crock in our basement, potato salad with the sharp bite of pickles in it, deviled eggs, peppers in olive oil, and, of course, cakes and pies. All of this laid out on a wooden picnic table, its cloth flapping in the delicious summer breeze, just as it had five years before.

And there would now be wonderful parties at our home again. One night a watermelon fight erupted out of nowhere. It started when my aunt Theresa left the kitchen for a while and someone with a slice of watermelon in his or her hands waited behind a door for her to return. When she did, that person shoved the watermelon in Aunt Theresa's face. In seconds all hell broke loose as everyone picked up pieces of watermelon and threw it at everyone else. Soon there were chunks of watermelon rinds and seeds ankle deep all over our kitchen floor. The place was a mess. But it was a good way to get over the past five years, to release some pent-up war fears, and to be thankful that all their siblings but one had returned safely.

Because the family was so big there would always be two seatings at our table. The women would serve the men their coffee and cake first—the cake was usually one of my mother's "from scratch" cakes, most often a chocolate cake with a walnut sprinkled, coffee-flavored icing—and then, when the men finished and retired to the living room to talk, the women would sit down and enjoy their coffee and cake leisurely. These were always wonderful evenings of talk and jokes and lots of laughter.

With everyone working now and settled into their new lives, it wasn't long before a happy time of marriages began. My uncle Veto married his lovely Pauline, and they moved into the downstairs parlor room next to the living room until they could afford their own place, which happened soon since both of them were working. Soon after, my aunt Theresa married a good-looking young man named Jim Rebar, who shocked our Italian family by liberally pouring ketchup all over his breakfast eggs. And then my aunt Viola, still my prettiest and favorite aunt, married a local man who was known to the family because he ran a nearby bar his father owned. He had been a sailor in the war and had spent his service time on a destroyer in the Pacific. His name was Ray, and in his sailor uniform, which he wore instead of a tux on his wedding day, he looked as handsome as Victor Mature and had a movie-star physique and smile to match. They were a beautiful couple. I was so happy to have all my family back together again. I couldn't wait for the Christmas holidays that first year after the war. I knew it was going to be the best.

First though, I was looking forward to my two-week summer vacation at my grandmother's house. My aunt Viola and my new uncle Ray were living there now, so I knew it would be a good vacation. Uncle Ray had quickly become a member of the family. He was fun, as I knew he would be. And it was immediately clear that he wasn't going to be a quiet in-law, laid-back and politely waiting his turn in our lively and boisterous family. Oh no, he jumped right in. At our house, instead of observing the family's male bonding time in the living room after having been served their coffee and cake in the "first shift" by the women, he would join the girls for their second shift of coffee and cake. Crossing his legs like them, smoking his cigarette in an overly exaggerated feminine way, joining in the gossip, he made the evening a lot of fun. And what made his behavior more amusing was that he was so obviously a very masculine man. He kept everyone in stitches. And he did something even more amazing: he listened to me, a kid, and even spent time talking to me and telling me things as if I were one of his best friends. One day at Grandma's house, when I asked him how you shifted gears in a car, he took me outside right away to where his new maroon Chevy coupe was parked and, putting me behind the steering wheel, coached me in the proper synchronization of the clutch and the accelerator. Patiently he talked me through the process of pressing down on one while easing off of the other. Because he wasn't critical, like my father, I got it in no time at all. So like many in the family I was immediately taken with him. Maybe, I thought, I had gotten lucky; and this new uncle would be the replacement for my uncle John. Maybe he would be the male friend I had always searched for, the one I could talk to, the one who would teach me all the things I wanted to know, the one to have adventures with, to learn things from.

By the time summer came and I left for my two-week vacation at my grandmother's house, my aunt Viola was very obviously pregnant with her first child. I had known all about the differences between the sexes for many years because of the secret times I'd spent with my next-door neighbor behind her garage. All it took for me to figure it out was one look at her private parts and one look at mine and it all became immediately clear. It was simple. So of course I knew why my aunt Viola's stomach was so big. But my parents, not knowing I knew the facts of life, discreetly left a book on the desk in our living room that explained the birds and the bees to a young person. I, of course, in my constant search for clues in the world of the big people, found the book and read it, using it to fill in the more technical gaps in my sexual education. Then I put it back where I'd found it, and days later it was gone. My parents must have breathed a sigh of relief that they had done their duty. I was amused at their innocence.

One night during that first two-week vacation after the war, my uncle

Ray and I shared our first secret. While my aunt Viola and my grandmother were busy in the kitchen preparing dinner, Uncle Ray asked me to go into the cellar with him. Though I never ventured into that dark place alone, I knew I was safe with my new best friend, so I followed him immediately, sure he had something interesting to show me. In the pitch-black at the bottom of the stairs, Uncle Ray pulled on the string of the sole light bulb hanging there. He walked forward, opened the door of the toilet at the bottom of the stairs, revealing its only object—a commode, and then stepped inside the toilet. I didn't know what I was supposed to see, so I just waited in the doorway of the toilet. Without a word spoken Uncle Ray unzipped the fly of his pants, pulled out his penis, and immediately began to move his hand back and forth on it. And within a very short time, something—a liquid I guessed—shot out and hit the wall behind the toilet seat. Having never seen a male ejaculate before I was surprised. And that was it. I followed him back up the stairs and into the kitchen where we sat down to our dinner. And not a word was ever said about what we had just done. I was still a year or so away from puberty, but I knew enough to know that what Uncle Ray had just shown me was not meant for casual conversation. And that made me realize that he and I now had an intimate secret of our own to keep. Uncle Ray never asked me to keep our secret. He didn't have to, for he knew he had already won me over. Having witnessed on any number of occasions my difficult relationship with my father, he sensed I was an easy mark. And he was right; I was an easy mark. I would keep our secret forever.

Soon, fully enjoying our secret intrigue, I began to share more of my secrets with Uncle Ray. One night after a party at our home when everyone was leaving, just like spies I had seen in the movies do, I slipped a note into his hand when we shook hands. I told him of my sexual explorations with the girl next door. We were strengthening our bond of secrecy every time we met. *Dice Niente*. Unbeknownst to everyone, an insidious form of evil clothed in charm, humor, and attractiveness had entered our family.

Within that year, when my first cousin who was nicknamed Junior was born to my aunt Viola and uncle Ray, my decade-long reign as the baby of the family ended. The next cousin born soon after was Sue Ann, the only child my uncle Paul and aunt Vi would have. And then my cousin John, named of course after the brother lost in the war, was born to my aunt Theresa and uncle Jim. I totally enjoyed playing with all my new cousins and was happy to give up my long-held position in the family. Now at Christmas time, all the children, me included, would have our own table. That would make the holidays even more fun.

The next summer when I spent my two-week vacation at my grandmother's house, my cousin Junior was old enough to be wheeled in his stroller to the bar where his father worked. Off we went one warm day, enjoying ourselves while we performed an errand: we brought Uncle Ray his bagged lunch that his wife had prepared. And there, because there were few customers in the bar at that time of day, Uncle Ray again instigated a masturbatory incident with me. Leaving Junior in the care of his bartender, he asked me to come behind the bar and into the toilet. While keeping one eye on the traffic in the bar to be sure no one would discover us, he exposed himself. Now though, he invited me to do the same. I, of course, did as he asked. I would do anything he asked me to do. I was now very close to the treacherous precipice puberty, a time when all sexual experiences were magnified and habit-forming. But I knew nothing of that then. As he had done before, he began to masturbate, though now he did so while glancing at my still-unresponsive penis. And as the time before, he very quickly climaxed. Soon after my cousin Junior and I returned to my grandmother's house. I was a quick study and, not too long after, I achieved my first climax myself, brought on by masturbation. I now knew what to do. Still I never told anyone of what Uncle Ray and I had done together. That was our secret. *Dice niente*. But our secret would reverberate down the years.

The changes in everyone's life after the war had been absorbed and made part of the normal. My mother still continued to prepare her wonderful meals despite her long store hours and my father would work double shifts at the steel mill whenever the opportunity arose so he could make the extra money. My sister spent many hours more than required at school, involved in her many extracurricular activities. I had a little more homework to do but nothing that wasn't easy for me to do. And I started to act in plays at school. We still went to my grandmother's house for Easter Sunday dinner and for Christmas Eve and Christmas Day celebrations. And all my aunts and uncles would do their best to make those days special. Everything was going along well.

Not so surprisingly, though, it was my aunt Florence who bucked the tide. Not too long after she returned home from the service, she began to exhibit strange behavior. I still listened attentively for those quick moments of information about the characters in my family's novel, those moments that happened out of nowhere and were gone as fast. What I was able to glean about my aunt Florence from the odd bits of conversation here and there was that late one afternoon, when she returned home from her new job in downtown Cleveland, she had arrived confused and frightened. When questioned by her brother Veto, who luckily happened to be home, she told him that strangers had been following her, stalking her, and that they were all speaking to her at once in a babble of loud voices. He and his siblings hoped it would be a one-time occurrence. But that wasn't to be. Soon her frightening voices followed her every day. They told her she was a bad person. She became paranoid and fearful of leaving the house. But the danger was there too. One day in the second-floor bedroom she screamed at one of her sisters, "LIE DOWN! THEY'RE LOOKING AT US!" But her sister saw no one out the window.

In one of those fleeting family moments, I thought I heard that Aunt Florence had met an officer while she was in the WAACS, that she had fallen in love with him and wanted to marry him. Did I hear right that his name was Steve? And he, though already married, had promised her he would get a divorce and marry her when the war was over. I must have heard correctly because years later I was told that one day she had taken my infant cousin Junior in his stroller to the Terminal Tower, pretending she was taking him to visit his father at his bar. She had been in touch with Steve and asked him to meet her there on the observation deck. And he had agreed to do so. When they met she told him that Junior was his son and that if he didn't marry her she would throw his child over the edge of the building. The observation deck of the Terminal Tower is forty-two floors up in the air. Steve must have realized that my aunt Florence was having mental problems, and he somehow got her back down to the street, my cousin Junior intact, and managed to get them both safely home. I don't think she ever saw or heard from Steve again. Still her voices continued. She could no longer close the door against them. Wherever she went now they were always there inside her head. Alarmed, her brothers and sisters made inquiries and, with everyone in the family pitching in to pay the bill, took her to a private doctor. But her case was a tough one. The first doctor she saw told her sisters and brothers that she was "tight as a clam" and would not tell them anything. *Dice niente.*

No longer able to work she spent her days and nights reading late and sleeping late, a pattern that would stay with her for the rest of her life. And smoking. She always smoked. Even when most all of the boys in the family had quit, spurned on perhaps by my father's cold-turkey quitting of his longtime, one-pack-a-day Camel habit in the early forties. (The boys would ask him, "How did you do it, Jim? Quit like that!" "WILLPOWER!" he would say. "THAT'S HOW I DID IT! WILLPOWER! THAT'S ALL IT TAKES!) In fact, my aunts Viola and Theresa and my aunt Pauline always smoked. For some reason the women in the family had a harder time quitting than the men. Was life harder on them than it was on the men? I remember once reading that among the ethnic groups in America, depression was highest among the Italian women. Was it possible that their lives were more difficult because of living with the Italian men who were often so righteous, men who lived by the phrase: "My way or the highway?" In the meantime, her brother Veto, the one who had always taken the most responsibility for her, continued taking her to doctors, though without finding any help for her or any answers.

Then in 1977, Congress passed a bill giving WAACs the benefits that all the veterans of World War II had. After that, she would always go to the Veterans' Hospital. And it was there, after many sessions with the staff psychiatrists, that she would finally be diagnosed as a schizophrenic. When I heard that word for the first time one day as it was casually mentioned, I rushed immediately to the new *Grolier Encyclopedia* my father had recently bought for my sister and me to help us with our school work, and I looked it up, for it was clear to me that no one in the family seemed quite sure of its meaning. But my *Grolier* was not much help. Then I checked out a book from our local library that was written by a psychiatrist at Menninger's Clinic. But it was not much help either. Schizophrenia seemed to be a rather large category for a large number of ailments. I knew the common idea of the word meant a "split personality." I had learned that much from the Hollywood movies I'd been watching for years. But that didn't help either.

Whatever the word's meaning, the hard, sad truth was that my clever, creative, and adventurous aunt would spend a good deal of the rest of her life right there in that Veterans' Hospital in Warrensville Heights, Ohio. And she would be treated with whatever hoped-for cure was the fashion of the day. Electroshock therapy came first. I'd seen *The Snake Pit* with Olivia de Havilland, and the horror of that being done to my aunt Florence frightened me. The treatment induced seizures, and the patient was totally disoriented afterward. What, I wondered, could happen to the brain? Couldn't it be damaged? It was scary. Then came the insulin treatments that also caused a massive shock to her system. Were they what made her look as if someone had blown her up like a balloon? The slim pretty woman I'd known was gone. Many years later would come the new chemical medications, and with those she would finally achieve a kind of balance. During this hopeful period, she often behaved quite normally and was able to leave the hospital and join the family gatherings. She still had to be watched though because she could—she'd already done it on a number of occasions—just wander off on her own. Still everyone hoped that this was finally the cure, and she was well again, for some do recover from this cruelest of diseases.

With another child on the way and needing more space my aunt Viola and my uncle Ray moved out of my grandmother's house into the nearby projects. The only time I now saw Uncle Ray was at family gatherings in our home, but my bond with him remained strong. On those nights at our house Uncle Ray would always find the time to be with me alone, usually in my bedroom. No one in the family ever thought it odd that he would do that. Though the masturbatory incidents ended … there was no place where we could be safely alone anymore …and because I imagine he was fearful of being caught … he would just talk to me about women and sex. And I remained a good listener. Once he told me that he had sex with his sister when they were growing up.

That surprised me. Soon though, Uncle Ray's life was busier than usual as was mine and I saw less and less of him. I still felt a bond with him, and still kept our secret, but I began to feel that he was not going to be the good male friend I needed. And with no one to talk to now, I was all alone.

But now that I had been taught how to masturbate I continued to do it ... daily... and it soon became my constant self-pleasuring activity, though I wondered if that were a good thing. My school buddies had always made jokes about jerking off, how hair would grow on the palms of your hands. Of course all the boys knew that wasn't true, that it had probably been a warning invented by an adult, hoping to keep young boys from abusing themselves. Then a girl in my class, Stella, whom I liked a lot, with whom I shared some feelings of alienation, suggested I might try going to church. She herself was a regular churchgoer and felt it was good for her. Wanting to try anything that would help me stop my daily sessions of self-abuse, I immediately went off to my local RC Church, St. Cecilia's, where I signed up for the First Holy Communion classes. Maybe, I was hoping, religion was the answer. I was turning for a friend to the head Savior of them all.

My father, as adamant as he was against the church and priests, did not make an attempt to stop me. That surprised me, for I thought he would surely try to persuade me away from the church. Perhaps he believed that I needed to figure it out for myself. So I held to my course. Unfortunately I was too young for the young-adult classes, so I was placed in the children's class. That didn't embarrass me at all. I would do whatever it took to be a good young Christian man. I had to find a way out of my painful childhood, and if that meant giving up masturbating, I would. So there I sat at the back of the church classroom, the tallest and the oldest person in the class, while Sister Mary Gertrude taught us our lessons. When the year was over and my elementary-aged classmates and I were due to take our First Holy Communion, I followed them as they walked two-by-two in their white suits and dresses up to the altar railing. I however was dressed in my new gray sharkskin suit, white shirt, a handsome matching tie and a new pair of shoes, the only off-note being the dirty smudge of downy hair on my upper lip; I hadn't started shaving yet. I didn't know who to choose to stand up for me as my godfather. I wanted Uncle Ray to be my godfather. But he wasn't a blood uncle and I was sure the family would want me to choose a blood uncle. Also I was embarrassed to say I wanted Uncle Ray for my godfather; I didn't want anyone to know how much he meant to me. So when my uncle Paul was suggested, I accepted it. Sister Mary Gertrude presented me with a wooden crucifix as a gift for being the best student, and I hung it on my bedroom wall above my bed as a constant reminder of what a good life should be, totally ignoring what I was really relating to.

I went dutifully to Mass every Sunday without fail after relating my impure actions and thoughts to the priest hearing my weekly late Friday afternoon confession. For my penance I always got the usual ten Hails Marys and Our Fathers. That wasn't a difficult penance. And for a while it seemed to work for me. But at the end of the year I knew I wasn't getting what I needed from the church. The praying, the usual ten Hail Marys and Our Fathers, and the weekly Mass attendance didn't seem to be helping. And I was masturbating daily again. The church and religion seemed a one-way street, with no response. I wasn't getting the love I was hoping to get from Jesus. What I was doing was relating to Christ's pain, to his agony on the cross, to the blood pouring out of the sword cuts on his body. His pain was my pain too. He was an outsider and I was an outsider. He wasn't loved nor was I. At the end of that year I stopped going to Mass and never went back—though I would not totally eliminate Christ and his pain from my life. Now I would place all my passion and hopes for the support I desperately needed and the confidence I so wanted in my schoolwork and in my many wonderful teachers.

Occasionally I would think about Uncle Ray and the secret we had shared and that I had still told no one about. Who would I have told anyway? Certainly not my father. He was totally out of the question and always had been. He was usually irrational, impatient, and he had a terrible temper. I never knew what his reaction was going to be to anything. And I didn't have a close relationship with any of my uncles and certainly not one that would have included telling them anything sexual. Nor did I have a close boyfriend I might have shared my secret with. So thinking it had no great meaning for me, I did my best to forget about it. Sometimes I did feel that Uncle Ray had used me. Maybe I felt that way because our intimate relationship of secrets shared had ended so abruptly. But being used was not a feeling I knew much about. And the words *abuse, molestation*, and *sexual manipulation* were not part of my vocabulary. It was, after all, the fifties. My life was getting busier so I let all that go. Besides there were many wonderful girls in school that I had crushes on.

I was still riveted though by the mystery of my aunt Florence—she who was so bright and so much more capable than anyone else in the family—and what had happened to her. While family members always made it a point to visit her, they rarely spoke of her. Was it the fear of mental illness being inherited that silenced them? I once heard that my grandmother, after one of her sons had been arrested—it wasn't a serious problem, but his arrest had made the papers—had hit herself in the head with a hammer. *Mea culpa ... mea culpa ...* Maybe they thought of that. But I was too young to be ashamed about my aunt Florence. And I was curious. I wanted to know what had caused her problem. How could someone be just fine one day and then totally different the next? That was scary. It meant we had no control over our lives, that what our teachers told us in school, that if we worked hard we could be anything we wanted, was after all a lie.

Her symptoms were obvious: she was withdrawn, she was sometimes hostile, she heard voices, and she seemed to be living in an ultimate loneliness, all true to the classic form of schizophrenia. But I was convinced that there must have been one incident in her life that had brought on her illness. By this time I had often been exposed to the wonderfully reductive Freudian theory used in many Hollywood films, and so I was into simple cause and effect. Everything had a reason. This was the New World. Finding the truth would set you free. So I wondered if perhaps her illness wasn't traceable to her father's ironhanded control or to the lack of equality in the treatment of the sexes. Maybe she felt her freedom was abused. Or maybe her family's teasing of her had deeply hurt her. Or was there actually something physically wrong with her brain, a chemical imbalance? I read somewhere that schizophrenia might be a disease passed down from mothers to children, an RH blood factor problem. Then I remembered my mother telling me that Aunt Florence had been born during the great flu epidemic of 1918. Maybe that flu virus had somehow gotten to her and damaged her brain. I had, in fact, read once that doctors thought that perhaps schizophrenia was caused by a virus. Maybe I had discovered the cause of her illness. But I could not be sure.

As I grew older I asked more questions about her and would occasionally get an answer, odd though it might be. The most romantic and the most movielike reason I heard always blamed her illness on the affair she'd had while in the service. This was the "It was the military service that ruined her" explanation. Because the man wouldn't marry her, she'd become angry and had turned that anger inward into self-destructiveness. Another time someone voiced the opinion that she had been raped in the service. There was no proof of that. To me, perhaps because of my problem with my father, her problem with her difficult father seemed a more likely cause of her illness. And I did have some support for that theory because I had read in a book that schizophrenia was not caused by a genetic aberration or a biochemical event but came about when a boy or girl needs to escape an unbearable pain. Hadn't her father forced her to give up the man who had asked her to marry him? Years later this theory was put forth again, when a friend who had a sister diagnosed with schizophrenia told me that the illness was a kind of predisposed condition. All it took to push these people over the precipice was one major bad crisis in their lives, one event that usually happens in their early to midtwenties that so shatters their already somewhat shaky grasp on reality that it is impossible for them to recover. That was exactly when Aunt Florence had become sick—in her early twenties. Other times I thought maybe she was, as the saying had it, "an oak that would not bend."

There were more explanations through the years of what had made her sick, some of them even amusing to a teenager. My favorite of those, often spoken by one of her brothers, was that all her problems came about because she was lazy, that if she had wanted to do the ordinary work a woman has to do she would have been all right. Mental illness brought on by laziness seemed pretty ludicrous even to me. That was, I decided, a particularly male point of view. And, too, laziness was an odd accusation for a person who had once been so adept at doing so many things equally well. No, I thought, if anything, she was a person who had been thwarted, who had never found the outlet for all her abilities, and who instead turned her anger against herself instead of searching for a more forgiving answer. She had judged herself in the highest moral court of all—her own—and her judgment was more severe than any normal court of law. The sentence: her vow of a lifetime of self-destructive behavior.

During one of her weekend family visits, Aunt Florence came to our house for a birthday party. The family, even larger now with the new in-laws and the youngsters, was even more boisterous and loud, with stories and jokes flying wildly about, each member trying to top the other, making it more difficult than ever to come forward with oneself. You had to fight for an opening. I enjoyed the passion of it all enormously, but it was hard to compete with my uncles, so I just listened. And that was all right with me, for I loved the stories they told of their childhoods.

Because I loved my aunt Florence I would always sit next to her at these gatherings. And this closeness allowed me to study her out of the side of my eyes. Where once she had been one of the most vocal members of the family, certainly on par with the men, she was now remote and withdrawn and never showed any enjoyment in the food or company at all. Her legs twisted pretzel-like around each other and, her head staring down at her plate, she slowly and quietly ate her cake and drank her coffee, all the while smoking one Lucky Strike after another. The only part of her body that showed any life at all was her crossed foot. It moved and twitched back and forth constantly like a cat's tail. The movement of that foot told me that there was an inner demon trying to get out. But what was it?

But what mesmerized me the most now was that my beloved aunt Florence was totally silent. She never spoke a word. Not one! How could she do that? How could a person not speak? Was it a conscious effort on her part? I was sure there are times in life when a person could not help but speak. Wouldn't a hello just escape your lips on its own? Or an automatic thank you when someone passed you a piece of dessert? But no, she sat there, never involved in the conversation, her glance always inward, never letting a word slip accidentally out of her mouth. This person who had once been so sassy, so quick, so bright, who always had a comeback, was now quiet as a nun who'd taken vows of silence. This had to be very hard to pull off, I thought. It must take enormous effort to keep oneself from responding normally to everyday life. I watched her vigilantly all those years, but she maintained her sphinx-like silence. Equally intriguing to me was the reaction of the rest of the family to her. By their behavior, you would think she wasn't even there. They carried on as they always had. Occasionally I would see someone glance in her direction, but that was all. But to me, the enormity of her presence and her silence was deafening.

One night, as I sat next to her at one of our family celebrations, I was rewarded for my patience and constant attention to her. The family was its usual ebullient self, totally enjoying itself and the food. And then, in an unusual moment of silence (did she time it purposefully to be heard or was it accidental?) my aunt Florence spoke. And I heard every word of it. What she said had nothing to do with the conversation at the table but only with the ongoing conversation she'd been having with herself for years now. She said, "I've done something wrong ... something very, very wrong." And in that lightning moment, the curtain between the ordinary lives we lead and the deeper hidden lives of despair and pain some of us also lead, was pulled back; and a hidden truth was revealed. It was a moment I had longed for. I repeated what she'd said over and over to myself so I wouldn't forget it. "I've done something wrong, something very, very wrong." That was all she said, and then the curtain quickly closed, and she was silent once more. What could she have done, I wondered, that was so awful, so devastating that it had caused a total rupture in her mind? I could think of nothing that would cause that kind of a break. But I was too young then to know anything of guilt and regret and of the toll they both can take.

There had been a slight bump in the conversation around the table, but then the conversation continued. I wanted to scream! Hadn't anyone noticed that she'd spoken! Didn't you hear what she said! Maybe it's important! But they didn't seem to be paying her any attention. Was it possible that I'd imagined what she'd said? No! I was sure I'd heard her correctly. Then without a word, she got up from the table, walked out of the kitchen and down the stairs into our basement. Why weren't her brothers and sisters paying attention?

But I was wrong. They were all aware that she had spoken and had then slipped away because someone, my aunt Viola I think, said to her brothers, "You'd better check on her." And in the sound of her voice was all the knowledge of how ill my aunt Florence was. One of my uncles got up and walked down the stairs into the basement. He soon called up for help. Two more brothers went down into the basement, and shortly after, they brought Aunt Florence back up into the kitchen. All I heard was a quietly muttered "She was standing over the sink with one of Rose's knives at her wrist." Luckily they had caught her in time. My father tried to shield my sister and me from what was going on by pushing us out of the room and into our bedrooms. But I crept back into the hallway next to the kitchen and watched as my uncles took my aunt Florence out of our house and back to the hospital. And I had collected another image to add to my photo album of indelible pictures that included the day I came home from elementary school and found my mother crying in my bedroom closet with the door closed, hiding in fear from my father; my uncle John whom I desperately needed to help me, lying sealed in a closed casket; my uncle Ray sharing an intimate secret with me; and now my aunt Florence standing over our basement sink, a large knife blade at her wrist.

What followed then were the sad years of her trying to kill herself, in one way or another, for whatever terrible thing it was that she had done. She tried pills but was always caught in time. Once, for what reason I couldn't imagine, she tried to cut off her tongue. Was it her sassiness she was trying to cut out? Or was she trying to make it impossible for her to articulate her own guilt or pain? Thankfully though, the tongue is a tough, thick, and ungiving muscle; and she wasn't able to do herself serious damage. Whatever her reason, surely this form of self-mutilation was one of self-hate, an internalized rage; for she was never outwardly violent, only inwardly on herself. Still I could never stop wondering what it was she had done that could have made her hate herself so.

One day when I was in college and visiting home for the holidays, my aunt Pauline, with whom I had begun to enjoy a more honest and sharing relationship, told me that all my aunt Florence's problems had come about because she had an abortion when she came out of the service. One story had it that she had even admitted to her sisters one day that she'd had an abortion. Certainly this would explain her feeling that she'd "done something wrong," and I thought it the most logical explanation. The next time I spoke with my mother, I asked her—we were also talking openly with each other then—if that were true. She said it was. And she said that she had been there on that afternoon in the girls' upstairs bedroom not long after Aunt Florence had returned from the army, when she told her sisters she'd had an abortion. But the doctors at the Veteran's Hospital had rejected that idea, saying there was no evidence it was true. But I think it must have been true. I think there was a cover-up. Abortion was a big taboo.

After my sister and I had both graduated from college, my father sold the store and built his dream home, doing most of the work himself, in Independence, Ohio. Some of the men in the family helped him, particularly Uncle Ray, who was knowledgeable about construction and who had always maintained a good relationship with my father. (I went home for the big day of the pouring of the long and wide driveway. Unfortunately, just as we were about finished with the last section of the driveway where it met the street, it began to rain. And who got blamed for the rain? I did. I was my father's scapegoat.)

One day during my early years in New York City, I had an unexpected call from my mother. She usually wrote me letters, often with recipes inserted in them, but this time the news was just too unbelievable, and it couldn't wait. It was about my grandmother, who could, it seemed, still surprise her family. Aunt Viola, while drinking her coffee that morning and reading the marriage license column of the *Cleveland Plain Dealer*, as was her habit, came across her mother's name. Aunt Viola immediately called my mother: "Rose! Did you see the marriage license column in this morning's paper!" My mother told her she hadn't gotten to it yet. "Well, look at it!" she said. Turning immediately to the marriage license page my mother saw what had so excited her sister. There in the marriage license column was their mother's name. She was stunned. Here was Grandma, receiving a bit of notoriety in the local newspaper for the second time in her life.

"Are you sure that's Ma?" my mother asked her sister.

Viola immediately replied, "It must be! It's the right address! She's getting married!"

"Did she tell anyone?"

"No! No one knows!"

This just wasn't done. After their husbands died, Italian widows grieved for the remaining years of their lives. They donned that ubiquitous black dress and never took it off. But there it was in print. It must be true. Shortly after the announcement in the newspaper, my grandmother abruptly began to close up the house on Thirty-fifth and Cedar Avenue, that house that was filled with so many good memories and some bad memories for me and the only house I'd ever known her to live in. My uncle Dutch, still single at the time and still living at home, was surprised to discover his bed dismantled when he came home from work one day, leaving him to scramble quickly for a new place to live. And in quick order, my grandmother married her new husband and moved into his house on the West Side of Cleveland.

My grandmother, it seemed, had more of a pioneering American spirit than anyone had ever realized. She had, after all, been an immigrant and had herself come to America to forge a new life, and without any fear of the New World, she had gone out into it and done battle. I only saw her in her kitchen cooking or at the market haggling over the prices or in a subdued mood in church. But she was much more realistic than my own mother, who was shy and retiring and only wanted to stay in her own home. It was my grandmother who told my mother in no uncertain terms that she had to allow me to be a boy and go swimming at a two-bus-ride-away pool if I wanted. She wasn't fearful like my mother. I should have known who she was then.

A few years later when I was on tour with a Broadway comedy that was playing at the Hanna Theater in Cleveland, I went to see my grandmother. Her second husband had died a year after she'd married him, and she was now living alone in their small house. As we had always done, we went shopping for groceries. Then I sat with her in her kitchen, having a cup of tea and talking. When it was time for me to leave, my grandmother followed me out onto her front porch, where she asked me when I was going to get married. I was twenty-eight years old at the time and totally engrossed in my theater career, which had taken off nicely. I thought about marriage but was not rushing into it, fearful I could not afford the financial responsibilities of it. She admonished me, "If you don't pick the seed when it's ripe, the birds will get it." I walked away from her, thinking about what she'd said and the wisdom of it. It had spoken to me. And it made me realize that I had hardly known this remarkable woman, who was so strong, vital, and forward-looking. I'd run to her skirts for the comfort I'd needed as a child, but like all children and all young people, I hadn't paid attention, involved as I was with myself and my own needs—that powerful "now" of life. And the truth be told, her generation did not talk much about themselves. They just got on with it. The past was past, and they had no time to look back. That was the last time I would see my grandmother.

My aunt Florence would spend much of the next two decades in and out of the hospital. As newer medications for mental illnesses came on the market, she seemed to improve. And often for a time she was much better. Out of the blue one day in the early years of struggling as an actor in New York, I received a savings bond from her. It was, I remember, very welcome. And it made me remember her other examples of caring—the circuses she had taken me to and the beautiful bedspread she'd made for me. Another time she sent me a box covered with seashells that she'd made in a crafts class. Then I would hear she was back in the hospital.

A few years later I received a letter from my mother, telling me that Aunt Florence was out of the hospital and was living in a group home. And even more shocking—she could still do that—she was planning to get married. My mother was ecstatic and wrote me in a letter, "Did I tell you that Aunt Florence has a boyfriend? She met him on one of her house-to-house tours of selling Avon products … she is doing wonderfully in this new work and is making a profit of 40 percent on all she sells! ... and they are buying furniture to set up a house. I pray she will find happiness."

But the marriage didn't work out. The family blamed the man. They said he was a mama's boy and not up to marriage. I wondered about that. My aunt Florence had always been a woman who valued her own freedom more than anything, someone always determined to do what she wanted, when she wanted. Perhaps I misunderstood her, but how was she going to suppress this willfulness in a marriage and do the work that had to be done together with another? When the marriage ended after a few months, she went back into the hospital again. I lost track of her whereabouts for a while after that.

Then in 1988, I received a very happy letter from her, telling me how much she was enjoying living in her new home. She had evidently been released from the hospital. "I'm so happy," she wrote, "to be out of the hospital after nearly twenty years. I can do things that I was never able to do before. Like taking better care of myself. Polishing my nails, wearing makeup, taking better care of my hair, etc." I was happy for her.

When many years later, after a long bout with brain tumors, my pretty aunt Viola died, I, not working at the time, made a trip back to Cleveland for her funeral. I was told that my aunt Florence would be at the funeral too, and I was looking forward to seeing her, for it had been a long time since our last visit. On the morning of the funeral, my uncle Frank and I picked her up at the shared home she was living in to take her to the church. Waiting for us in the living room of the home, she was, as usual, smoking. She put out the cigarette when we entered the room, and after I'd kissed her and said hello—she barely responded—we walked out to the car, where she got into the backseat behind me and we drove off.

In her backseat solitude she immediately lit another cigarette, rolled down her window a bit for the smoke to escape—that was thoughtful of her—and smoked her cigarette in that same sharp, militaristic manner I'd always remembered. (I read in later years—still learning whatever I could about my aunt Florence's condition—that a large percentage of schizophrenics smoke and that the nicotine somehow calms their brains.)

We drove on. No one spoke. She was still an inward-looking person. Wanting to figure out where she was now mentally after all these years, I surreptitiously sneaked glances at her. The color of her skin was alarming. She'd evidently been sitting in the sun, covered with the formula everyone had used during the war years before commercial suntan lotions came on the market: baby oil and iodine. (Was that where she had stopped in time?) That old home remedy had left her face badly streaked (that was the iodine) and cooked looking (that was the baby oil). Figuring that she would never instigate a conversation, I decided to break the ice and ask her a question, hoping that she would respond. I also wanted her to know I didn't think of her as someone who was a freak—that is, a crazy person. So I said to her, "Aunt Florence, it's so wonderful to see you out now and living on your own." She smiled at me as she continued blowing her cigarette smoke out the back window of the car.

But I wanted a response out of her, something that would tell me where she was now. So I took the bull by the horns and went right to the point. "What happened? How did this come about after all these years?"

She didn't take my question as an intrusion into her privacy at all. She simply said, "I don't cry about things anymore."

There it was again—that unknown pain of whatever it was that had happened to her many years before. I didn't question her anymore. If the painful past was truly over, I was happy for her.

After the funeral Mass at the church and the internment of my aunt Viola's body at the cemetery, the immediate family gathered at my uncle Frank and aunt Clara's home in Brook Park. It was now the family gathering place in Cleveland. There was a table full of the usual foods for such an occasion— the local deli platter of cold cuts, a salad, plus the wonderful breaded veal cutlets my aunt Clara always made; and as the family sat in the living room talking with amazement about the many old friends who had shown up at the funeral, people the family hadn't seen in years, my aunt Florence, out of nowhere, started telling jokes. She hadn't related to the family reminiscences at all. Perhaps her history was different now, made up of the years spent in a mental hospital, the years of making your family out of strangers, out of your fellow inmates, and of sitting around with them in the dayroom, telling jokes to alleviate the long sad hours of their lives. And so that was how she related now, how she contributed to the group.

I was surprised by what an accomplished comedienne she was. Then I remembered that she'd always been wonderfully funny. I'd spent hours laughing with her when I was young. But this was somehow different. Her timing was immaculate. Her delivery dead-on. She was a pro. Like a good comic, she never laughed at her own jokes, just kept them rolling on, one after another, allowing a small pause at the end of each joke to let her audience laugh yet never missing a beat, never faltering once while searching for a word and never ruining a punch line. It was a remarkable performance. Being a professional actor I was very appreciative of her good timing and pacing, and I was knocked out by her performance. One after another, the jokes came in finger-snapping time. She was on a roll, and I roared with laughter, tears of release running down my cheeks.

She was on for a good half hour. But after my initial delight in her performance, I began to notice that there was an odd disconnectedness with her audience. She never related to us at all. The deadpan delivery, a great asset for a comic, was connected to her own deadness. Comedy itself is a form of disconnectedness, but this was different. She was performing by rote; she was robotlike, mechanical. She wasn't aware of her audience at all. We could have easily not been in the room. And it was then I realized what a terrible toll the years of illness had taken, for not only had she lost all those years, but she could also no longer relate to anyone as a human being. She lived now, as she had perhaps for many, many years, only in her own head—stuck there, a prisoner there of her own thoughts, regrets, and guilt. Her whole world was bounded by her brain—the same brain she'd battled with all her life. Is that kind of unrelenting inwardness what we mean by insanity?

Later as I kissed her good-bye in the driveway of the home, she said to me, "I know they all think I'm crazy, but I'm not." I laughed so that she'd know I agreed with her, but it was a line that had been spoken so often by truly crazy film characters that it was a cliché. Was she so delusional, I wondered. Or was she sharing with me, her nephew who had always loved her, her real truth? I didn't know what to believe. What of the years of self-destructiveness? The many attempts at suicide, the self-mutilation? Were these not signs of a mentally troubled person? The doctors had said early on that she was a schizophrenic. Wasn't that true? And if she weren't crazy, did that mean that she'd chosen this awful life she'd led? Why would anyone choose a life of such inactivity and boredom? That seemed the worst part of it to me, the constant sameness, that inability to get out of one's head and enjoy the world, to enjoy the sheer wacky serendipity of it all. No, she had been a person with serious mental problems, no matter how one defined them, and she had now somehow come to a better-managed place in her life, probably due to newer medications. Uncle Dutch drove her home.

When most of the guests had left, and it was just my aunt Clara, my uncle Frank, my sister, and myself who were left, I learned something horrible. At some point my sister and my aunt Clara had gone into a bedroom to talk. I continued talking to my uncle Frank, paying no attention to what they were doing. After a while, when my sister came out of the bedroom, she sat next to me on the sofa and began to whisper something in my ear. At first I couldn't understand what she was saying. When I glanced at my uncle to excuse my sister's whispering, I noticed an odd look on his face. Then I heard what Aunt Clara had told my sister in her bedroom and that my sister was now whispering to me. It seems that Ray ... I can no longer call him *uncle* ... had been sexually molesting his son's daughter, his own granddaughter. The girl, a beginning teenager, had told her father what her grandfather was doing with her, whereupon the father, that same Junior that I had wheeled in his stroller to his father's bar so many years before, called the police and had his father,

Ray, arrested. The family didn't know much more than that. Or if they did, they didn't want to talk about it.

All the lightness of my body fell in upon myself. All the possible good that human beings can achieve drained out of me. I felt a deep heaviness. While trying to hide my own feelings so as not to give myself away, I remembered what he and I had done, how he had betrayed my innocence. I was happy for my cousin that she had done what I had never been able to do. Still I felt a great sadness for her, for I knew from my own experience what she would now go through. And then I felt terrible guilt. If I had told someone what he had done with me years before maybe this wouldn't have happened to her. But I had been in thrall to him. He and I had a bond. I couldn't tell. And maybe I was still in thrall to him. My sister had finished telling me what she knew. Then the subject in the room changed. No one wanted to talk about what Ray had done. It was too sordid. Too ugly.

Over the next few months I asked more questions. I wanted to know what the outcome of the court case had been. It turned out the judge had only sentenced Ray to a mandatory number of classes about sexual abuse. And that was it. No jail time. I was sorry to hear that. It seemed too lenient a sentence to me.

Because of what Ray had done to me, I had always lived with a subtext of darkness under my outwardly cheery persona. At times I retreated to my apartment like a hermit, in a state of deep depression, unable to connect with others. Later I realized that I had been partly traumatized. I could do my work, but there was deadness in me. I always thought I had not let what Ray and I had done affect me. I mean, worse had been done to many others. I could ignore it. But I had never forgotten it. I had only forced it down inside me, out of sight, while I got on with my new and exciting life.

Then one day, with a man I met at the gym, I made an attempt, without realizing it, to recreate the sexual scenario I had shared with Ray. It was an aborted and unsuccessful attempt, and I quickly left the man's apartment. But as soon as I walked out onto the sidewalk, I had an immediate flashback of what Ray and I had done. Still it would take a few more aborted experiences before I really began to connect the dots. And those experiences led to great feelings of worthlessness and inadequacy and years of self-destructive behavior. Finally, unable to do my work, I went in search of my first therapist. Then I got a job out of town and had to take it. Then I found another therapist on my return to town, but that was a bust. It wasn't until the fourth therapist I found that I really got to my true feelings. After making the realization that what I was working on was my relationship with my therapist and that through that I would be better able to get to my feelings, we began to make progress. And so it was that one day, at the end of a particularly bruising session, when Bill asked me what I would have done if Ray had done to a child of mine what he had done to me. I said, "I WOULD HAVE KILLED THE SON OF A BITCH!" It had taken me a long time, but I was finally able to admit to the truth and to admit to the degree of anger I felt for Ray. I was no longer in thrall to him. And now he had hurt another innocent person in the family.

I needed to know how the girl was doing. And just as I feared, she would go through a very bad time. Always an honor student, she dropped out of school before she finished. Then she was bulimic and gained a great deal of weight. Then she was anorexic and shrank to a skeleton of herself. Then somehow she got herself together and finished school and worked toward her PhD in—what else?—psychology. Last I heard she was finding some peace with herself. I hope and pray so. Some people say abuse is only as serious as you think it is, that it is only a matter of perception, perception being everything. Maybe for some. But not for me. I say abuse is an adult leading a child into an unwanted sexual act and is therefore a taking away of an innocent child's authenticity; it is nothing less than the murder of a soul. It isn't so much the sex as it is the betrayal. How can one love when love itself has been used as a weapon against one's own person? And there is something more horrendous: what if I turned around and did the same to another young person? It was possible. As Auden said, "Those to whom evil is done, do evil in return." If I ever did that I would slash my throat from ear to ear.

I didn't see my aunt Florence again for ten years. My mother was now living with my sister in Minneapolis—my father had died a year before—and when her brother Veto called her to tell her that her sister Florence was in bad shape, she decided that she wanted to travel to Cleveland to see her one remaining sister and her brothers. (When my Aunt Theresa was dying of lung cancer a few years before, I was playing in *That Championship Season* at a theater in Detroit near Battle Creek, Michigan, where she lived. On my first day off I went to visit her in the hospital. She was in terrible pain, but she did her best to ignore it and to be the sweet dear aunt I had always known. That was the last time I saw her.) The plan was I would fly from New York City, Mom would fly from Minneapolis, and we would meet in Cleveland. So Mom, at eighty-eight years of age and always uneasy about flying, with a pacemaker, poor leg circulation, and arthritis, bravely made her first solo flight.

First Mom and I, with her brothers Frank, Dutch, and Veto, visited her brother Paul in East Liverpool, Ohio. Macular degeneration had taken its toll on him, and he was now close to being totally blind. After a pleasant luncheon we drove back to Cleveland, where Mom saw a number of her friends, and then we went to the hospital to see my aunt Florence. I could tell it was the one visit that Mom dreaded. Aunt Florence had been back in the hospital for a number of years now. The group home was no longer viable because she needed more care. And, too, she now had cancer that had started in her breasts and was working its way through her body. When the doctors suggested a double mastectomy, her response—some of the old sassiness was still there—had been quick: "I've had these breasts all my life, I'm not going to let anyone cut them off now." Soon thereafter, the cancer moved into her shoulders and then her lungs. Uncle Frank and his wife, Clara, visited her often, as did her brother Veto and his wife, Pauline. They prepared us for the great change in her looks.

We were told to wait outside her room while the nurses got her ready for our visit. She wanted to look her best. Fifteen minutes later, when we were all finally ushered in, I hardly recognized my aunt Florence. Chairs were pulled around the bed. Mom kissed her sister, a sister whom she'd almost raised herself, and then sat silently. She was shaken. Trying to break the silence and hoping to inject some humor into our visit—humor was after all the common ground she and I have always shared—I said to my aunt Florence, whose hair was now thin and dusty looking, "I see you don't color your hair anymore." And she said her first words. "I never colored my hair." She said this very matter-of-factly and without any sense that I was gently kidding her. Then she was silent. There was some talk of what a nice room she had, of the many pretty clothes in her wardrobe. I studied her face. She was indeed greatly changed from the last time I'd seen her. Her lower jaw, practically nonexistent, was a problem; it constantly fell out of its socket. She would hold it up in place with her hands, hands that were now so arthritic that they remained tightly closed in a permanent fist. She did have the use of her two index fingers, one of which she constantly brought up slowly to her right shoulder. Did the shoulder bother her, I asked. She nodded her head. Later Uncle Frank told me that the cancer kept her in constant pain even though she was medicated. And he also said she seemed unaware that it was cancer.

Her lunch came. Uncle Frank helped her eat it—he'd done this often before—while we sat there trying to think of the right thing to say. She didn't eat much. Some applesauce. Nothing else appealed to her. She made a big point of being sure that the uneaten cup of yogurt be given to one of the nurses. This was evidently a daily ritual of hers. We sat a while longer, trying to pull out the person we once knew, that person who could be so challenging, so alive and bristling, so funny, that person I had so admired, but that person was no longer there.

We'd been in her room for maybe forty minutes or so when the nurse came in to give her a pain pill. And shortly after taking it she started to drift off, and we knew it was time for us to leave. I was the last one out of the room, and at the door, I turned and blew her a kiss, hoping for a last response of some kind, a smile perhaps, or even a good-bye, something that I could remember of her always, of the clever and creative person my aunt Florence had been. But all she said was "Close the door! Close the door!" I knew immediately it was because she didn't want anyone to see her as she now was. I did as she asked and walked out of the room.

Two months later, on August 30, 1998, at the age of 80, she died. And she took to the grave whatever it was that she had done that was so terrible. Her doctors had once described her as "tight as a clam," and that's how she wanted to remain. She even demanded her records be closed forever. *Dice niente.* That was the centuries-old religion. There was even an Italian proverb that said "Vita privata, vita beata." "Hidden life, happy life." But I didn't believe that, for without the means of talking, of communicating who you are, your humanity is denied. And the control you think you have over your own life is a false one. Don't we all want our true selves known, at least to one person? Isn't that what intimacy is about finally? The choice my aunt Florence had made was the choice that causes anger, whether directed inward or outward.

Though the war hadn't been fought on our own soil and though we had won it, it had destroyed more than we realized and was now taking, years later, another toll. It had helped ruin my aunt Florence's life. It had also hurt my uncle Frank, who had missed out on a high school education, something he would always feel had handicapped him, limiting his opportunities. My grandmother had lost a son, my uncle John, whose loss had also devastated me; for he had been my hope; and his death had left me characterized as a sissy. It also meant that my search for a role model to help me get over that hateful word would have to begin again. And that search would lead me to a sick person who would abuse me. Not all the victims of the war were on the battlefield.

My grandmother who had given me the gift of unconditional love died in 1973 while I was working in a Broadway play, so I hadn't been able to return to Cleveland for her funeral. She had fallen and broken her hip and as so often happens, while she was recovering in the hospital, she developed pneumonia and died. It wasn't too long after she died that my mother sent me a photo that had appeared in the *Cleveland Plain Dealer*. Grandma's big home at Thirty-fifth and Cedar had burned to the ground. The magical mahogany sliding doors that led into the living room and that mysteriously disappeared into the wall from the main hallway were now no longer. And the wide smooth banister I'd slid down so often to be caught at the bottom by one of my uncles or aunts was also gone. As was the dark basement where I had been so cleverly manipulated and used by my uncle Ray.

Also gone were some good memories too. There was my adored grandmother slipping me giant Hershey chocolate bars in her pantry. There was the happy return of my uncles and aunt after the war and the return of jitterbugging in the living room. There were the many wonderful Christmas dinners when I helped my grandmother make her killer ravioli, carefully pressing the tines of a fork all around the edges of them, and the hundreds of gifts under the Christmas tree, the top of which always touched the ceiling, many with my name on them. I will always have those memories too.

Grandma's Killer Ravioli

- 3 ½ to 4 cups unbleached all-purpose flour
- 1 tsp. salt
- 4 extra large eggs
- 1 tsp. olive oil

In the middle of her scrubbed wooden dining table, Grandma made a mound of
her flour (the following recipe makes about 1 lb. of pasta dough—enlarge as
necessary) that already had the salt sifted in.

Make a well in the flour and then add the eggs and oil. With a fork, beat the eggs lightly with the flour. Gradually pull in all the flour until it's absorbed. Knead the dough, which is a stiff dough, for about 10 mins. If the dough is too sticky, add a bit more flour; if it's too hard and doesn't mix well, add a few drops or more of warm water. The dough ball should be elastic and a little sticky. Wrap dough in plastic or put in a covered bowl. Allow to rest for 30 mins. at room temperature.

Rolling the dough: Grandma had a broomstick that she wielded like a lacrosse player, deftly and quickly with the palms of her hands. A rolling pin will work too. (Grandma never, of course, had a pasta machine; but you can roll the sheets out that way too.) Place dough on floured surface. Knead for 7 mins. or so till dough is smooth. Cut dough in half and roll out very thin, to about a 1/16" thickness.

My grandmother rolled out the dough so that she could cut her 5"x5" squares out of it. She would place a dollop of the filling on the lower half of the square, fold it over, and then cut the corners off, leaving a five-sided ravioli. Then with a fork I would seal the edges together and poke three sets of holes in the top of each ravioli. These ravioli would then be boiled gently in salted water for 10 or 15 mins. or as long as the thickness of the dough needs. Remove carefully from the water with a slotted spoon.

Drain. Place on plate, top with sauce, and serve.

To make small ravioli: Cut dough in half and roll out. On one-half, drop a teaspoon of filling about 2" apart until dough sheet is filled. Take second rolled out sheet of pasta and cover first. With fingertips, gently press around each mound to form a little square. Cut squares with a ravioli roller cutter.

The Ricotta Filling

- 16 oz. whole milk ricotta
- 6 tbs. freshly grated Pecorino or Parmesan cheese
- 1 egg
- ¼ tsp. salt
- 1/8 tsp. freshly ground pepper
- a handful of freshly chopped parsley

Mix and set aside.

(Additions to the filling: You can use an ounce of *soppressata*, the pork sausage, cut and sliced into 1/4" pieces. Or you can add meat to the filling—ground round, veal, or pork—and cooked finely chopped spinach. Or whatever filling you'd like to try … fish, vegetables, etc.)

CHAPTER 8
E Polvere o Merdo

∷

By my midteens I knew my mother's repertoire of sayings and proverbs, in both Italian and English, for every occasion and situation. And though I'd usually heard the phrase before, I always looked forward to hearing it again to experience its comforting repetition. And Mom, like a great comic with a long-before established routine that had been honed and worked for years, always got her laugh. If I had a pimple on my face and complained to her, her response was always the same: "It's the badness coming out in you." I was a boy, so, of course, there was always the possibility of built-in badness.

My father could never find anything in the house: his work clothes, his lunch bag, and on and on. And there would always be that moment when frustrated in his search, he'd blow his top: "RO! WHERE THE HELL'S MY LUNCH!" Mom's first response, not wanting to give away the game too quickly, was always "I saw a dog running down the street with it!" To which Pop would always respond, while he continued to poke around in the refrigerator and getting angrier by the moment, "COME ON! DON'T BE FUNNY!" At which point my mother would casually walk over to the refrigerator and remove his lunch bag, which was, of course, right in front of him the whole time, saying as she did it, "If it was a snake it would have bit you!" Big laugh from me. Pop's response to this would be his usual half-playful/half-serious raised hand in warning while he said: "You know, sometimes I'd like to …" We all knew the completion of that sentence: "…smack you one!" But the tension had been broken by Mom's humor, and he would join in the joke even though it was on him. And as far as I know he never hit my mother; he only threatened to, which is the same thing.

But my favorite saying of my mother's was one that amused me to think of as our family motto, though I suspected a deeper truth in it that I couldn't yet articulate. The phrase was *E Polvere o Merdo*. And this is what it meant and how it came about: When my grandfather was a young man in Italy, he set about one day to make gunpowder so he could go hunting. Now I don't know the exact ingredients of gunpowder, but I believe you need saltpeter, charcoal, and sulfur. So as Grandpa was burying, in a hole in the ground, some tree branches—those of the pear tree being the best, I believe, to make charcoal—and as he was adding his other ingredients to the hole, a neighbor, who was out for a walk, peered into the hole and asked him what he was doing. My grandfather explained that he was making gunpowder. Whereupon the neighbor, an older and more experienced man, told him that he was going about it all wrong, that it wouldn't work. To which my grandfather responded, "E Polvere o Merdo." It'll either be gunpowder or shit.

I envisioned this expression on our family's coat of arms: E POLVERE O MERDO! GUNPOWDER OR SHIT! This saying surely indicates the genetic strand of fatalism that the people in Southern Italy, who had been conquered, raped, and enslaved at one time or another by all the powers in the Mediterranean region, still harbored. I could hear this fatalism too when my mother would sing in that high, almost whining sound of the *Mezzogiorno* (the southern part of Italy) her favorite pop song of the day, "Che Sera Sera," as she went about her daily tasks. Though sung by an upbeat, chirpy, all-American Doris Day, Mom knew its true meaning and, of course, related to it; for it was the pop music version of our family motto: what will be, will be. While the "getting on with it" was a positive and good way of living, I heard the deeper feeling underneath it, the sound of resignation, the awareness that life was not a matter of choice, that it was predestined. And along with that, there was also the warning that if you reached too high, if you tried to rise above the modesty of your circumstances, fate would intervene, and you would suffer a terrible fall. Best not to be that most reviled character: a "big shot." And best not to dream or wish too high. Whenever I wished for the impossible, a vacation in New York City or a piano of my own, my mother would often say to me, "Wish in one hand, *merdo* in the other." It was useless to dream for it only left you with a mess.

But I was an American boy, full of the trees and plants and flowers of the fields of northern Ohio. Near the main thoroughfare, Kinsman Road, there grew a favorite tree the school kids called the monkey-ball tree. I think now that it must have been a light-barked buckeye. Once a year it produced a large round seed that, when opened, released a fibered inside that dropped down an unsuspecting friend's back on the way to school could cause great scratchy discomfort. There was a wild bush that produced a bright red berry that made an excellent poison ink. And there were the many milk pod bushes with the big seed pod that, when squeezed open, emitted into the air the thousands of silky flying seeds. I was also enthralled with all the wildlife that lived on the southern shore of our great lake. Once, while at summer camp, a sleek fat black king snake slithered across our path in the woods. I ran after it, but it disappeared quickly in the undergrowth. Near that camp was a long-abandoned castle that reeked of the smell of skunks. We boys would run inside and stay inside for as long as we could bear the smell. It was a test of endurance. On a summer's night we always caught as many lightning bugs as we could, dropping them into a bell jar, and then screwing the punctured top back on. It made a wonderful lantern. I never tired of catching grasshoppers and squeezing them a bit, making the creature release a strange, tobacco-colored liquid. All of this enthralling life that existed around me made me feel the possibilities of my own life. I had luck on my side. I could take risks. I could be anything I wanted to be.

So when I would say to Mom, in anticipation, that something she was preparing looked really good and she would answer—with that universal shrug endemic to all mothers who know they cannot create masterpieces in the kitchen every day—"E Polvere o Merdo," I always laughed because with Mom's cooking I knew it was never the *merdo*.

Mom, of course, did all the cooking in our home, as most wives did in those days; but my father always liked to say he could cook too, the implication being that he, if the truth were known, was as good, if not a better, cook as my mother. My sister and I would look at each other with raised eyebrows but would never dare pursue the matter. All we'd ever seen him cook were steaks. He could do that all right. And once, when Mom was on a rare break—not a vacation, mind you, but a week's stay in the hospital to pass a murderously painful kidney stone—Pop had to cook. Usually what he did was warm up food that Mom had prepared before she'd left or broil steaks, of course, or prepare—and this was his specialty—*Spaghetti Alio e Olio*. This dish was the mainstay of the Italian male's small repertoire of meals, for not only was it delicious but it was also simplicity itself to prepare. All you needed was olive oil, garlic, pasta, and few red pepper flakes. And Pop did it well. There was one occasion though when what Pop prepared was a major disaster.

Looking back now I realize with a bit of a shock that I had more than my share of health problems when I was growing up. I had chicken pox and the mumps. I had scarlet fever when I was in junior high school. I got over it by listening in my darkened bedroom—I wasn't allowed to read—to the daily soap operas on my new RCA Victor radio, the very one I was thrilled to notice on Barbara Stanwyck's bedside table in *Sorry, Wrong Number*.

I had a serious case of ringworm on the soles of my feet, caused no doubt by my love of running barefoot outside during the summer months. After Dr. Menzalore had cured me, he told my parents one day that it had been a serious case, that I'd had "one foot in the grave." I was startled to hear that. I hadn't realized how close I'd come to having my blood totally poisoned. But I mutely accepted this news as truth, for it came from Dr. Menzalore whom I was very fond of.

I recovered from those illnesses and thought no more about them. But there were two conditions I had all the years I was growing up. I was always anemic and I always had hay fever. For the anemia, Dr. Menzalore gave me weekly shots of iron and told me to eat bananas daily so as to improve my appetite. There was nothing wrong with my appetite. I ate everything in sight and in larger quantities than anyone. So it was a big shock to me that I was anemic. How could that be? Perhaps it came from having shot up in height so quickly. I was hitting six feet at the beginning of my teens. Whatever its cause, I would have it all through my teen years.

Nothing much was made of these problems by my parents. Wisely they didn't want me to dwell on them and, I'm sure, thought I'd outgrow them all; and eventually I did. But it was the hay fever that caused the major fracas in our family, for it couldn't be ignored. It wasn't unseen like the anemia. I was the prisoner of monumental sneezing sessions that went on forever and that, because of their frequency, turned into a family ritual, laced with the usual humor. Everyone—well, except for my father who was not amused—would start to count the number of my sneezes as soon as an attack started. Most sessions lasted ten or twelve sneezes. On some occasions I would go to thirteen, fourteen, and fifteen sneezes. And on peak occasions, when the pollen count was at its highest, I would go to nineteen or twenty sneezes. These were major events in our household that could not be ignored, for I would be overwhelmed by a volcanic physical cataclysm that could not be stopped and that sapped all my energy leaving me limp as a piece of cooked spaghetti.

Mom, forever trying to defuse the seriousness of it and thereby minimizing Daddy's reaction, would always count as I sneezed, seeing if I was going to break a new record. But this never deterred Pop from his usual reaction. Frustrated no doubt by my exhaustion and his inability to do anything to help me, he would get angry. When I'd go into the first sneeze, with everyone looking on, holding their breaths and hoping it would be a short seizure, Pop would always say, "Here he goes!"

And then, about the time I was on the verge of the eighth sneeze, he'd start getting really angry, and he'd yell at me, "ENCORA!" AGAIN! And then the pleas to stop would begin: "BASTA! BASTA!" ENOUGH! ENOUGH! When I'd finally stop, wilted and droopy, he'd always say, "AH, FINALMENTE! FINALLY YOU STOP!" That made it seem as if it were my fault. And then, as I was beginning to breathe normally, would come the final invective: "MANNAGGIA

L'AMERICA!" Pop was not always rational in his understanding of the way life worked.

I listened intently for all these Italian phrases. Italians have, of course, some of the same curse words we have in English, words that relate to the body parts and their functions; but they also have a more creative sense of curse words, phrases that in translation seem innocent to an American but that had great meaning for them. One of these phrases I liked in particular was *Va fa Napoli!* I sensed immediately what it meant the very first time I heard it. I could tell from the rhythm and stress of it and the way it was used that it meant "Go to hell!" But for my father and his friends, and this was what so amazed me, hell wasn't the hell we knew from the Catholic Church; it was the city of Naples! In other words, wishing someone to go to Naples was like wishing them to go to hell. What could Naples be like, I wondered, if that was how these men thought of it?

But "Mannaggia l'America!" made me think more deeply. Was it possible that America was not perfect? That's what I heard in the phrase. Evidently, among Pop and his *paesani* there was enough of an undercurrent of negative feelings about America to have invented a phrase that said it all. It said that America was sometimes at fault, that life here was perhaps not what they had expected; the streets were not paved with gold, and if you wanted to achieve anything, you had to work your butt off. And somehow America was implicated in my hay fever.

My attacks went on all through my teen years. Pop, at his wit's end, finally gave in and let me go for allergy shots. He was persuaded to do this by our good friends Ange and Jen Cerchiaro, the same couple who had helped my father with the down payment for our store and home. They were originally from Pittsburgh and had come into our circle of friends through the close community of shoe repairmen in Cleveland, most of whom my father knew.

Despite the difficulties I had encountered in my search for a man to emulate and admire, I still continued to look and hope. I knew I was supposed to love and respect my father, and I did love and respect him, but I knew unconsciously—for I never could or would articulate such a thought or even imagine it—I knew that I never wanted to be like my father. His amount of anger, of irrationality, of being judgmental and narrow-minded, all cast with his 100 percent certainty, was frightening to me; and therefore, I felt he had nothing to teach me. I wanted a more open world, a larger and more accepting world, one free of prejudice and constant hurtful criticism. I wanted someone who had pride in me, someone who said something good about me. I wasn't a terrible kid. I knew that … well, sort of. I couldn't be sure. I was getting crossed signals. But I'd never caused my father any trouble; I was one of the good kids. Education was the all-important passport to a good life. I didn't dispute that. But I liked school, not to please Pop but because school was where I got my stroking.

Pop's face was another mystery to me, and I would spend hours trying to read it, trying to see if I could figure out what he was thinking and feeling, and to discover there on his face my own wholeness and comfort in the world. But it was not an easy face to read. And when he would stare off into space, as he often did, his ice-blue eyes miles and miles away, I'd always ask him, "What are you thinking about, Daddy?"

And I'd always get the same answer: "Nothing! Nothing!"

I always hoped he'd tell me something about himself. Perhaps he was thinking of his town in Italy or maybe a dream he wanted. But he never shared that far place he went to so often. At other times his face was an impassive, rock-hard mask of a face, a face of withholding that often looked ready to burst from dissatisfaction. I suspect my father adhered to a philosophy of child rearing common at the time. It stated that you should only love your children when they're asleep. I assumed if you loved them when they were awake you would spoil them, and that, you must avoid at all costs.

My sister and I were always held up as having been the best kids in the family. The example of this always given was that if my father or my mother told us to sit in a chair, we would dutifully sit there until told we could move. When I first heard that story of a young boy I no longer remembered or related to, I thought, *Of course I sat there. I was too frightened of my father to move.* This did not, it seemed to me, make for a good child, only for one who obeyed, not out of love but out of fear. So much for some family stories.

My father (and my mother too, for there was nothing in her simple beginnings that would have taught her) did not know one of the great secrets of parenting and of the world: that if you tell a child they can do something, they can and will do it. All they need is someone to hold out that promise to them, to accept the possibility of success as the simplest thing in the world. "Of course you can do that, my child. You can do anything you want." And to make that secret work, you have to lie a bit, for in truth, you don't know the child can do what you say he can. Who among us knows the future? This is the best lie in the world, and all parents should indulge themselves in this lovely fib. And oh, how I longed to hear those words.

But fear of provoking my father's anger held my mother back, and my father was held back by his cold belief in the truth, in life as it is and not as it might be. To him there was nothing more beautiful than the brutal truth. Life as it ought to be was a lie. This is how it is. Period. Don't mess up your head with a lot of junk, fantasies, and silliness. His certainty of this position was 100 percent. And it never occurred to him he might be wrong. A philosophy arrived at through his childhood experiences in the hardscrabble southern part of Italy, it was only strengthened by his experience in America, where he would have no choice but to labor physically all of his life. So I was, in my attempt to understand him, always willing to give him the benefit of the doubt. And I could see the beauty in a kind of rough but simple truth, that there is a virtue in recognizing things for what they are.

But I could always detect an underlying resignation. I could hear it in his voice, in the way, when I expressed a dream, he would say knowingly: "Well, you'll find out one day …" That was his version, though a less humorous one and therefore a more meaningful one to me, of my mother's *E Polvere o Merdo*. And though it was a thought uncompleted I fully understood what wasn't said: I would find out one day that life wasn't the fantasy it was in the movies we saw; that it didn't usually work out so well, that you can't always have what you want. Was he only expressing that fatalism of the Italian character that came out in a kind of dismissiveness about life, or was it the summation of a man who remembered that he was only allowed to go to school for three years and then, despite his pleas for more schooling, had to work on the family's farm? Was it because his mother had died when he was young, leaving his grandparents to raise him … as his father took a mistress? Was it partly the result of being called up for active duty in the First World War? And when, after a year in Sicily, being sent north to Genoa, where—I was convinced—his political education had been made firm? Genoa, a northern city, was alive with the new thinking of the left, the ideas of anarchy, of the need for people to take their fate into their own hands. These were ideas my father immediately related to and which he held dear for the rest of his life.

Because he wasn't the firstborn son in the family, he would not share in the land and the farm that his father would leave. That meant he had to find another path to make his way in the world. When the war was over he joined the elitist, separate corps of the police, the *Carabiniere,* and found himself fortuitously stationed in Rome for three years, where his political and cultural education would continue. I have a treasured photograph of him standing next to a Grecian pillar in front of an obviously painted backdrop of a landscape, dressed in his full regalia as a member of the *Carabiniere.* He is wearing a large ostrich-plumed hat and has a saber hanging at his side on a wonderful golden swash of fringed material. And in Rome his love of the truth would become even more ingrained and instilled in him, a truth so brilliant in its piercing light that it would level all the lies before it and become the most beautiful prize in the world. In a world of problems and poverty and class struggle, this youthful truth he found would be the rock strength of his whole life. And so one learned not to indulge in fantasies such as the average person did. And I surmised that God, though he never said this in so many words, was also one of those fantasies.

This truth-telling extended to me, his only son. If I didn't measure up or disrespected him, he showed his displeasure, if not in words then certainly in the rock-hard set of his face. I looked and looked for reasons to exonerate him, to make him human. But what if, I thought, his behavior was just the animal arrogance of the human, our survival-at-all-costs ego? I couldn't figure him out, and my response to him was as preordained as was his response to life. And I could never learn anything from my father because there was always this red fiery wall of angry criticism that stood between us, impenetrable and constant. And to this day criticism returns me to my childhood, and I become once again that angry son who feels nothing but his own hurt and anger. A legacy from a father who didn't know the secret lie.

Perhaps I should have been one of those sons who fought back. But something in me couldn't do that. This was my father and I respected him. But my anger was building. He could have just once told me I'd done something well, but he never did, never could. If he had I would have felt closer to him. But try as I might and knowing he was doing his best (oh how these thoughts held me prisoner as a young man!), I still couldn't look up to him. And still desperately needing a male to emulate, I turned to Jen Cerchiaro.

Jen was a handsome, unusually tall man, his height topped with a head of wavy silvery Cesar Romero hair that he combed straight back. He was also, unlike my father, always elegantly dressed. So I did my best, within my limited means, to dress like Jen, even buying a pair of blue suede slip-on moccasins, just like he wore, shoes much too sophisticated for a school kid who had no wardrobe to go with them, but shoes—the soft, elegant adult feel of them—I remember to this day. Jen moved in a more steady, reasonable, and more accessible pace than my father; and most importantly, he listened to me.

His wife Ange was a handsome dark-haired woman, with distinguishing thick natural eyebrows that she never plucked or penciled-in like other women did. She was also my mother's best friend. Always beautifully dressed in the latest fashion of the day, the "New Look" of the '50s—Jen's income allowing her to do this—she was something of an anomaly in our community, where the housewives generally wore wraparound house dresses all day long (dusters, my mother called them). Intelligent, strong-minded, and opinionated, she also had a wonderful knack for making you know—with a kind of playful, tough, sergeant-with-a-heart-of-gold manner—that she cared about you. I never minded any mild criticism from her. I considered her my friend and buddy.

Ange's gifts to me at Christmas and birthdays were always different and exciting. One year she gave me an album of the Vienna Boys Choir; another, a beautiful cashmere sweater. She treated me to my first airplane ride. The plane was one of the Viscount prop planes with engines by Rolls-Royce. It was the newest technology in airplane travel. And though it would soon be made obsolete by the jet engine, it was a sleek beauty of modern engineering, and as I walked toward its shimmering silver body waiting for us outside the airport gate, my excitement grew. We were flying from Cleveland to Pittsburgh to visit her family, one of whom—her youngest sister Florence, or Babe as she was called—would become very influential in my life. Soon after we were up in the air, we flew into a violent rainstorm with lots of thunder and lightning. I was sitting next to the window, watching the wings of the plane flap wildly. Fascinated by the whole adventure I didn't even think of being sick, as were many people on the flight. But my friend Ange wasn't even concerned. She sat in her seat as cool as could be, reading a fashion magazine and smoking a cigarette as if nothing were wrong, letting me, a young fellow on his first flight, know that this was the way it was sometimes and that we'd be just fine.

We visited Ange and Jen in their beautiful home in Warrensville Heights at least once a week. Because Jen owned and operated the two best shoe repair stores in the city, he had done quite well financially, especially for a shoe repairman. Once settled into their beautiful living room, Jen and I would listen to his favorite radio shows of the day: Jack Benny and Allen's Alley. They were not my father's favorite shows because they were language based, and he didn't quite understand the humor of them. Then we'd usually play a few games of Chinese checkers, which he'd taught me to play. After that, his wife, Ange, would always serve coffee and dessert, which if I were lucky, would be her wonderful torte cake—a blissed-out sugar confection made of whipped cream, meringue, nuts, and fresh strawberries.

Ange and Jen had no children of their own. I often wondered if that was why they were able to show so much love to me and to other friends' children. Did they give us all the love and the nonjudgmental caring they couldn't shower on their own children? Wherever their love came from, I was the one who benefited. I adored them both. And I appreciated Ange even more so when she took my side and would go up against my father, which she often did.

Seeing how debilitating my hay fever attacks were, my good buddy Ange butted heads with my father, trying to convince him that I needed allergy shots. And her persistence finally won my father's permission, grudging though it was. And so, twice a week, on Tuesday and Thursday evenings, Ange would drive me in her black Buick coupe—the car General Motors advertised for the "strivers" of America—to the office near Shaker Square of a kindly elderly white-haired doctor who called me lad. I was quite taken with that. No one had ever called me lad. It was always my father calling for me: "VINCENZ!" Or Mom yelling for me: "SONNY!" But no one had ever called me, and so pleasantly, lad. It was right out of an MGM all-American movie, and I was Mickey Rooney, and the doctor was Harry Davenport, surely the kindliest doctor there ever was. The shots went on for a good year or so, but unfortunately, my marathon sneezing sessions never stopped. Pop was getting increasingly frustrated at this lack of improvement. He told Ange that the doctor was stealing his money. "HE'S A CROOK! JUST LIKE EVERYONE ELSE!" To my father, most people other than the working man, were "CROOKS!"—people who had their hand in your pocket. At the top of this list were the politicians, next were the priests, and then the doctors.

Ange tried to argue with him. "You have to build up his immunity! It takes time!"

"All that crook is building up is his pocketbook!" was Pop's answer.

And then Pop, looking for someone to blame, for God forbid he had any part in it, would accuse Mom of being the guilty party: "He doesn't get this from me! He gets it from you! From your family!"

Here was that great irrationality of Pop's again, falsely accusing Mom. But she never sneezed. And no one in her family had allergies that I knew of. It was only my nose that was continually red and sore all through the late summer and early fall months of my teen years. And it was only me who went through handkerchiefs by the hundreds, though this was a great help at birthdays and Christmas, for everyone always knew what to get me as a gift.

And so it had gone for years and years: me having marathon sneezing sessions, Pop frustrated and getting angrier and angrier, Mom counting to see if I'd broken the old record of numbered sneezes, and my buddy Ange taking me twice a week for my shots to the kindly white-haired doctor who called me lad.

Frustrated that the shots were not doing me any good and that he was wasting all that money, Pop decided to take action. He'd cure me himself. While hunting one day in the woods near our home, woods that are now suburbs of Cleveland, my father noticed the huge amounts of goldenrod growing in the fields. And seeing all this bounty available and free for the taking, he hatched a plan. (In those days everyone thought the cause of hay fever was goldenrod; they didn't yet know that the main culprit was ragweed.) Unbeknownst to the rest of us, he gathered basketfuls of the golden weed, brought it home, and, after tying it up in bundles, hung it upside down in our basement, right alongside the *pepperoni* and *provolone* he was curing. I discovered this one day when I had to go into the basement for an item needed in the store. I couldn't believe my eyes. Alarmed, I ran up the stairs to tell my mother of my discovery.

"What's all that goldenrod doing in the basement!"

"Your father put it there."

"Why!"

"I don't know why. He won't tell me."

"But that's what I'm allergic to! Is he trying to kill me!"

"No! No!" she answered, trying to calm me. "And don't be so dramatic! It won't bother you!"

"How can you say that!" I protested in my best exasperated Jack Benny voice. "Our house has the highest pollen count in the whole state of Ohio!" But my reasoning fell on deaf ears.

When school started, there was still no answer to what Daddy was planning to do with all the weeds in our basement, which had now grown considerably in quantity. Then one early October evening, when I had interrupted our dinner by launching into one of my marathon sneezing sessions, this one a record-breaking thirty-one, my father had finally had enough. "THAT GODDAMNED DOCTOR!" he said. "HE'S NOT DOING ANYTHING! I'M GOING TO FIX YOU ONCE AND FOR ALL!" Whereupon, he jumped up from the table and quickly ran down the stairs and into the cellar. I looked at my mother, who only shrugged as if to say, "Don't ask me." Soon though, my father's plan to cure me of my hay fever became clear.

In a few minutes, Pop reappeared on the run, carrying Mom's biggest spaghetti pot, the one she only used for big family parties. And he headed straight to the stove with what was obviously a very heavy load.

"MOVE THOSE POTS!" he yelled at my mother.

"What's that?" she asked.

"NEVER MIND! DON'T ASK QUESTIONS! DO WHAT I SAY! NOW!"

Knowing that in this mood there was no point trying to reason with him, Mom did as she was told and made room on the stove for her big spaghetti pot. Pop set it down over two burners and lit the flame under it.

Fearing the worst, I ventured a timid "What's that, Daddy?"

It was a question repeated by my mother, who was now close enough to look into the pot. "What's that mess?"

"THIS IS GOING TO CURE HIM!" my father said.

Mom, incredulous, still looking into the pot, said, "Those weeds are going to cure him?"

"THAT'S RIGHT!" he told her.

Not able to contain myself, I jumped up and ran to the stove and peered into the pot. Then my sister followed. We were now all staring into this huge pot, just like the witches at the beginning of *Macbeth*—which we'd been reading in school—who, by staring into their brew, had prophesied the tragedy to come. But I was not aware yet of the similarities of these two brews.

The pot was filled to the top with water and weeds. And it was obvious that Pop had been cooking this concoction for a while now on Mom's second stove in the basement, the one used for the big dirty jobs like canning, for the weeds had started to break down into a sludge-like, murky consistency, a slimy, ugly brew.

My sister's reaction—she was in college now and could voice the most learned opinion of us all—was "Yuck! What is that?"

Pop ignored her and ordered Mom to get him a cup.

Mom balked. "A what?"

"WHAT'S THE MATTER WITH YOU! ARE YOU DEAF? GET ME A CUP!"

Again Mom bravely ventured a question. "What for?"

Pop's arm rose up quickly. There was that gesture we all knew the meaning of. Mom did as she was told.

I couldn't take my eyes off the glutinous mess in the pot. What could my father possibly have in mind? It was too frightening to contemplate.

Mom quietly brought him the cup. Pop dipped it into the pot, pushing aside the scum on the top and the longer pieces of stems that hadn't broken down yet, and filled it with the dirty-gray liquid beneath. Then he handed the cup to me and said, "Now, drink it!"

"What?!" I said.

"DRINK IT!" he repeated.

In shock, I still managed somehow to say, "I can't drink that!"

"YES, YOU CAN! AND YOU WILL!"

I knew that if I resisted him he would only become more stubborn, and our tug-of-war relationship would be reactivated in a second, so I kept silent.

"YOU WILL DRINK IT EVERY DAY, TWO OR THREE CUPS A DAY, AND YOUR HAY FEVER WILL GO AWAY!"

Now the light dawned on all of us. I was struck mute by what lay ahead of me.

Mom was the first to respond. "Are you crazy?!"

"NO! I'M NOT CRAZY! I'M TIRED OF THAT DOCTOR STEALING MY MONEY! THIS WILL BUILD UP HIS RESISTANCE TOO! THAT'S ALL THAT'S IN THE SHOTS HE'S TAKING! THE SAME THING! YOU THINK IT'S SOME MYSTERY? I'LL MAKE IT FOR HIM AND CURE HIM! YOU'LL SEE!" Then he turned back to me and pushed the cup forward again. "COME ON NOW! DRINK IT! IT WON'T HURT YOU!"

What was I to do? I thought it would be better to get it over with, for there didn't seem to be any other way out of this one. And I knew, too, that my father didn't mean me any terrible harm. It drove him crazy to see me sneeze, to know that I was sick, that I had a health problem. So slowly I raised the cup to my lips and took a sip of the disgusting slimy brew. Then I dropped the cup and ran into the bathroom, where I made retching sounds as if I were throwing up.

I could hear Mom saying to him, "YOU'RE CRAZY! DO YOU KNOW THAT?!"

But Pop was determined. "I'M NOT CRAZY! IF ONLY HE WOULD DRINK IT, IT WOULD CURE HIM!"

"Daddy," my sister said, having regained her collegiate reasoning, "you have the right idea, but it doesn't work that way. It has to be in the bloodstream. And in a form that won't make him sick."

"BUT IF ONLY HE WOULD TRY!" It was hard for Pop to let go of an idea once he'd gotten hold of it. And one, like this one, that he'd spent so much time and effort on.

"TAKE THAT POT DOWN INTO THE CELLAR," Mom ordered, "AND WASH IT OUT!" She had the high road now. "THAT'S MY GOOD SPAGHETTI POT FOR COMPANY! I'LL KILL YOU IF YOU RUINED IT! AND THROW OUT ALL THOSE WEEDS!" I came out of the bathroom in time to see Pop, his tail between his legs as he carried the pot back into the basement, still muttering, "If only he would try it …"

What was there to say about Pop's wacky ideas? We were stunned into silence and sat back down at the table to try to finish our dinner. Mom broke the silence. "I guess we know how that concoction turned out. It wasn't the *polvere* but the other one, you know, the *merdo*." I tried to laugh at Mom's joke, but somehow I couldn't summon my usual enthusiasm. This had been a close call. I would need a little more time before I could turn Pop's latest weird idea into one of the family's favorite stories about him.

Later I remembered a story I'd heard about my father. As a young boy in Italy, he had come down with a serious illness. Perhaps it was diphtheria or maybe malaria. There was, at the turn of the twentieth century, an epidemic of malaria in the southern part of Italy. And having no cure for whatever it was he had, the family sat by helplessly as his temperature climbed. Knowing they could do nothing more for him, they left him to sleep, hoping for the best yet fearing the worst. Young people often died. Infants even more often. It was a part of life. It was fate, as common and expected as the cycles of the seasons they lived by. And they accepted it.

During that night of high fever, my father, in a delirious state, woke, got out of bed, and walked into the kitchen. On the table, marinating in olive oil, garlic, and parsley, was a big plate of the very hottest peppers from their farm that his grandmother had prepared that day. Without thinking, he ate them all. In his feverish state, he wasn't even aware of how they burned as they went down his throat. Then he returned to his bed and fell into a deep sleep.

When he woke the next morning, the fever had broken and he felt better. He got up and asked for breakfast. Everyone said it was a miracle. My father, never much of a believer in miracles, said it was the hot peppers that had cured him. They had, he said, burned the infection and fever right out of him. And perhaps they had. So for all his remaining years, my father would always sprinkle hot red pepper flakes over all his food. Sometimes his plate of food would be so covered with red pepper you couldn't see what the meal was. And no amount of shock or alarm on anyone else's part could ever dissuade him from this practice. He knew it worked. Hot pepper warded off disease and kept you healthy. So he had tried to cure me in the same way. The natural way. And maybe he was right. He did live to be ninety-six years old and was perfectly healthy till the end.

Of course we shared the hay fever–cure story with all the family and friends. It was too good to keep quiet about. It was further evidence of Pop's *pazzo* (crazy) ideas. But Pop was stubborn to the end, and he'd always say when the story was told, "If only he had tried it, it would have worked!" But to me in later years, it would come to symbolize my father perfectly: he wanted so desperately to do the best for me, yet he often went about it in the wrong way.

When my buddy Ange heard what he'd done, she let him have it. Shaking her head in disbelief, she balled him out good. I was secretly glad she did. She was standing up for me! No one had ever had ever done that before. And for some reason, Pop accepted her criticism. And he allowed her to continue taking me for my twice-weekly shots for the rest of my high school years, though they never seemed to have any good effect on my hay fever or curtailed my marathon sneezing sessions. In that, Pop was right.

The legacy of stories about Pop, I can see now, were almost all a comment on his being an immigrant, for that was what was being laughed at: his "old ways" and their idiocy up against the new ways of the New World. This caused an imbalance in my life, for it said to me that my father, the immigrant who spoke with an accent, was somewhat laughable. I often wondered if the family's reaction to his behavior might not have caused my father some pain. Surely always being the butt of the joke must have hurt him. But he never let on that he was hurt if it was so. He was always a good sport about it. One day later in life, my mother told me that because he was laughed at for his accent by his English language classmates when he had first come to America, he quit the classes. That didn't sound like my father at all. It didn't square with the tough guy I knew, who just kept on going no matter what anyone said. Was Pop more sensitive than he ever let on? I think he was. And it would take me years to realize that my father was so much more than a stereotype. He was highly intelligent and extremely capable and he was also a proud man. To be reduced to a laugh must have hurt him deeply.

A year or so after the hay fever incident, when I was a freshman in high school, Jen—because Ange and her two sisters had gone off on a long-planned trip to Florida—was at our home for dinner. When we'd finished dinner and coffee, we all walked Jen through our living room and out our back door, down the porch steps to his black Buick. A discussion ensued about learning to drive. I now had my learning permit and could drive as long as an adult accompanied me. My father offered his usual skepticism about my abilities: "Well, we'll see what kind of a driver he is." Whereupon, Jen said, "I know he can drive without any problems right now. Maybe in city traffic it would be a bit harder, but on the highway he'd be fine." I was knocked out. Imagine! A compliment! Someone expressing confidence in my ability! This had never ever happened to me! No family member had ever complimented me.

Then somehow the conversation veered abruptly away into a totally different subject: death. My father and Jen were discussing a hypocrisy endemic to the human being: how one said terrible things about the living but the minute a person died one never said anything unpleasant about them. Jen, who had a wonderfully sardonic side to his nature, a ruefulness that was the leavening of his character, was saying as he got into his car, "It's true. When you're alive, everyone calls you an SOB, but when you die, all of a sudden you're a wonderful human being."

That conversation on our back porch as Jen was leaving stayed with me. First of all I'd received my first compliment. Then I'd heard some adult words about death and the hypocrisy of humans. But the main reason I would remember that conversation on our back porch was that it would be the last time I saw Jen alive. He drove from our home to another friend's home, where, after drinking a Coca-Cola, lay down on their sofa for a while. And it was there that he suffered a fatal heart attack. Had he had a premonition—I was always looking for answers—or had it just been a coincidence that his last words were about death?

Jen was only forty-nine years old when he died. And that was too young. Our community was shocked. What could possibly have happened to him? One person said that a trip to Italy a few years before to see his mother and finding her living in sad poverty had deeply depressed him. Someone else said that it was all the Cokes he drank that killed him. Everyone knew how dangerous Cokes were; why, if you put a nail in a glass of coke it would disintegrate! But I didn't believe that explanation either. People needed, I surmised, an answer—no matter how ridiculous—for the shocking and unbelievable intrusion of death into a still relatively young life. But as always there was no easy answer. And I had again lost someone who had been wonderful to me, had taught me games with a great deal of patience, had shared his love of humor with me, had shown me a more reasoning way to deal with life, and had even complimented me and been supportive of me. Would people say that he was wonderful now that he was dead? It hardly mattered to me. I'd always thought he was.

The funeral was held in Pittsburgh. I wanted desperately to go. So Mom stayed home to take care of the store, and Daddy and I drove to Pittsburgh for the funeral. We left our home early in the morning while it was still dark, and we arrived in Pittsburgh in time to join the cortege as it wound its way from the funeral home to the cemetery on a hill overlooking the surrounding valleys of western Pennsylvania.

This was the second funeral in my life that caught me unawares. Again I was blindsided by a depth of emotion I still didn't totally understand. But now I was sixteen years old, and I was aware that Jen was someone who had meant a great deal to me, someone whom I had emulated and had hoped to keep learning from. And the truth now was that time had run out for me; I had no one else to turn to for my role model. I looked at my buddy Ange, who stood unmoving and silent at Jen's graveside. What was she thinking? Or was she so traumatized she couldn't think or feel? And for some reason it was her stoicism, her pain that released my heartbreak and made me start to cry. Embarrassed to be the only one sobbing, just as I had been at my uncle John's funeral, I left the graveside and climbed into the back of a limousine, where no one would see me crying and from where I watched the proceedings. When the graveside ceremony was over and Jen had been lowered into the ground, everyone returned to their cars, and we all silently moved down the hill and returned to Ange's parents' home, where my father and I had been graciously invited to stay the night.

Our bedroom was on the second floor of their home, past a beautiful stained-glass window where the stairs made a U-turn to the second floor. I had never slept with my father before. After we had both fallen asleep, I was awakened by my father, who had rolled over to my side of the bed and had thrown his arms around me. Embarrassed at first by this unusual show of affection on his part, I tried gently to push him away without wakening him. But every time I did, he, still sound asleep, rolled right back over to my side of the bed and once again wrapped his arms around me, hugging me closely. My father, always so strange to me, so removed and separate, was now showing affection to me, I thought, for what I'd felt that day. But then, in the darkness of that strange bedroom, it dawned on me. It wasn't me he was hugging; it was my mother.

How often I had wondered if my parents actually loved each other. I saw no sign of it growing up. There was very little outward affection between them. And my father's playful swat at my mother's behind didn't look like love to me; it looked more like a warning for her to behave. There was always a ritual hello or good-bye kiss on the cheek. But that was all I ever witnessed. Did they really love each other? I couldn't tell. Yet here, in this strange bedroom in Pittsburgh, my physically unaffectionate father kept returning to his accustomed embrace of my mother—they slept spoon fashion, it seemed—even though I constantly pushed him away. Finally I relented and let him be, trying to sleep myself. And though I had realized his embrace wasn't meant for me, I was comforted by the knowledge of his affection for my mother. It seemed he could show affection … just perhaps only in his bedroom and at night.

Ange returned to Cleveland to pick up her life. She hoped to keep their two shoe repair shops running. But she soon gave up the one in the Higbee's department store in downtown Cleveland and concentrated on the one at Shaker Square. There, working behind the counter of the shop, taking in shoes for repair, she was the most handsome and elegantly dressed woman in any shop around the square and certainly in any shoe repair shop in America. I worked for her in the shop on weekends and in the summer too, behind the counter. She had taught me how to mark the shoes for what repairs were needed. On those days when she closed the shop she always let me drive her new dark-green Chevy Coup home to our house, where she usually stayed and had dinner with us, my parents' generosity keeping an open door to her always.

Though she made a strong attempt to get on with her life, it wasn't working. I'd watch her, as I had my aunt Florence, as she made futile attempts to eat but would finally push her plate away with apologies to my mother. Then she'd light up a cigarette and nurse her cup of coffee. It was plain for us to see that she was sinking deeper and deeper into a depression. Drooping over her plate, quieter than usual and often deep in her own thoughts, her spark for life—that wonderfully contentious way she went about it that I had always adored—was gone.

To keep herself going, to persuade herself she was still alive, she went on compulsive shopping sprees, once buying three new fur coats. But these new luxuries never satisfied. Then she began to change the furniture in her home over and over, finding any reason to send it back, searching for absolute perfection, anything to help her start anew, hoping in this way to change the past—an impossible task. My mother and father and all of her friends were alarmed by her behavior but could do nothing more for her beyond providing a place and a table where she was always welcome.

Her grieving went on for too long. Had she felt guilt for being away when

Jen died? I'd heard that their last conversation had been an argument over the phone, an argument she had ended by hanging up on him. I still listened to everything, hoping to piece the puzzle together, but there seemed to be no easy answer. Ange got worse and sank deeper into her depression, which was now being mixed, her friends suspected, with sleeping pills and alcohol.

Finally dysfunctional and unable to care for herself, she was introduced reluctantly to the same treatment my aunt Florence had first been given: electroshock therapy. It did not seem to help her. She retreated into her home, not answering her doorbell or the phone. My parents, upset when they couldn't rouse her, fearful she might have had an accident, would often drive up to her home after they'd closed the store. Knowing she was home because they could see a light in her bedroom and not being able to rouse her, they would place a call to her sister Florence in Wilkinsburg, who would then drive to Cleveland to deal with her sister's problems. It was on her many trips to Cleveland that I got to know this remarkable person who would change my life.

I'd heard that while an undergraduate at Westminster College, Florence had shocked the student body by refusing to join a sorority. The sorority she had wanted to join had blackballed her because they thought she was Jewish, a mistake they perhaps made because of her very strong Roman nose. Another reason they might have made that mistake was that there were very few Italian American girls at that mostly WASP college. When they discovered their mistake, they reinvited her to join. But she would have none of it. And that was why one morning in assembly, she stood up and told the whole student body that she would not join any sorority that discriminated in any way at all.

Besides her deep moral sense, she was the possessor of a most unique, resonant, perfectly placed and beautifully modulated alto voice, which, coupled with her intelligence and curiosity of the world's events, made her an early player in the radio and then TV broadcasts of the day. I discovered that if I held my hand over the air vent in the back of my RCA Victor radio, I could pull in the weak signal of WCAE from Pittsburgh all the way to Cleveland, and I could listen to *The Florence Sando Radio Show*, her commentary on local and national events every weekday at twelve thirty. When WDTV, the pioneer TV station which was later folded into KDKA-TV, came on the air, she was one of the first news broadcasters in America, perhaps even the first woman to deliver the news on TV. Also an actress who appeared regularly at the Pittsburgh Playhouse, her achievements were remarkable enough for her to have been included in Who's Who Among American Women.

On the weekends she came to Cleveland to prop up her sister; she was fun and outspoken in a way I'd never heard before. In her car one day—she drove a snazzy green Ford convertible, the fabulous '49 Ford with the round propeller-like grille, the aerodynamic one!—as we were on our way to the Cleveland Museum of Art to see a Matisse exhibit, she got me to join her in a duet of "Anything You Can Do I Can Do Better." When I graduated high school, this remarkable woman, knowing I had enjoyed acting in high school, suggested I go to the Carnegie Tech Drama School in Pittsburgh. And so my fate was set.

Finally it was decided that Ange would move back to Pittsburgh to be close to her family. And so, as soon as Florence could get her sister's household goods packed, Ange was gone from our lives. My mother, who counted her as her closest friend, would see her only rarely now when Ange would make an occasional visit back to Cleveland to see her friends. But slowly these visits ended, as Ange, making a great and heroic effort to pull herself together, decided to become a visiting nurse, which she remarkably accomplished and did for the rest of her life, greatly rewarding her patients, I'm sure, with her wonderful ability to take charge in a strong but loving way.

Years later, when I was living on my own in New York City, I often spent the holidays at my parents' home in Florida. When I wasn't working, it was a great place to have a bit of a vacation. And it was there during one of those breaks that I witnessed my father sneeze with a fury and violence that practically knocked him off the chair he was sitting on. His sneezing was operatic, a volcano erupting. It started with the initial intake of breath, the foreshadowing, which began the fear for the rest of us. Then there was the buildup to the explosion and then the climax itself, a letting go that was as convulsive as it was loud. It was an attack more Verdian than Puccinian. It didn't last as long as my attacks of hay fever, but it was even more violent than my eruptions had ever been. And it was then I realized that my father had always sneezed that way. When I suggested to him that "if I'd gotten my hay fever from anyone," it was surely from him. And my father, stubborn to the end, refused any such thought. "NO! NO! IT'S JUST SOMETHING IN THE AIR!" He didn't have allergies, of course, for he was perfect.

But an interesting thing happened to me once I left home and set out on my own; I no longer sneezed. I seemed to have left all my allergies behind in Cleveland, left them in the fields of Ohio and in that home behind the store that I grew up in. But my ancestors' fatalism, that fatalism that echoed in my grandfather's phrase *E Polvere o Merdo*, would haunt me still. Perhaps I could turn that motto around and make it mean that everything has a use. After all, *merdo* was manure, wasn't it? And manure was useful on the farm. Maybe that was what my grandfather had meant. Perhaps it was a motto of bravery, a motto of practicality. Could I make it be that? I would try.

Spaghetti Alio e Olio

(I offer this instead of Pop's hay fever–cure recipe. This pasta dish with garlic and olive oil is the Italian male's quick standby favorite meal.)

In a pot of boiling saltwater, cook the amount of pasta you need. Spaghetti or linguine is best for this.

While the pasta is cooking, pour a small amount of olive oil into a saucepan, perhaps ½ of a cup.

Add 2 or 3 large cloves of chopped garlic.
Add a shake or two of red pepper flakes.
Add some salt and black pepper.

(Instead of salt I like to use 2 or 3 anchovy fillets. They dissolve in the pan, and no one will ever know they're there. But they give a wonderful subtle added taste that is better than plain salt.) Cook the garlic till it is golden.

This sauce will only take as long as it takes the garlic to become golden—a couple of minutes—so time it to be done when your pasta is cooked. Then drain the pasta, throw the sauce over it, mix in some fresh parsley, and serve immediately with fresh grated Parmesan or Pecorino-Romano cheese.

If you need a bit more sauce for more pasta or to slow down the cooking process of the garlic, add a little of the pasta water to the sauce.

I also add broccoli to the recipe now. I throw the washed flowerets into the boiling pasta pot just as the pasta is nearly done and then cook them together. It's a good healthy variation. And sometimes I add some lemon juice, which with the grated cheese added before eating, makes a brighter, lighter sauce and taste.

My mother always broke the long strands of spaghetti in half. I do too. This is heresy to Americans who love to slurp and snap the long strands of spaghetti into their mouths, but it makes the spaghetti more manageable and is much easier on everyone's shirts and blouses, especially on the days when tomato sauce is being served.

Mom was, in fact, creative with her use of pasta. It was not an inviolable product. It was meant to be used as you wanted, broken up in half for a sauce or broken into 1" pieces for pasta and beans if she didn't have anything smaller on hand. Or used broken up in chicken soup if she had no *pastina*. The slight change or flavor and texture was welcoming, as is the sense of improvisation in the kitchen that makes one feel creative.

CHAPTER 9
Merdo Can Be a Good Thing

::

When the long pent-up anger toward my father—the anger that I'd been respectfully holding inside of me for all my growing up years (I always dutifully kissed my father on the cheek in greeting and when going to bed at night), the anger of all the years of him withholding his approval of me alongside the constant criticism and belittling of me—when it finally exploded, it happened at that very same porcelain-topped kitchen table one night as we sat down for dinner, just as we had forever, back to the beginning of time. But this night would be different. It would be surprising not only for my reaction—I had never erupted in anger toward my father nor had ever had a fight with him—but also for my father's. And I would understand immediately what I'd never understood before.

My high school graduation party took place at our home. There were the usual guests—my aunts and uncles, along with our wonderful neighbor Josie, who had come to my commencement ceremony. For my party Mom made her stuffed shells, the one meal she prepared that she really liked. Uncle Veto presented me with a bottle of wine for my graduation besides, of course, the usual envelope with cash in it. And it was, as is so often the case, that mundane bottle of wine that became the catalyst for the release of my father's anger and mine. Mom asked me to open the wine. I found the corkscrew in the drawer next to the sink and set to work. It was a very dry cork. I was able to get the corkscrew into it but it wouldn't budge.

So Pop got up to show me how to do it. "Give it to me!"

"I'll get it, Daddy. The cork's too dry. That's all."

I attacked the cork again but with no success. And now the corkscrew was losing its hold as the cork began to crumble. Pop was at my side, anxious to get his hands on the bottle to show me how to do it. And naturally we got into our usual tug-of-war relationship.

"You're making a mess! Come on! Let me show you how to do it!" And he tried to grab the bottle away from me.

But I held onto that bottle tightly; it was my life. "No! I'll get it!" I couldn't give in to him, not on this night, the night of my high school graduation. Surely I deserved some respect.

He tried to grab the bottle again. Then Mom joined in. "Leave him alone, Jim! He can do it!"

That only made my father angrier. "Come on! Give it to me! You're making a mess!"

And then the moment came when I could take no more of his constant criticism of whatever I did, the moment when I needed to claim my own identity and be my own person. I slammed the wine bottle down on the counter. "I AM SO DAMNED TIRED OF YOUR CRITICISM! GO AHEAD! YOU OPEN THE GODDAMNED BOTTLE!" And I walked away.

I had never sworn at my father. Shocked by my words, I sat down in silence in my chair at the table.

Pop, though somewhat taken aback by my outburst, was now concentrated on opening the bottle but was having the same bad luck with it that I had.

Mom saw this. "Look at the mess you're making! Let your son do it! He was doing it right!"

And that was when my father himself exploded in a monumental anger and said to his wife, "EVERYTHING HE DOES IS OKAY WITH YOU! BUT WHAT I DO IS ALWAYS WRONG! THAT'S THE WAY YOU'VE ALWAYS BEEN!"

I was struck dumb. Had this always been what stood between my father and myself, this elemental Freud? It was laughable. Were we such a cliché? Was my father jealous of me? Was I competition for him with his wife? Is that why he treated me the way he did? Had he resented me all these years because my mother had favored me too much? I never thought she had. I always thought she was just overprotective. But obviously he thought so. The depth of his anger told me exactly how strongly he felt. So despite all his powerful certainty and his famous willpower that enabled him to do whatever he wanted, he, too, was human; and he, too, had also lived at the effect of life. It made me wonder if my mother wasn't partly to blame for his treatment of me? But there it was. Out in the open at last.

School was still the only place where I got the stroking and support I needed; but by my senior year it, too, had turned sour. And my last year of school would be the worst year of all. By that time I was a confirmed outsider, though certainly not by choice. I kept up a good front, my cheerful nature covering my inner turmoil, my feelings of inadequacy. But I was withdrawing.

Perhaps sensing my pain, my best friend moved his allegiance away from me to my next best friend. I was deeply hurt. With grown-ups I simply felt overpowered. I became whatever they wanted me to be. They defined me, not myself. And that made me a prisoner locked in a hell I saw no way out of.

In English class we had read Willa Cather's short story, "Paul's Case." It was the story of a young man who finally throws himself in front of a moving train when the dichotomy between the reality of who he is and his grand illusion of himself finally catches up with him. I related to his story. Just as he had learned to reinvent himself and "dress the part" from his actor friends, I had also reinvented myself. Desperate to be someone, I transformed myself into a "playboy." Having the use now of my father's new four-door black Buick sedan, the one with the portholes on the side and the sluggish Dynaflow transmission—my father continued to drive his overhauled '39 Buick to work and to the market—I drove myself to school every day, hoping to impress my schoolmates. Along with the new car, I had also accumulated a sharp wardrobe that consisted of more V-neck cashmere sweaters than anyone. When I had a date, I took her to the theater and to a nightclub where, surprisingly, we always succeeded in being served liquor. This first role I created, a desperate means of survival, just as the role-playing later in the theater would become, turned out to be very successful. Unconscious, I never made a total connection in my mind between Paul's story and mine, yet it reverberated in me and remained with me always. And I wondered, for I was also suicidal, if my ending would be the same as his?

I had also read a recently published book called *The Outsider*. I related to it too, for it described me. I was that pathetic outsider described in the book. It's funny how we find exactly what we need to find, out there in the world to corroborate our own experience. I also related to a popular recording called *Tubby the Tuba* ("Alone am I, Me and My Together") that Danny Kaye had recorded. I played it over and over. Because it ended on an upbeat note with "Tubby" being accepted by his orchestra mates, it assuaged my frightening feelings of aloneness. In journalism class, when we wrote our own obituaries, I fantasized another great role for myself—that of a famous drama critic, dead in his luxurious mansion on the Riviera, married to wife number seven.

While I might have fooled others, I couldn't fool myself. I never shied away from the downside of what was happening to me. Like Paul, I would look into "the dark corners." When I needed to go into the basement storeroom for an item for the store, I would stand in the same place near the basement sink, where my aunt Florence had stood, and like her, I would check out the large knives. How, I wondered, does one slash one's wrists, and does it hurt? Somewhere I heard that if you did it under water it was less painful.

Every morning I drove to school as usual so that my schedule looked normal to my parents, and then, after parking across the street from the school and watching my classmates enter after the final bells had rung, I would speed away to downtown Cleveland. My schedule was always the same. My first stop would be the Art Museum, where I'd wait under Rodin's *The Thinker* for the museum to open. I'd then spend an hour or two in the galleries, being particularly fascinated by El Greco's twisted and tormented *Christ on the Cross.* Though the church no longer offered me any solace, I still related to Christ, though not the Christ of the church, the Christ of redemption, but the Christ of pain and art; for the two were becoming intermingled. I was now Christ reincarnated and I felt His pain. And while it was secretly rewarding to be godlike, to know I had powers of perception no one else had, this reward came at the heavy price of pain … His and mine.

After an hour or so at the museum, I'd then head downtown to one of the great movie palaces at Playhouse Square. A movie was always a good mood changer. But as the senior year wore on, I would more often drive down Parkway Boulevard to Lake Erie, and standing out on the boulders at the end of a breakwater that jutted far out into the lake, I would wonder if drowning was the best way to kill myself. But wouldn't that be hard since I knew how to swim? Maybe I could use my father's double-barreled shotgun. But an inner voice would always break my suicidal reverie. Was my greediness to see it all, to experience all of life, winning out over my depression?

Finally I would drive back home, planning my arrival at my normal coming-home-from-school-time. And no one was the wiser—not my parents or my teachers in school. Being one of the A students, one of the "good kids," they always accepted my faked sick notes from my mother and hoped I was feeling better. They were sure I would never cut school. One day, just by overhearing a conversation our admission teacher was having with another student, I found out that I was one day shy of having to repeat the semester. That was a shock! Wouldn't my father be happy if that happened? I made sure I never missed another day till the end of the semester, and luckily, I was able to graduate with my class. Still I made the honor roll and in a first experience of irony I was voted the best dressed.

I often had a corresponding vision that came to me during those years. I saw a very long sliding board, down which we humans traveled when we died and moved into the next world. At the bottom of the long slide, there were thousands of dead people watching the newcomers arrive. When the newly dead hit the bottom of the slide, the already dead all pointed at the newcomers and laughed uproariously at them because they had taken life so seriously. How ridiculous they were! And how they laughed at me as I slid to the bottom—another poor, self-involved, vanity-driven human. Our life was laughable and meaningless; translation—it was stupid to care, to make an effort. What's the point if it's all useless? And I promised myself that I would graduate, put all this behind me, and I would not take anything too seriously ever again. I would keep my problems to myself, for there was obviously no help from others who were all imprisoned in their own worlds.

I had hoped to be one of the contestants in my class to win the Honor Key, an award that went only to a few students, the ones who were best all around, who had excelled both in academics and in extracurricular activities. I was the first-page editor of the school paper, I was in the Dramatics Club and the Radio Club, and I had been on the honor roll every year. But though I had been the first student in my freshman class to be inducted into the Honor Society, I was abruptly thrown out of the National Honor Society at the end of my freshman year. What got me thrown out of the Honor Society was the senior play *You Can't Take It With You*. I had been asked by the seniors to join the cast of the play as Eddie. It was an honor to be asked, and I was naturally delighted. On the last night of the weeklong run, the other cast members came to me and said they wanted to put back for the last performance some lines of dialogue about having a baby that our principal, deeming them inappropriate for a school play, had cut. I enthusiastically went along with the conspiracy. After all, we lived in America, the land of free speech, didn't we? And the lines were innocent ones, I thought, and would not offend anyone. I (Eddie) say to my wife (Essie), "Let's go upstairs and make a baby." And so on Saturday night the lines went back into the play, and they got the big laugh everyone had hoped for.

Monday morning I was called into the principal's office, where I was told that because of my involvement in the incident I was being thrown out of the National Honor Society. None of the other graduating seniors in the play had anything to lose, so they were not reprimanded. It was only me. And it was a harsh punishment, for it meant I could no longer be considered for the Honor Key, for one of the requirements of winning it was membership in the National Honor Society. That was a blow to me. My beloved school, John Adams High, a proud symbol of public education, rich in its racial and cultural diversity, whose teachers I adored and emulated, and the only place I had succeeded, had come down hard on me. And I broke down and started to cry, which prompted the principal to deliver a lecture to me on how I "mustn't be too sensitive, for that could make life difficult." That was easy for him to say; he didn't have my father. But there was no recourse to due process of the law then, and I had to accept my draconian punishment.

Still when it came time to graduate, not being a member of the Honor Society did not keep the principal from denying me the honor of being one of the two commencement speakers. I was surprised. If I was persona non grata as far as the school was concerned, why was I being allowed to speak for my classmates? But I said nothing, for I was too embarrassed to let anyone know what had happened, and I went along with the program. Weeks before, I had submitted a speech that had been approved. It took as its theme William Ernst Henley's poem, "Invictus."

> *It matters not how strait the gate,*
> *How charged with punishment the scroll*
> *I am the master of my fate,*
> *I am the captain of my soul.*

But I no longer wanted to give that usual uplifting speech, that clichéd one that always said, "Commencement means a new beginning." I didn't believe we were the "masters of our fate." I was neither the master of my fate nor the "captain of my soul." Others were. So I felt I couldn't say that. I wouldn't be honest if I did. I was speaking of my own life, of course. What other experience could I speak from? I saw no way out of my life except through suicide.

In the Masonic Auditorium in downtown Cleveland, a powerful spotlight blinding my view of the audience and my notes, I stood in front of the largest high school graduating class till that time in the history of the state of Ohio—375 students—and told them that we were not the "masters of our fate" nor were we the "captains of our soul." I told them that we were a very young form of life that was just a few thousand years out of the caves, that we were a form of life living on a planet that was whirling around in space, not knowing who we were or why we were and that, in the face of such overwhelming fears in order to survive, we had created a false scenario for ourselves. And furthermore, I said, "Of what use are we humans? The worms are more important; they aerate the soil so plants can grow. And the bees are necessary, for they propagate the plants and trees that bear fruit. Without them we couldn't live. But what good are we?" I answered my own question. "Not much at all that I can see. We only harm and destroy the beautiful world we've been given, and we do it with great arrogance and great certainty." Then I sat down.

Immediately after the ceremony, in the lobby of the Masonic Auditorium, my father had an argument with my mother because she couldn't remember where he had parked the car. He made no comment about my speech. Nor did anyone else—not my family or my friends. I began to think that no one had even heard it. But one person had heard it. And that person was someone I had never met before: the mother of my prom date. While I waited for her daughter to come down the stairs of their home on that longed-for night, she took me aside and presented me with a little book titled *As A Man Thinketh*.

She had even taken the time to write an inscription inside. "If you will read this book over and over, you will become the master of your fate and the captain of your soul." I was so happy that someone had actually listened to my speech and had heard it! And I thanked her for her gift, which I still have. Then her daughter, Carolyn Reiser, one of the prettiest girls in our class, came down the stairs. My good friend Carmie had fixed up Carolyn and me. Like me, Carolyn had no prom date either. And, oh boy, had I lucked out there. Carolyn was a knockout in her beautiful, light spring-colored prom gown. I helped her on with her matching stole, and as we headed for the main door of the house, her father, who had been sitting in a chair next to the door, reading the evening paper and who hadn't said a word to me, dropped the paper to his lap and, looking straight at his daughter, said, "You're a ship sailing in uncertain waters." Wow. What a weird thing to say to your daughter on her prom night. I imagined W. C. Fields was sitting in that chair.

As I opened the door on my dad's car that I'd spent the afternoon vigorously washing and polishing, I asked Carolyn what her father had meant, and she just said, her eyebrows shooting up to her hairline, "Oh, pleeeze!" I ran around the car and slid into the driver's seat, and off we went to our prom—first to the dance in our high school gymnasium and after that to a downtown nightclub where we sat in a tufted leather booth, the boys in their white formal dinner jackets, the girls in their pastel gowns pinned with the corsages the boys had worried over, drinking Tom Collinses, and listening to Dorothy Dandridge sing very sexy adult songs. After that we went to the home of my wonderful friend Riki Gordon—who had taught me by her own behavior so much about being passionate about life, of caring about it, and of participating in it—where, thanks to Riki's gracious parents, my close friends and I had our final party.

But before entering the house, my beautiful prom date and I spent a feverish hour in the backseat of my father's Buick trying to devour each other. I don't know what came over us. I certainly hadn't planned on it. And none of our other friends had stayed outside. It was just something that had overwhelmed us. Maybe we were in the grip of the force of our pent-up feelings of not being in control of our own lives, of our anger and pain. Maybe if we went to this wild place we had never been before we could wipe out all the past, all those years of not being free, and maybe we could now finally be ourselves, our unrestricted selves. Or maybe it was just hormones. Whatever the force was that propelled us, it released an overwhelming passion of necking and petting that hopefully proclaimed the end of youth.

Two days after the blowup with my father over the opening of the bottle of wine, I left home. I'd been secretly planning it for weeks. I had saved enough money from working at my friend Ange's shoe repair shop on weekends, and with it I bought a plane ticket and a two-week hotel reservation on Martha's Vineyard. I knew nothing about Martha's Vineyard; it was the suggestion of the helpful lady in the travel office at Shaker Square. The morning I was to leave, I got up very early, packed my bag, and quietly, so as not to disturb my mother and father who were still sleeping, walked out into the living room and called a cab to take me to the airport. Mom heard me on the phone, of course; she never missed anything happening in her house, and she immediately came out into the kitchen to see what was going on.

"What are you doing?"

"I'm calling a cab."

"A cab!" We never called a cab in our family. People with money called cabs. "Why?"

"I'm going away."

"Where!"

"To Martha's Vineyard. I have a ticket. I'm going to stay two weeks."

"Where?" Like me, she'd never heard of Martha's Vineyard either.

"Martha's Vineyard. It's an island off Cape Cod."

"Just like that you're going?"

I hadn't really thought through the consequences of what I was doing. I just knew that I had to find a place away from my home environment, a place where I could breathe my own air freely and deeply.

My mother said nothing and immediately disappeared into her bedroom. Now I was worried, for I thought she was waking my father up. When she returned in a few minutes, I was surprised by what she said to me. "Your father will take you to the airport."

I guess they had decided quickly there was no stopping me. But what I most certainly didn't want was my father being any part of my first day of freedom. I wanted no interference from him.

"He doesn't have to do that," I told her. "Anyway, I've called a cab. It'll be here soon."

Then Pop, hastily pulling on his pants and buttoning his shirt, walked into the kitchen. "I'll take you to the airport."

I couldn't believe how quickly they had both acquiesced to my plan. Still I couldn't let him drive me to the airport. "I don't want you to. I've called a cab."

Seeing how determined I was, he knew immediately there was no use trying to change my mind. And I think he understood. He had often said to me, "Twenty-one years old and you're out!" I always thought he was trying to get rid of me, but years later, I realized he meant it as being helpful, that the sooner and faster I got on with my own life, the better for me. So though I wasn't twenty-one yet, he had to go along with my need for being responsible for myself. He offered me some money.

"Here. Take this. You'll need it."

But I was too proud to take his money on this, my first foray into manly responsibility. "I don't need it. I have my savings." And he backed off for the first time and did not try to force his will on me.

A horn blew. I walked to the window overlooking the store. It was my cab. I grabbed my suitcase, said my quick good-byes to my parents—no good-bye kisses this time—and ran down the stairs and out the door to the waiting taxicab, the first cab I'd ever called. I hoped and prayed I was leaving my inessential childhood behind as I rushed toward the beginning of my longed-for real life.

Mom, ever aware, knew exactly what was happening, and as she followed me down the stairs to lock the door behind me, she said, "Your father carried you to school on his back when you had ringworm on the soles of your feet and you couldn't walk. He carried you to school, put you into your chair, and then picked you up at the end of the school day. He didn't want you to miss one day of school. Do you remember that? You must have been seven or eight years old."

I hadn't remembered that. But my mother never forgot anything, and she used that story that early morning to make peace in the family. But I was already out the door and on my way down the driveway to the cab.

She called after me, "Call me when you get there! Reverse the charges!"

I said I would.

And in my powder-blue, butchered linen suit, my blue suede slip-ons on my feet (the shoes I'd bought to emulate Jen), I stepped into the yellow cab, into a world where I could say and do what I wanted for the first time and where I was hoping I would be perceived as a grown-up, maybe even someone with some dash in his person.

At LaGuardia Airport in New York City, I had a three-hour layover while I waited for the flight to Martha's Vineyard. I jumped into the second cab of my life outside the airline terminal and told the driver to take me into Manhattan because I wanted to see the Broadway theaters. He didn't question a young man's unusual request, and off we went to midtown Manhattan. Once in Times Square, my driver took me up and down all the side streets where, for the first time, I saw for myself all the fabled Broadway theaters that I longed to see—the Shubert, the St. James, the Music Box, the Palace, the Booth. From my fifteenth year or so, I had regularly sneaked away from home on Saturday afternoons and had attended matinées of touring Broadway shows at the Hanna Theater or the Music Hall. I had seen the national companies of *Guys and Dolls*, *Oklahoma*, *South Pacific*, and *Brigadoon*. I saw Sam Levene in *Light*

Up The Sky, Katharine Cornell in more than one play (she always gave the first performance of her plays in Cleveland), the wonderful Thomas Mitchell in *Death of a Salesman*, Katharine Hepburn wooing and winning the audience in *As You Like It*, and the Lunts, who were fascinating to watch no matter how unmemorable the play. I saw Helen Hayes, a deft comedienne, and Eva LeGallienne and Charles Boyer, so good on the stage in *Red Gloves*. I saw one of the first performances of *Picnic* and was stunned by the beauty of Janice Rule but even more stunned by the talent of a remarkable, unknown actress named Kim Stanley, who was playing the tomboy younger sister. Tallulah Bankhead played the Hanna Theater in *Private Lives* before opening on Broadway. I saw the national company of *Streetcar Named Desire* and bought a copy of the play, reading it at night in bed and thinking—especially during the last scene, when Blanche is taken away to a mental institution—of my aunt Florence. I went to Severance Hall to hear a Wagnerian concert played by the Cleveland Symphony Orchestra and saw, by chance—I didn't know who she was—the great Kirsten Flagstad in one of her first concerts in the United States after the war.

When our tour of the fabled Broadway theaters was over, the cab driver drove me back to the airport. I paid him the ten-dollar fare and added a grown-up tip of a dollar. Though I never touched my feet to the pavement, I had seen my dream, and it was real. But it would have to wait for seven more years till I finished college and did an enlisted stint in the army; I didn't want anything to get in the way of my dream once I'd embarked on it.

The hotel on Martha's Vineyard turned out to be filled with elderly people, so I made friends with the staff, mostly college students. When my two weeks as a guest were up, and urged on by my new friends, I asked George and Martha, the couple who ran the hotel, if they could use an extra person on the staff for the summer. And happily they said they could. I would do whatever was needed: I would wash toilets, change beds, pick up new guests at the wharf in the hotel's limousine, and even wait on tables in the restaurant. I was ecstatic. And I had an amazing summer, learning a great deal about life from the somewhat older staff members. Surely this glorious freedom was the way life was meant to be.

Mom called every week to see when I was coming home, but I was having too good a time with my new friends—spending our off times on the beautiful beaches of the island, having clam, lobster, and corn roasts—to think of leaving. My real life had begun. Every morning I woke up singing and ran headlong into what new adventure and joy the day would bring. Years later when I mentioned that summer, all my mother said was, "That was a hard time when you went away like that, without any warning. Oh, what parents have to go through."

I returned home in time to pack my bags and leave for college. With Florence's help—she coached me in my two audition pieces—I had been accepted into the Drama Department at Carnegie-Tech in Pittsburgh. And making my new life even more hopeful, I had also been awarded a tuition scholarship. I was now on my way to being an actor. Why had I been bitten by the acting bug? Surely it was a need to transform myself. And if that weren't totally possible, then the many different roles I could play—I had already created one successfully—would give me a respite from myself and offer me the chance to be what I couldn't be. Or, and this was the better reason, the chance to be the person I really was, the chance to be me. And in that way I would survive.

There was also the possibility that I was helped in that choice by all the movies that Pop took me to, the only activity we ever shared that was peaceful. Pop loved entertainment, and he absolutely adored the movies. The family story about him was that before he had married he would, on his day off, go from one movie theater to another all day and evening long. He absolutely loved the kind of entertainment that Hollywood was churning out, particularly the musicals. He got a great kick out of Carmen Miranda and Jimmy Durante. And he pronounced Hedy Lamarr and Dolores Del Rio the most beautiful women in the world, and he spoke forever of the day he had seen Jean Harlow exit the stage door of the RKO Palace Theatre in downtown Cleveland: "She was so beautiful! And she had no makeup on! No makeup!" That impressed Pop.

So all through my high school years, Pop and I went to the movies, sometimes three times a week. Mom either had one of her headaches, or she was always too tired to join. In those days all the theaters had the same schedule: one bill on Sunday, Monday, and Tuesday; a less popular bill on Wednesday only; and then a new bill on Thursday, Friday, and Saturday. And if that wasn't enough to satisfy our cinematic cravings, we had our choice of three local movie theaters: the nearby Imperial, the Shaker on Lee Road, and the Colony at Shaker Square. We could go to a movie every night of the week if we wanted.

And though these were peaceful evenings with my father, they still held some danger for me because I knew and dreaded what was going to happen. Pop, exhausted from his long day of work, would sit down in his seat, watch the film for about fifteen minutes, and then, just as I feared, he would start to fall asleep. What followed was a routine that I knew well, for it never varied. First his head would slowly drop into his lap. Feeling himself falling asleep, he'd try to fight it, which resulted in him snapping his head up violently and back, almost into the lap of the person sitting behind him. Awake for a dazed and surprised moment but unable to stay awake, his head would begin rolling around, first to his left and then to his right and then finally back into his lap. Embarrassed by all this, I would poke him awake with my elbow as quietly as I could over our shared armrest so no one would see me and know that I was with this person. He would then jerk his head up, saying loud enough for everyone around us to hear, "I'm not sleeping!" I would be mortified. But soon the head rolling would begin again. Finally after two or three bouts of the head rolling, he would go into a deep sleep, from which he would never wake. The danger then was that he would start to snore, which he did sometimes. When that happened I would slide down into my seat as far as I could while still jabbing him with my elbow. It was a painful way to watch a film. And probably the reason I prefer going to movies alone now.

At the end of the movie, when I'd wake him, he would always jump up startled, oblivious to what had happened and to anyone or anything around him and he would lurch up the aisle in front of me in a mad dash to get to our car in the parking lot before the others. I would follow a few steps behind him so as not to look as though I were with this odd person, my father, who was a stranger to me and an embarrassment. Why did he never refuse me when I suggested we take in a movie? I know he loved the movies. But he could have begged off and had a good night's sleep. It was only later that it occurred to me that our movie going was the only activity my father and I shared that was without contention. And maybe, because of my father's love for the movies, if I became an actor, I might finally please my father, maybe even win his approval.

This image of my father always on the run would stay with me forever. I always wondered what he was like at work. But he never spoke to us at home about the steel mill. Once, just once, I entered his mysterious work world. His old '39 Buick had broken down, and he had called Mom, telling her that he needed me to pick him up when his shift was over. So when I got home from school and got the message, I immediately left for downtown Cleveland. As I drove across the Clark Street Bridge, I could see below me the Cuyahoga River valley, the valley of dirt and grime where the factories and the hundreds of giant smokestacks poured their poisonous billows of iron-ore wastes into the air, making it dense and smoky and smelling of sulfur. I quickly closed all the windows to keep the smell out. This was where my father worked. Somehow I found the main gate of his enormous factory, the gate of the Otis Steel Company—or was it the Republic Steel Company then? Or maybe it had already become the Jones and Laughlin Company by that time. By whatever name it was called, it was still a place I knew I never wanted to work in. I parked close to the gate and waited for my father.

My timing had been perfect, for within a few minutes, at four o'clock on the dot, a loud whistle blew; and workers immediately began pouring out of the factory. And the very first one out, as if he'd been shot out of a cannon, was my father. He was running toward the car, just as he ran unconsciously up the aisle of the movie theaters of my childhood and as he ran from one activity to another all his life. Did he want so desperately to get away from this polluted valley where he spent half of his life? Or was he just concerned that we get away before the rest of the traffic poured out of the parking lot and headed across the bridge? He had been impatient his whole life and had always hated waiting in any line. With a thick rope he had in the trunk of his car, he tied it to the back bumper of the new Buick. Then telling me to drive cautiously, he got behind the steering wheel of the old car, put it into neutral, and off I drove slowly to our home. And that image of my father—of him running from the hated, dirty mill, and running constantly all through his life, lost somewhere in his own head, oblivious to the rest of the world—would always be the imprinted movie of him in my mind in all of my growing-up years, which were his working years, of course.

In the fall, a miracle happened. As terrifyingly empty of needed emotional sustenance as my senior year of high school had been, college was the total opposite. It was an experience of coming home to a world of learning and openness, a release of all that had impeded me before. I had entered an amazing new world, a world of the tabula rasa, where you could wash away all that had gone before and start anew. And you could do it with a large number of young people just like yourself, who had also been crippled in their childhoods—some more so, some less—and who were, like you, looking for a way to overcome their givens, to turn them into something productive. Childhood, it turned out, was just a short prelude to your real life, to the real you; it was a signifying prelude but a prelude nonetheless. I had gone from being a suicidal teenager to being a totally alive, involved, committed student of the theater. I was amazed at how one could go around a corner and one's life could change—just like that!—in a moment. I no longer identified with Paul of "Paul's Case." I wasn't alone. I had found my community. Every morning when I woke up, the world was created anew. That life could change for the better that quickly was a lesson I would never forget even though I was entering the biggest gambling casino of them all: the theater.

A few months into my green first year as a "dramat," as the drama students were called, I sat down in the main stage theater to watch a production of Chekhov's *The Sea Gull*. I was totally innocent of it. I had never heard of the play, let alone the author, Anton Chekhov. During my first weeks at college I had often peeked into the main theater to watch the seniors rehearse the first play of the semester. Sometimes I sneaked in and sat down for a while and just watched. I could have sat there and watched for hours on end. I was drawn in by the deep serious concentration of all the members of the cast and the director as they worked out bits of stage business and their characters. They were so involved it was palpable to me. I couldn't wait to be up there with them doing that. As soon as the curtain rose on opening night, I was catapulted out of my body and my seat. I was up on that stage, along with all those overwhelmingly alive and feeling human beings. I was one of them! Laughing and crying with them! The out-of-body spiritual experience I'd looked for in church but had never found now happened to me in a theater. There was no real time; three and a half hours passed in a flash. One moment I was waiting for the curtain to go up, and the very next it had come down at the end of the performance. But in that flash of time I had felt great sorrow and joy, great yearnings and love. And there was even a young man to relate to, a young man who, out of desperation at his lot in life, kills himself. I had seen life as it really was.

I was hooked. Not by any glamour or stardom, but by what I was learning about people; for the work of the theater is to explore character, to find out what makes people who they are, what motivates them, why they are driven to do what they do, and how they care and feel and dream and love. It was about us. It was the stories Mom had loved to recount of the people in our past, and it was a way to try to understand my father and myself. And it was so joyous that I realized that great art, no matter the subject matter, could never be depressing. It was always exhilarating. Was that possibly true of life too? That the horror of it, the pain of it, could also be exciting? For it was all experience, all a learning process, and it could all be used. That was the important thing; it could all be used. I prayed that would be true. Just as my parents had always saved everything to be used, I would do the same. I would not waste anything from my past, not the good or the bad. I could use the loss of the Honor Key, reciting the lines that were cut in the senior play, the sad loss of a needed uncle, my mother's fears, and, most of all, the pain I felt from the lack of connection with my father that had caused me to look to others for a mentor which had led me into a bad thing. It was all fodder for my work. I would mine the gems of childhood, blending them into my creation of character. And I would come to cherish that young man who, while suicidal, also had lots of guts.

For my freshman acting class, I created a pantomime in which I stabbed myself repeatedly in my stomach, hara-kiri style, all to the exalted vocalize of Villa-Lobos's "Bachianas Brasileras No. 5." The idea of suicide, a "Hamlet" idea, was still with me; but now it was turned into a performance, something usable. Art, the home of the imagination and the opposite of the authoritarian demands of "willpower," would be the antidote to the deaths and loss of my role models, Uncle John and Jen. I had turned a corner and found my place in the world! In that first year, I read William Saroyan's *The Time of Your Life* and found, in the preface to it, these words: "In the time of your life, live!" That's what I would do. And I was so happy!

Stuffed Shells

Have a marinara sauce prepared.

Cook the amount of large shells you need, allowing six or eight per person, in a pot of boiling water. Do not cook all the way. Remove them from the water a few minutes before they would be done (10 mins. or so). Strain and cool.

In the meantime, mix your stuffing:
- 1 lb. ricotta cheese
- 3 whole eggs
- 2 oz. shredded mozzarella cheese
- 1 tsp. finely chopped Italian parsley
- ½ tsp. salt
- ½ tsp. pepper

On a flat workspace, stuff the shells with the mixture and then place them in a baking dish in rows. Add some sauce. (Be sure to keep some for the table.) Sprinkle some grated mozzarella cheese on top.

Cover and bake for 15 mins. in a 350° oven.

When they are done, plate them and top with some of the set-aside sauce and serve.

CHAPTER 10
Citrus Trees, Mango Jam, and Key Lime Pies

∷

Where is that porcelain-topped kitchen table that, when turned on its mysterious axis, magically opened up to double its size? That table around which our family drama played out; on which we had our daily meals and daily lessons; on which we made the hundred pounds and more of our Italian sausage that we sold weekly in our store; on which, as I watched wide-eyed, the cornucopia of candy and cookies was sent overseas during World War II; and on which, one evening of disaster, I so bruised my head, trying to avoid my father's constant backhand? Mom thought it went into the basement of the home Pop built in Independence, Ohio, and was probably left behind there on my parents' next move to Florida. Or perhaps it wound up in the basement of one of Mom's brothers' or sisters' homes, as did her original high-legged, off-the-floor stove, that kept, my mother said, "the steadiest temperature of any oven I've ever had." It went first to her brother Frank's basement and then out to his son Frankie's home in Long Beach, California, where I believe it is still working perfectly.

But the table disappeared from my thoughts, for I was long gone. Once college and a stint in the army were over, I headed straight for New York City and to my life in the theater. And there I threw myself passionately into my work. I was determined to be lucky and I was. Within three months, I scored my first New York City acting job, an off-Broadway production of *La Ronde*. I was on my way. My hope was that my new life would help me escape my past and the conflicted relationship with my father that had led to the constant search for a replacement for him and that had taken me into a dark place. I hoped I had also escaped the servile involvement with family, the fatalism, the need to be right, the overpowering certainty, the intolerance and prejudices. It had all eaten me alive. I wanted a confident life, a tolerant one, a life of creativity, a generous life of giving without the claustrophobic narrowness of my givens. And I hoped, too, that I could now easily revisit the past and make good use of it to enhance my delineation of character, to use it as the underlying subtext of each new character I attempted to bring to life. And by doing so, I would not only survive but I would also thrive. Actors, in their attempt to flee themselves, to create themselves anew, have, paradoxically, no choice but to use themselves. And the great father-son themed plays I would work in, plays like *Death of a Salesman* and *Da*, would help me forgive my own father and accept him too for who he was.

If we all have one great love in our lives and one great city, New York was my one great city. It was the city that called the many young people from all their separate Clevelands; it was the place where they would now be the immigrants and where they would reinvent themselves. They were all outsiders, like me, and an amazing number of them had also been crippled by their families and their fathers. As for the one great love, I hoped it would also come, but first I had to establish myself as an actor.

I would change my name. In order to assimilate, to move up, I would get rid of the hated *Romeo* and the constant unwelcome queries of "Wherefore art thou?" and "Where's Juliet?" as soon as the large influential talent agency I'd signed with asked me to. I would become my middle name and my first name: Paul Vincent. And this would deeply offend my father, who would say to me one day when I was visiting Florida and still struggling as an actor, "If you hadn't changed your name, you would have made something of yourself!" It was another humiliating backhanded slap in the face to me, for I certainly didn't consider myself a failure ... not then anyway. But I had known that changing my name would offend him, so I wasn't surprised. I also knew that a small part of me had done it exactly for that reason: to deny him, to deny the father who had never given me the emotional support I needed.

On another trip to Florida, he again reminded me that I was a failure in his backhanded way when he abruptly told me, "It was your sister's fault that you got mixed up in show business! It was because she was acting too!" It was true that my sister had also pursued the idea of acting when she was in college, but she hadn't been the one to influence me. Truthfully I had probably influenced her. I had always acted in the school plays; she never did. I was the one who discovered live theater and would, on occasion, double-date with her to a stage performance. No, if anyone had influenced me in that decision, it was my father. And though I had always hated the blame game and did my best to avoid it, I couldn't resist it this time and I said to him, "No, Daddy, it was you who influenced me because of all those movies we went to when I was growing up." That silenced him. But of course, there were many strands of my history that had led to my choice of career. But I didn't care about any of that. I had found where I belonged, and that was all that mattered to me.

Every day of my new creative life, I set out with great joy and anticipation, flying down the five flights of stairs of my, twenty-eight-dollars-a-month, walk-up Greenwich Village tenement apartment. ("Down! Down! I come, like glist'ring Phaethon!".) Once on the street, I entered the surging flow of the many other young searching people, all connected by our shared nervous ambition that pushed us on. I would search for my own truth in this new creativity that would prove to be, I hoped, stronger than the suicidal despair of my youth. I interviewed with Lee Strasberg for his private acting classes. Again I was lucky, for he accepted me into his classes immediately. I couldn't believe it. It took some beginning actors years to be admitted to his classes. And in his classes, after performing my first scene with a partner, Lee told me that my "sensitivity was my money in the bank." He had demolished the lie of my high school principal, who had told me to avoid being sensitive. I was home. I was the monarch of my own thoughts and actions.

Then one day in a Greenwich Village bookstore, I picked up a book of Gustav Jung's writings, and it fell open miraculously to a section titled *"Imitatio Christus."* I quickly read that section and was amazed to learn of the error Jung felt many people inadvertently committed. He wrote that we were not to relate to or to imitate Christ's pain. That was, of course, exactly what I had done. I hungrily read on. Jung believed that Christ's message was that we should all follow our own path of life, just as Christ had followed his. This was Jung's famous path of "individuation." I immediately began to let go of the pain of Christ I had so imitated as a young person and began instead to follow my own path of individuation.

The professional acting world is, of course, a world fraught with minefields, many of them outward mines, many of them inner mines. Few will become one of the 5 percent of our union who make a killing in the theater, though one could surprisingly make a decent living in the theater if one worked constantly. And there are no rules to success in it. You begin by thinking that pure talent will win out, but then you realize that talent is a common commodity. One needs something more. Besides the luck, of course, one must have a 100 percent commitment, an iron constitution, a total belief in one's talent and a killer-shark instinct that places you first. Most important of all, you need a unique watchable quality. It is a world in which the ordinary, simple pleasures of life will always come second to the neurotic need to "make it," neurotic because its proof of success is based on your childhood. And without that proof of success and stardom—the only way one can assuage the pain—one can never quite be a complete person, an authentic person. If success isn't achieved, one will possibly lead a life of childhood repetition—

that of rejection, self-loathing, and disappointment. And then one can become a ghost, many of whom one can see walking around the streets of New York City. Of course there is no guarantee that success itself will give you the new life you want, but one doesn't know that yet. Only the very strong and the very lucky can break out of this descent into hell and find a useful life. What would save me, I hoped, would be my good training and my commitment and focus on my work, for that's where the joy was for me.

Pop had fallen in love with Florida instantly on a previous short vacation that happened because I was contracted to perform in a play in Miami Beach for a month. I asked my parents if they would like to go down with me and have a vacation while I worked. They had friends there to visit, especially their friend Sara who was now living in Hollywood, Florida. Pop was excited by the idea. So I flew to Cleveland and drove them down to Sara's home in Florida. Once there, my father was immediately thrilled by the climate. He quickly realized that southern Florida's climate was similar to the one he had left as a child in Italy and that it was perfect for him, for he could enjoy, year-round, his favorite retired recreation—gardening. There was another great benefit he saw too: no snow. My father hated snow passionately. At one Christmas Day dinner in Ohio, his new son-in-law—my sister's husband who was a minister's son—gave the blessing, something we had never done in our family. As soon as he was finished, my father, looking heavenward, jumped in with his blessing: "PS, thanks for the goddamned snow!"

And within weeks of his return to Independence after his visit to Florida, Pop sold the new home he had built and prepared to move to Florida. Mom was not so willing to move. First of all, she was reluctant to leave her beautiful new home. Second of all, she didn't want to leave all her family behind. Her umbilical cord to all her brothers and sisters, a number of whom she had helped raise, was still intact. But Pop got his way. Mom acquiesced to his wishes as she usually had all through their lives. And in quick time, their belongings were packed up and stored to be shipped later. On his arrival in Florida, my father quickly found a very pleasant home and purchased it. My parents were now legally residents of Florida.

Pop was ecstatic with his new life. Florida was all he had hoped it would be. Very soon he would begin grafting fruit trees, turning his new backyard into an orchard. I now had a place to go for some much needed R & R between jobs. And when I arrived at their new home, the first thing I had to do was to follow my father out into his garden to see what was new. Joyously he would run to show me the orange trees he had grafted, his new lemon tree that produced juicy lemons the size of grapefruits, the grapefruit tree that had been on the property that had never produced grapefruits but that was now producing the best grapefruits I'd ever tasted. He considered that a good omen. He even had a mango tree that provided a delicious fruit new to him. There was also an amazingly fruitful avocado tree. And in the far corner, a small banana grove. That was an experiment. In another corner of the yard in full sun, he had planted a vegetable garden. Though it was a bit too hot for his newly planted fig tree, that was all right with him. He was happier than I'd ever seen him.

But my mother wasn't happy. The move had been hard on her. The estrangement from her family and the loss of her good friends brought on a major depression. She wrote to me in a letter on August 29, 1969, "Oh, Sonny, if you only knew how I hate it here. I don't even look like the same person. How far we are in travel and phone calls. It makes me sick. Daddy has taken me away from all my family and my friends. I can't make anyone understand how I feel. I told Sara how I felt and she said, then I shouldn't have come to Florida. So you see no one cares about the other person. In plain English they don't give a damn! So what the hell am I doing here? I don't do anything. I don't sew, I just can't. I try to do things and I make so many mistakes … when I cook … and I can't write checks. I was so happy up north, even if I just stayed in the house. This is just a dumping ground for all sorts of drug addicts and Hippys [*sic*] and widows looking for a rich husband and there's a lot of robbery going on here. I just want you to understand me. Your father is outside in the rain trying to pour the concrete on top of the tool shed he built in the backyard. I'm sick of cement and concrete. I'll send this mess now and please take care of yourself. I'll try also. Much love, Mother and Dad."

But she couldn't take care of herself, and she became immobile and depressed. Their doctor suggested a psychiatrist who, in turn, suggested electroshock treatments. I wasn't told any of this at the time. True to my parents' behavior, they never told my sister or me any of their problems; they didn't want to bother us. We had our own lives. About five years later on a Christmas holiday to their home, my father finally did tell me. By then my mother was fine, so, you see, it wasn't a burden for me.

I was, however, stunned by the news. Was there a condition among the women in our family of depression? I remembered my aunt Florence, who had endured many of those treatments, and didn't I hear once that my aunt Theresa had a nervous breakdown? I also flashed back to my mother hiding in fear from my father in my tiny bedroom closet. Why did she always have to give in to my father's wishes? I remembered, too, a fiftieth wedding anniversary party given her and my father by my aunts and uncles in Cleveland. She dutifully played the role of the good wife, posing pleasantly for photographs with my father, graciously accepting all the attention; but when I sat with her for a while apart from the others and congratulated her on achieving this wonderful milestone, of having made a good life for her husband and her children and of now being able to enjoy some of the rewards of all that work, she said to me, "But I'm alone." "You have your husband," I said. She replied, "You don't understand. I am all alone." My heart broke for her. But America was changing, I told her, and people were no longer staying in marriages that didn't work. I asked her if she'd ever thought of leaving him.

"How could I do that?" she replied. "I made an agreement for life. That's how I am."

I knew that would be her response.

Then she said, "Anyway, that's how all these men are. They don't change." She continued, "They just mellow with age."

I was sure she was thinking of her own father, who had been a tyrant in his home too and around whom she'd also had to tread silently.

I hoped for her sake that was true. Then slowly, things began to look better for her. She made a number of new women friends—women friends had always been important to her—and that made her life better, for she now had them to talk to. Finally she came to enjoy her life in Florida. And there was much to enjoy: the beauty of the setting, their simple but comfortable home, and the bountiful garden that provided them with an overabundance of fresh vegetables and fruit. Every year they would send my sister and me a big box of their amazingly sweet grapefruits. When I would visit for a holiday or just to take a break, I would occasionally see them walking hand in hand, something I had never seen when I was growing up. So all was okay, I thought.

But it wasn't. A few years later I was staying with them while working at the Coconut Grove Theater. After lunch, my father and I went outside to sit and relax on the patio he had built under his avocado tree. And there, looking out through that clear, pristine late-afternoon light into that primeval garden called Florida, thinking all was now well with my parents, I said to my father, hoping to enlist him in a good father-son conversation about his life, a conversation we had never had, "Things are good for you both now. You have a nice home, a beautiful garden, and a very good life. You deserve it, Daddy. I'm very happy for you."

And my father, the anger and the fierceness still powerful, said to me: "I SHOULD NEVER HAVE MARRIED YOUR MOTHER! SHE HAS POISON IN HER BLOOD! SHE KEPT ME BACK ALWAYS! I WANTED TO DO MANY THINGS, BUT SHE WOULDN'T GO ALONG WITH ME!" With my father, one had always to be careful where one stepped, for one could still touch a hidden land mine. His outburst shocked me. And I wondered when the mellowing my mother had spoken of was going to happen.

Where had this particular anger come from? What could he possibly be talking about? I said something lamely about Florida and how Mom seemed to have gotten over her problem.

"It's not just Florida," he said immediately. And then what had been bottled up for years came bursting out. "It's everything! She was never any good. I gave her everything, but it didn't help. You know what's wrong with her? She's weak! A weak mind! Her whole family is sick ... the same way. They're okay ... but they're weak. All of them. They got no ambition, you know. I hate that. I despise it. No ambition. And they all gamble. 'Course your grandfather liked to gamble too. So maybe that's why. I would have left your mother long ago but for you two kids. How does it look people should say 'Their parents are separated!' Huh! No good. But we were no good together! She wasn't the wife for me. I should have married someone else ... someone with ambition. Everything I wanted to do, your mother was against. She didn't want me to build the house. She was sick then too. No! I should have married someone else!"

So the home I had grown up in that I always thought was perhaps not the happiest home nor perhaps the most loving but a home I could often enjoy turned out to be the home I had always feared. I thought all along I was the problem, that my mother had loved me too well, more than her husband; but that wasn't, it seemed, the real problem for my father.

Yes, it was true that Mom was hesitant to try new things. Her fears always came to the fore. And yes, she was a person who was only happy in her own home. She never asked for a more grand life than she had; it was always enough for her. Then I remembered an apartment building that my father had wanted to buy. It would have been a good investment, but Mom didn't want the added responsibility of it. Pop was probably hoping he could start a small real estate empire that would have allowed him to quit the steel mill. I remembered him referring to himself once as a working jackass. But Mom saw it only as more work, and she had enough to do as it was. And maybe there were other things he wanted to do that I knew nothing of. My father wanted to grow, to expand himself, to do new things. Had he been educated, he would most likely have been a professional of some kind. Though he always read and spoke English at home, I think he felt his bad English had kept him back. Still he was able to constantly teach himself new things. What he had hoped for in a wife, and didn't feel he had found, was someone to support him in the kind of life he envisioned for himself.

Yet hadn't my mother worked without complaint for all those many years in the grocery store he put her in charge of, running up and down the stairs all day long, while cooking and cleaning her house too? And wasn't she the one who held everything together, the one with the sense of humor to calm the waters, the one who entertained us to make us forget the problems, who spread her love out on the dinner table every night? What more could she do? What more could he have wanted? And the phrase "poison in her blood"—why, it was medieval. So my father had lived with frustrations. Maybe she was partly to blame, but surely she wasn't all to blame. Did he not share in the choices they had made? And where was his famous willpower? Why hadn't he relied on that and accomplished what he'd wanted, no matter what?

Trying to cajole him out of his black mood and choosing the path of humor as I had been taught, I said, "But just think, Pop ..."—I had never called him *Pop* to his face, but I did now, hoping to lighten the mood, to Americanize him, and make him that pal he never was—"if you hadn't married Mom, you'd never have had Angela and me."

Without missing a beat, my father said to me, "THAT'S ALL RIGHT! I WOULD HAVE HAD TWO BETTER CHILDREN! TWO MORE AMBITIOUS CHILDREN!" That was more than a slap to the face; that was a punch in the stomach.

Here in the backyard of their wonderful retirement home, looking out at the beautiful garden he had nurtured, here in that paradise, instead of a wonderful father-son conversation, a grown-up conversation that would have brought us closer together, there was nothing but bitterness and regret and anger. My father, ignoring the sweetness of our surroundings, only spoke of his deep dissatisfaction not only with his wife but also with my sister and me. Did he not realize how hurtful what he had just said was? Did he not think that saying what he'd said would not permanently hurt our relationship? I saw no remorse in him at all. Nor did he ever try to lessen what he'd said later. My father never questioned himself. He just spoke his mind. Always unaware of his own actions, certain he was right, he had often struck out and blamed others without thinking, his anger blinding him, making him unconscious. I was happy my sister wasn't there and didn't have to hear it. But I did hear it.

How does a son respond to that? One would be justified to take an axe to one's own father for such a deep-to-the-soul destructive cruelty. Outside of the meanness of the remark, there was its falseness, based on his failure to see me clearly, for the truth was that I, just like him, seethed with ambition, but had been, so far, thwarted in my attempts to achieve all I wanted, also just like him. Even though I had always worked as an actor, there were still the times I did consider myself a failure. How could there not be? I had never, as a successful theater friend had once glibly said to me as if my life meant nothing, "gotten that part I needed to put me on the map." Still I consoled myself by working and receiving praise from my peers in the business. He had purposely found an area in which I was vulnerable.

I might have responded by reminding my father of how he had limited me by not letting me have the piano lessons I so badly wanted. That still rankled. Or given me the dog I so badly wanted that would have shown his love. I could have told him how, because he had often backhanded me across my face, I had grown up fearful of anyone coming close to me. I could also have told him that because of him I could never learn anything from a critical person. I could have gotten back at him by telling him how he had failed me, betrayed me really, by making me look elsewhere for a father figure, for a man to emulate. I could have told him how he had never said that magic phrase to me—"You can be anything you want to be"—and how that lack had torn away at my confidence. But I knew that my father would deflect any remarks I made by reminding me how much he had done for my sister and me. I could already hear him saying, "Well, we parents do our best. I gave you everything you needed." I knew who he was. There was no point.

But he was my father. He had brought me into the world. Without a decent education, he had worked hard and struggled valiantly without ever faltering. He had been fearless, perhaps even heroic. We always knew we could rely on him. Life never ground him down; he kept on always, never complaining. It was Pop who was the rock of our family, who gave our lives the needed focus. It was Pop who was determined that my sister and I have a college education so that we could have a better life than he'd had.

Was my father the more sensitive one of my parents? Was his 100 percent certainty just the other side of his fear of failure in the New World? We humans believe with the most certainty those things we can least prove. It's both our greatest quality and our most troubling quality. Had I misread him all the time I was growing up? Had his powerfully held beliefs overwhelmed his better qualities? After all, he was the one who always cried at the movies, not my mother. He was the one who had quit English classes when they'd laughed at his accent, and he was the one who was hurt by my mother's inability to back him in his dreams. He was also the one who, when misfortune fell on any of his friends, was the first to go to them to see what help he could be. He was the one saddened by the news of the deaths of his *paesani,* his childhood friends, all of whom died long before he did, and who, when Ciccio died, had locked himself in our bathroom and cried for hours. And he was the one who, no matter how many times I pushed him away, kept wrapping his arms around me, thinking I was his wife all through the long night in Wilkinsburg, Pennsylvania. Certainly mercy, the mercy all humanity needs, was his due.

My father had given up much of his dream so I could have mine. How could I hate him? But I could not turn this latest transgression into one of those funny family stories about my father. I told no one what he'd said. I wanted to forget it. Despite the years of trying to understand him, to respect him, to love him, so that I could defuse the anger and certainty and see him whole, the sting of his words on this occasion would last for a long time. Mean words spoken can never be retrieved. It occurred to me that he might have felt we were having a grown-up conversation, that we were speaking the truth, for it was apparent he still believed that the truth, no matter how hurtful, was beautiful. That was who he was. That was what I had searched for in his steamer trunk and had never found. I knew it now.

I got up from the chair next to my father and walked back into the house, leaving him outside by himself. I didn't tell my mother what my father had said, but ever aware (had I not seen her peek through the back window at us as we sat in the garden?), she sensed something had happened or been said that day that had bothered me and she told me, "Don't worry about us. We'll be fine. We'll repair ourselves and go on. You take care of yourself. You do what you have to do to have a good life. That's all we want. You're our whole life, you know." That was Mom, always trying to make everything okay.

My father's remarks, while they had hurt deeply, closed a door for me. I would never look to him again for the approval I needed. I didn't have to kill him; he had killed himself for me. I felt that I'd finally left behind that loving and naive little boy who was so needy of his father's love and approval, that boy I'd always been.

When the run of the play I was appearing in was over, I returned to my Emerald City and my own creative and fulfilling life. But I would continue to visit my parents in Florida. I didn't want to abandon my mother. And as my father aged and was less able to do the maintenance work around the house, I took it on. I painted the inside of the house and the outside a number of times. I climbed onto the tiled roof to scrub away the mildew with bleach. I fixed whatever needed to be fixed. And I also pruned the many fruit trees in the front and backyard. My father, sitting mostly in his easy chair watching TV, left me alone.

On one of those Christmas holidays in Florida, when I wasn't working—a condition that was becoming more frequent as I got older and was less in demand—while my mother and father and I were sitting in the living room after dinner watching TV, the phone rang. Being the closest to the phone, I answered it. After I said hello and heard that same innocent word spoken from the other end, my stomach tightened and twisted. It was Ray. I hadn't talked to him or seen him since my aunt Viola's funeral four years or so before. I never asked anyone in the family about him. I didn't want to ever hear from him or about him again. Once, I had heard it mentioned in passing that he had remarried and had moved down to the west coast of Florida, from where, I now surmised, he was calling.

This was a moment I had long been dreading. I knew he had always stayed in contact with my parents. And I felt sure that at some future time I might have to talk to him. What I didn't know was if my parents knew about his sexual abuse of his granddaughter. Now protecting them from unpleasant news as they had once done their best to protect me, I had never mentioned it to them. But I suspected that my mother might have known, for she stayed in contact with her brother Frank and his wife in Cleveland. I also thought that if she did know she would probably not have told my father about it, not only because of his age—he was in his nineties now—but also because it was the kind of thing that would have made him very angry. What should I do? I had to make up my mind quickly. If I spoke to him I was giving him the benefit of being decent to an undeserving person. I didn't want to do that. For a moment I thought to myself, *Hang up! Hang up! Don't talk to this bastard! Don't give him the benefit of your kindness. He doesn't deserve it.*

I glanced across the room to my mother. And I knew from the look on her face that she knew who I was talking to and that she also knew what had happened. Then my curiosity got the better of me. I wondered what he wanted. I suspected he was calling to wish my parents a happy holiday. And when he asked if he could talk to them, I looked at my mother to see if she wanted to talk to him. Silently she shook her head no. I was so glad. I told him, and it pleased me no end to do so, "They don't want to talk to you." And he said, very calmly: "I understand."

My, my, I thought. How decent he's being. He's expressing in a very rational way his awareness of the awfulness of what he's done. I found that even more reprehensible. How dare he be so cool and collected? And not be apologetic at all either. Well, I thought, at least he's not pretending what happened hadn't happened. Then I thought that even though I never wanted to hear his voice again, this might be my last opportunity to confront him. Many, many years had gone by, and he and I had never spoken about what he had done with me. Maybe this was my last chance to tell him that the sexual activity he had involved me in had not been without consequences. Would he have any remorse about that? Or would he deny it? I didn't care. I needed to do it. And very quietly, not only because I didn't want either one of my parents to hear me, but also because the memory still held its heavy darkness for me, I said to him, "Do you remember what you did with me?" Calmly, without any shame or remorse in his voice, he said he did remember. Oh, he was being too civil.

Now I was becoming angered by his lack of remorse, and I said to him, still being as quiet as I could, "Aren't you aware that when an adult makes a child join them in a sexual act that it is confusing to the child and takes away the child's autonomy, his own sense of himself? That it is harmful for the child?"

Totally ignoring what I said, and in an attempt to justify his behavior, he replied, "I only did it so I could get to your sister."

That really incensed me. It was a bald-faced lie. My sister was nowhere near when he had masturbated in front of me and had then asked me to join him. Why would he say that? Was it because if he had admitted to it, he would have had to admit to homosexual tendencies, which he obviously did have, never mind the pedophilia? I was sickened by his attitude. I didn't want to continue talking to him if he was only going to lie. Had he learned nothing after his son had him arrested? Had he learned nothing in the classes he had been forced to attend? What kind of a monster was he? He had fooled us all with his charm and manipulative behavior. Maybe he was a sociopath. He seemed to fit the pattern: someone who has no guilt about his bad behavior. I decided there was no point talking to him, for he would never admit to his guilt. And since I had dealt with what he had done to me and had come to understand my feelings, I didn't really care about him anymore at all. He no longer had anything to do with my life.

But the actor in me was interested in motivation and character. I wanted to know if he knew why he was the way he was. Was it, I asked him, that in the navy he had been part of masturbatory scenes on board ships? He said no to that. Then I remembered how he had once told me he had sex with his sister when he was growing up. I reminded him of that. He said it wasn't true and denied ever telling me that. I was sure he had told me that. And I didn't think the youngster I was then would have even been able to make up something like that. For starters I didn't know his sister. My mother had once told me that he and her sister Viola, after staying with my parents on one of their visits to Florida, had driven up the east coast on their way north and had stopped at his sister's home somewhere along the way. And when he knocked on his sister's door she had refused to let him in. I'm sure it must have been her sister Viola who told her that; no one else would have known. And now he was telling me it wasn't true. He was lying of course. Then he quickly changed the subject and started making accusations about my family members to obfuscate and justify his behavior. I had heard enough. Obviously he wasn't going to take any responsibility for what he done. And there was no use talking to him. I would never get from him what I wanted. And the conversation, though all of it had been quiet and restrained, was making me sick to my stomach. I cut him off in the middle of his rambling accusations and told him I didn't want to hear anymore. I said good-bye and hung up the phone. I was no longer enthralled to him. And that's how it ended. Not with the more theatrical confrontation scene one imagined but with a more Chekhovian ending, the more real ending. I had been holding my breath through the whole conversation. I needed air. I opened my lungs and breathed in a gulp of life-giving air. It was over.

When I returned to New York after that holiday, I truly felt I could let go of all that had happened to me in the past. Reassessing my life, I knew that I had sacrificed a lot to have my dream. I had never had children, fearing always that I couldn't afford them. And that had kept me from having lengthy relationships, which were usually with my leading ladies, for, conveniently built into that relationship, was its ending when the show closed. Now though, the fear of getting a girlfriend pregnant over, I was having the best relationship I'd ever had with a terrific woman. We were in our second year of living together, and it was going well. I seemed to have come finally to a place of peace about my life and myself. I even liked myself. And I looked forward to continue working as an actor, playing an interesting part now and then, for it was still the exploration of character that interested me. That was the work of the actor and the joy of being an actor. I had had what I had always wanted: an entrance into a wider world of knowledge and understanding. And thankfully, I still had my insatiable curiosity about everything; I still wanted to learn.

My mother said that she and my father would repair themselves and go on. And they did. They were able finally to enjoy, because they were both healthy and long-lived, a good decade more of a very pleasant retirement in Florida. My father, after years of ignoring his music, went back to playing his mandolin and his clarinet. His fingers were rusty and no longer had the agility needed, but he would sit and pluck his way through his library of music. And Mom would often join him, singing their old songs in that high whining sound of the *Mezzogiorno* she'd always sung in. One Christmas, they sent me a cassette tape of them playing and singing Christmas carols. Their table was always still welcome to their friends. And during the winter months, relatives and friends from the north would often visit. So Mom did finally come to love living in Florida, enjoying the ease and the bounty of it. These were wonderful elongated years, years of reward for all their labors.

Had the American dream finally then turned out okay for Pop? That was a question I had never asked him. But did he, to himself, I wondered, ever admit to being caught between reality and his own expectations as we all are? Wasn't that what he was thinking about when, searching his face as I so often did growing up, I would see his white-blue eyes drift away into another world. Of course it hadn't all turned out as he'd wanted. Of course he was sometimes bitter. Wasn't his love of the movies more than just a love of entertainment? Wasn't it the love of the image of an America that had a happy ending, an America that had strong and warm family values, a place where one could realize one's dream? That must have greatly appealed to him. America was the right country for him, for it was based on that presumption of innocence that lies at the center of our American lives, an innocence which he had. And wasn't it also based on our great dual spirits of self-reliance and generosity, both of which were also a major part of his character?

Hadn't he also been taken in by the fantasy? Hadn't America itself put a wedge between my father and myself? It not only hurt him, the immigrant, in its attempts to stereotype, to limit a person; but it hurt me too, for I accepted the limiting. I was always embarrassed by my father, by his accent, his old-world ways. America had come between us. It had taught me an ethnic self-contempt. Why else had I created a role to play, the well-dressed sophisticated playboy, if not to escape my givens? *Mannaggia l'America!*

But I do think that I had sometimes pleased my father, though he would never admit it. My mother told me how he loved watching me on the daytime soaps. That he had, in fact, become addicted to them because I was on one of them. And she also told me that once when I opened in the National Company of a Broadway touring show in Cleveland—I even got a hand on my entrance in my hometown—that he had run joyously up the aisle and had accosted Hermione Gingold, of all people, who happened to be in the audience that night, and told her, "THAT'S MY SON!" She must have been taken aback. So I did give him some proud moments ... though he would never tell me that.

My parents made two trips to Europe during their retirement years. And both times they visited my father's family in Italy. He told me he might rent a little house, stay there for a year maybe, but both times they were back within a month or so. I asked him why. He said, "They're not democratic there. If you're a professor you can't cut your own grass. They still have big-shot ideas. No. America is the best country."

And Mom was right too about Pop. I noticed that the balance had shifted. She was now an equal partner in their relationship and was no longer afraid of Pop. She spoke her mind, and it was a sharp mind, for she didn't miss a trick. And she now gave him orders that he meekly obeyed with a smile that said, "See how she bosses me around now?" It was a hard-won victory, but she was there.

Pop was determined to live to be one hundred years old, being the magnificent specimen of man he was. I always remembered how he would crack the shells of walnuts with his teeth. When my mother would tell him to use a nutcracker so as not to hurt his teeth, he always replied, "MY TEETH ARE STRONG! NOT LIKE YOU AND YOUR CHILDREN'S TEETH! I HAVE ALL MY OWN TEETH AND NO CAVITIES!" It was true; he had all his own teeth almost to the end of his life, when they all had to be pulled because they were so worn down as to be of no use. And he would come close to that century destination, missing it by only four years—a feat due, I'm sure, to his good genes and to Mom's healthy, simple, fresh food, that peasant diet he had grown up on and continued eating all his life, a diet we now acknowledge to be one of the healthiest of the world.

The Christmas holidays of '95 were upon us. My mother told me that he had been constantly asking, "Are the kids coming for the holidays?" So my sister and I made plans to travel south. Once there, we wondered why his favorite TV programs no longer intrigued. And why he started to push away his food, a man who had always taken such a great pleasure in having a robust and appreciative, though always intelligently moderate, appetite. Still he joined us in the usual celebrations on Christmas Eve and Christmas Day dinner. My sister, in order to spend part of the holidays with her children, left the day after Christmas. The holidays over, he immediately started to drift away. Sitting in his favorite reclining chair, staring into space, he began to slide his hands back and forth, one over the other, over and over. I brought him, as I did every year, a dozen of his favorite chocolate-covered cherries. He refused them for the first time in his life. Only half with us now and mostly silent, he was making preparations for his death. But we didn't know that. A few days later he stopped talking and eating. Then when he became incontinent we realized he needed around-the-clock care, so with the help of his doctor, we moved him into a hospice.

Still, I didn't know how close he was to dying. I kept trying to get that information out of someone at the hospice so that I could warn my sister that the end was near and she could fly back down to say good-bye to him, but no one would give me an answer. Finally on his second night in the hospice, a nurse, just in passing, said to me (I was still listening, you see, doing my boy's work, learning about the universe), "I don't think he has long."

"What do you mean?" I quickly asked her.

"Usually once they're here, it's only a matter of days ... three or so."

I called my sister immediately. She flew down the next morning.

Pop hadn't spoken now for days. I wondered if he was angry with us for moving him into the hospice and was reverting to his usual method of punishment: withholding. But I don't think it was that. I think he was in preparation mode for his death and had gone inward, away from us.

The next day, all together as a family, we walked into his room. I noticed immediately that his left hand had turned black, due, I surmised, from a lack of circulation.

I said to him, "We're all here now, Daddy."

He said nothing.

Nor did anyone else. Both my mother and my sister stood silently at his bedside. I tried to read my mother's face. There were no tears. She just looked defenseless, not knowing what to do or say. Perhaps she was just numb or in shock. What did it mean to her that her husband of some sixty-nine years was dying? I couldn't read my sister's face either. Was she sad? Did she feel anything watching her father die? I wondered why they were both silent. Were they concealing their feelings as we had so often done in our family?

Was there nothing they wanted to say to their husband/father before he died? No last words?

It can't end like this, I thought, in this ambiguous silence that had always permeated the past and that could be so misunderstood. Words must be spoken, I thought! Feelings conveyed! We must talk to one another finally! And not just out of bitterness and anger. Somehow we must scream through this silence of withholding and say what is really important and forget past hurts. Certainly I have grown. I have learned. I have forgiven. In some cultures, the son breathes in his father's last breath to take his father into his soul. I could not let my father die without hearing an expression of gratitude and love. So I said to him—this man who had mystified me all my life, who had been a tyrant in our home, whose fierce certainty had struck a fear in me, this man who had never paid me a compliment—I said, "We love you, Daddy."

He said nothing.

Then I shocked myself by adding, "Do you love us?" I desperately needed an answer to my question, but I also wanted to give my father the opportunity to achieve his humanity.

To my question, my father immediately nodded his head yes. Born in 1900 and forged in pre-Freudian southern Italy, my father had no use for self-awareness. The idea of it, though he could enjoy a laugh at his own expense, would forever elude him. He was a natural man, his behavior as elemental and unquestioning as the earth and its seasons. Though he had impeccable manners when needed, he often belched, burped, and spit openly. They were natural things, you see. And I suspect that sex was natural to him too. That it was no big deal. Just something everyone did. Enjoyable, yes, but don't make too much of a fuss about it. What was, was. To look for more, to fill your life with the illusion and fantasy of what could not be known and seen for sure, was a waste of time. "To see things as they are is to drink from an endless cup" and Pop did that.

My father died that night. I think he had waited to die until we were all there. Because my father had always said whenever the subject of death came up in our house, "I don't care what you do with me when I die! Dig a hole in the backyard and throw me in! When you're dead, you're dead!" And so, since he had been so happy in Florida, I scattered his ashes in some of his favorite places. And my sister planted a tree for him in a memorial garden. I spent most of the following year with my mother in Florida until we all decided that she would be better off living with my sister in Minneapolis. Still working occasionally, I was loath to leave my beloved New York.

Looking back now, I think that in many ways the fifties were a better time than people think today. Yes, there are new benefits now, especially in the greater openness and knowledge our young people have. And that's good. But the fifties may have been the last innocent time of childhood in America. And there was something to be said for that. And the idea of the melting pot felt better to me than the present one of pluralism. The differences we all so loudly tout about ourselves are only skin-deep, are only cultural. We are all the same underneath that superficial exterior. We have all the same needs and wants. We all want to be loved. We all want someone to know us well. Plurality breeds a kind of exclusivity, an us-against-them behavior. I don't like belonging to select groups because, by their very nature, they immediately exclude. I don't like walls between people.

If pain is the creator of human memory, there also exists alongside it another form of memory—that of joy, of love—for I remember the good times as well as the bad. The child is born to love, to feel secure, and to bask in the warmth of the love it feels. I felt heart-bursting, overwhelming love when I was a child for my family. I can still feel today the warmth of my grandmother as I folded myself into her deep skirts that always smelled of flour and cooking as she stirred a pot on the stove. And though she never said it in so many words, I knew she loved me. And it was she who forced my mother to give up being overprotective and let me go swimming at the Cumberland pool. What would I have done without her? And there were all my aunts and uncles who shared their joy in being alive despite their poor beginnings, who shared their delight in jitterbugging, in going on family picnics, and who, two years in a row, saved all their state sales tax stamps so that I could have a real boy's two-week stay at the YMCA summer camp. There was my aunt Florence who shared her excellence and pride in what she created, who took me to the circus, and who introduced me to the pop music of the day and who showed me how fragile we humans are, how easily it can all go wrong. And I will always remember my uncle John, who came to our house on the eve of his departure to fight and die in World War II, specifically to bring me, a kid who had very few toys of any kind, a new pair of roller skates, and who promised me that on his return he would teach me how to ice skate and how to box.

My heart ached with love too for our good friends. There was Josephine, who squeezed my cheeks hard in a *pizzicotto* kiss and who always filled me with warmth just with her smile, who told my mother once she always felt I was partly her son too. And Ciccio, her husband, our own Caruso, who gave up a professional career to fill all of our lives with the glorious sound of his voice. There were Daddy's *paesani* who loved to entertain us all with their music and stories. And Ange and Jen who opened up the possibilities of a wider life to me, of new worlds of travel and humor and style, and of whose love and support gave me my first feelings of acceptance. I thank Sara, whose good humor always bathed us in human warmth and the joy of life, even when I threw up all over her sons' bed. And I will never forget Ange's sister Florence, my liberator, who pointed me in the direction of a new kind of life, a life of openness, of consciously thinking about what it meant to be a human being. And there was the girl next door, my conspirator in a blood pact, who taught me so much so gently and so easily.

I loved too my gods and goddesses, all my wonderful teachers in school: Ms. Follin, our elegant journalism teacher, who foresaw a fine future ahead for me; Ms. Sugarman, my French teacher, who brought a joy and excitement to the knowing of another language; Ms. Gaffney, who let me sit quietly in her room one day, crying my eyes out because of a missed A on a report card (what would I tell my father?) while she sat quietly grading her students' papers; Ms. Lodwick, my wonderful English teacher who gave me an A in my senior year "despite the many days I'd missed"; Ms. Lee, our dear radio teacher, whom we all sensed was a kindred, sensitive and caring person, someone we could always drop in on and talk to; and Sister Mary Gertrude at St. Cecilia's who saw something good in me and oh, so many more ... all my heroes. How they sustained, encouraged, and supported me and constantly wished the best for me, always pointing me in that higher direction. I ran zealously to all of them, greedily taking what I needed to grow, to drink in their wider vision, their knowledge. How rich I was in the variety of people who came into my life and were willing to share themselves with me, the first-generation son, asking nothing in return. I never thanked them for the meaning they gave my life, the meaning of doing for others, but I do now. And I praise them now, my human bridges who saved me.

Of course underneath it all was the constancy of my parents and their hard work. My mother who always managed to set a table with the most remarkable and wonderfully tasting food. And for whom friendship was so important. She knew and cared about everyone on our street, for our small grocery store was a window into the lives of our neighbors. She knew their problems with their children and their husbands—it was the wives who did the shopping—and related their stories to me. And even when a new A&P opened on Kinsman Road and made a serious dent in our business and most of our customers now came in only for a quart of milk, a loaf of bread, or a bottle of wine, she still shared, with her favorite customers, her pickled eggplant, her roasted red peppers, her eggplant parmigiana, her Christmas cookies; and they shared in return their barbeque sauce or their sweet potato pie. And when one of her customers was sick, Mom would tell me to watch the store for a short while so she could run over to their house with a plate of food. When my parents sold the store, they were left with a couple of thousand dollars of unpaid credit that Pop and Mom had extended to some of the better customers. Most of them always paid up at the end of the month, but a few hadn't. My parents let it go.

And Pop, always on the run to get it all accomplished, often difficult and filled with contradictions, whom I would work hard at never reducing to a caricature or a stereotype because he was so much more than that, gave me the best of him—his passionate joy in life, his love and appreciation of music and of the physical world, not only in what it produced but also in its sheer visual beauty that he always wanted me to feel, saying, "LOOK! LOOK! HOW BEAUTIFUL!" That joy in life is his greatest gift to me and the one that means the most, for it would sustain me through all my years.

His death opened the floodgates of memory for Mom. In the year after he died, she said to me one day, "They wouldn't have let me marry him in Italy, you know. His family was higher socially than ours. They owned land. They had the first electricity in the town." I was glad they'd met in America. Another day as she was preparing a meal, she said, "He raised me. He taught me everything I know." She was speaking of the not-very-worldly eighteen-year-old girl she'd been when she married him. She'd dreamed of being a schoolteacher but had settled instead for the life of a housewife, mother and storekeeper, a "career woman," as she once said jokingly. And then one day came her final thought: "He lived a clean life, never any problems, never any trouble. He was respectful of others and never intruded into their lives." She had been rethinking who her husband was since he had died, too. And she was telling me, that he was a person of some nobility and decency.

So thanks to my father, I got the education he never had, which allowed me the luxury of doing what I wanted with my life. And I sense, as I write about him, that he was more like me ... and I am more like him ... than I ever thought. He, after all, also set out on a risky journey into the unknown, just as I had done. Weren't we the same, after all, both pursuing a crazy dream? And by totally pursuing my dream, wasn't I paying homage to my father's dreams that were sometimes thwarted?

Just as the alchemists of old had tried to turn base metals into gold, I would use the pain of the past to turn into the gold of creating the emotional lives of my characters; and in doing this, unlike the alchemists of the past, I could succeed. Instead of willpower, I would use imagination and feelings to transform the wounds of childhood into creative work that would hopefully enrich the lives of others and tear down the barriers of prejudice and difference that exist between people. I could turn my grandfather's useless *merdo* into life-enhancing manure. And that would be a good thing and would be all I would need as a human to thrive on ... my life's work. And I could happily live with that. And I would tell the family stories of my father with humor and with love. And I, too, would come to see the beauty of recognizing the world for what it really is and how that *is* an endless joy.

-the air and paper doodle I had constantly drawn
all my life without knowing its meaning that
looked like this:

was, I finally realized, a circle of my wholeness crossed out.

I now draw that circle of wholeness without the
the cross through it.

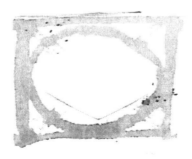

MORE OF MOM'S RECIPES

Stuffed Artichokes (my favorite)

This is the way my mother always prepared this remarkable vegetable, which is actually the large flower bud of the plant harvested before it blooms. Some people prepare them without the breadcrumbs, but I am partial to them stuffed. What you get used to, I guess. They can also be baked, but Mom always cooked them in a pan on the top of the stove. And be sure to eat the heart of them, the best part. When we were children, my sister and I didn't want the fuss of cleaning the choke so we always handed the bottom of the artichoke to my father, who always accepted them without any protest. Wicked of him. Stupid of us. By the time I was in high school I knew better and guarded the heart of my choke zealously. By the way, the heart can be eaten raw, slivered with some oil and lemon juice or in a salad. And you can, if you want, clean the choke before you cook them. You need to spread the leaves open widely, go down with a grapefruit spoon, and remove the fibers in the deep center. Then, as some do, you can fill the cavity with more stuffing. I like to do it myself when I eat one. Gives you a better sense of the total vegetable and its glory.

For 4 artichokes:
- ¾ cup bread crumbs
- 1 tsp. black pepper
- 2 cloves garlic, chopped
- A little salt
- ½ cup grated cheese
- A little oregano

Cut bottoms flat by removing the stem. Cut off ½" off the top. With scissors, cut off the points of the leaves. Spread leaves apart. (Some people boil the artichokes in water for 5 mins. to make them easier to open. You can force the leaves apart enough for the stuffing.)

Push the breadcrumb mixture down into the leaves well and into the center. Use the mixture equally among the artichokes.

In a pot with water halfway up the artichokes and with the artichokes standing upright against each other to keep them in place, squeeze juice of a half lemon in the water and drizzle a bit of olive oil on the top of each choke.

Bring to a boil and then lower the heat a bit and steam with a lid for about 50 mins. They're done when you can easily pull a leaf away from the bulb.

(If baking, in a dish covered with tin foil and the same amount of water, an oven at 375° for 45 mins. to 1 hour should do it.)

Roasted Red Peppers in Olive Oil

(A dish of these was present at every meal in our home. They add a zesty taste to any meal and go well with any meat sandwich or dish.)

- 6 red peppers (you can add a yellow one if you'd like) Wipe them clean. Do not use water on them.
- 2 cloves sliced garlic
- parsley (a few sprigs)
- salt (a sprinkle)
- olive oil (1 tbs.)

Place peppers on a cooking sheet and put in oven at 500° (or you can place them under the broiler), Keep a close watch on them and turn them so that all sides turn black.

When that is done, place the peppers in a brown paper bag. Leave for 10 mins. Then remove from the bag and peel away the burned skin. Remove the stem part, take the seeds out, clean and tear or cut into strips. Place in a container and add the garlic, olive oil, salt, and parsley. Set aside and let marinate.

The combination of these flavors produces an unexpected wonderfully tasting condiment. If you'd like, you can add onions to the mix, which have to be sliced and sautéed.
You can also add some anchovies if you like them, but if you do, be sure to wash off the salt. You can also add a hot pepper to the mix. It has to be treated the same as the bell peppers. And you can add a small amount of capers if you'd like.

Pickled Eggplant

Besides the red peppers in olive oil, Mom always had a crock of her pickled eggplant in our cellar. And when family members arrived, they would often grab a plate and sneak down for some of them. You'd have thought gold was being stored in our basement.

In a large crock (we had a ceramic crock that was about a foot and a half in diameter and about two feet high), layer thinly sliced eggplant. Between the layers, add chopped garlic, oregano, hot green peppers, and salt.

Place a round board on top that fits the whole opening and a brick or rock on top of it to add pressure. For two days or so, pour off the water that collects.

On the third day, add white wine vinegar. One quart of it. When that seeps down, add another quart. Eggplant must always be moist.

To use, remove eggplant, slice in strips, add a little olive oil.

(If you want, Mom always sliced her eggplants, 20 or so for the big crock, and then placed them in a slotted wooden vegetable basket with salt between the layers, a heavy object on top, to remove the water from them before putting them into the crock. It's an extra step, but you will have less to drain off this way.)

Fried Smelts

There would always be a platter of these quickly cooked little silverfish on the table for Christmas Eve. And they would disappear the moment they hit the table. I loved them. It was another one of those "betcha can't eat just one" dishes.

It Italy, fresh sardines are used, but they are not readily available in the United States, so smelts are the usual replacement. If you ever find fresh sardines or anchovies (even more rare), use them.

If fish are whole, remove head and eviscerate. Wash thoroughly under cold running water.

On a flat plate, combine one cup of flour, salt and pepper, and some chopped parsley. Dredge smelts in this and set aside. In a heavy skillet, heat olive oil over medium-high heat until almost smoking. Oil must be hot so fish will not absorb too much oil. Sauté fish without crowding for 8 to 10 mins., turning frequently. Remove and drain on paper towels.

Place fish on a platter, sprinkle with a bit more parsley, add lemon wedges, and serve immediately. This is a great finger food.

The Famous Christmas Baccala

Before refrigeration and the means of transporting fresh fish that we have today, the only method of preservation was to dry the fish in the sun and then salt it heavily. And cod leant itself wonderfully well to this process, as many countries and peoples discovered, each having their own way of preparing this versatile fish.

We always used dried cod because that was the tradition, and we always wanted to maintain that connection with our ancestors, but today you can buy cod in vacuum-packed bags that doesn't have to be soaked for days. You can even buy it fresh, but somehow that's cheating to me and a disregard for your ancestors and history, for even here in America, dried cod was crucial for the survival of the early settlers.

Soak the dry cod (cut it in manageable pieces) in cold water for 2 or 3 days, changing the water every six hours or so. Toward the end of the process, cover the bowl and refrigerate. It can, of course, be cut into individual sizes before soaking. Fish will become plump and soft. Rinse again, pat dry with paper towels, and cook.

There are many ways to prepare *Baccala*. It can be fried, sautéed, baked, stuffed, even roasted.

This was the way my mother always prepared it:

Prepare a tomato sauce in a deep frying pan, with a chopped onion, 2 garlic cloves minced, 1 can of imported plum tomatoes, and a bit of oregano. This is close to a puttanesca sauce, just missing the capers, which you can add if you like. *(Puttanesca,* a colloquial term for prostitute, was believed to have originated on the Isle of Ischia near Naples.) Cook the sauce for 15 mins. or so. Add the *Baccala*, which needs little cooking at the end of the process. Add black olives and a few anchovies. Cook for 20 mins.

Braciole or Stuffed Meat Rolls

Braciole was usually prepared for Christmas Day. It is a typical Calabrian tradition. With its colorful and intriguing stuffing, a whole egg that is sliced through, it was a special, festive preparation that I always looked forward to when the holidays came around.

- 1½ lbs. top round steak, sliced ¼" thick
- 4 hard-boiled eggs, peeled, one for each roll
- ½ cup dried breadcrumbs
- 6 tbs. freshly grated pecorino or Parmesan cheese
- 4 tbs. fresh Italian parsley, finely chopped
- 3 cloves garlic, finely minced
- 1 tbs. olive oil
- ½ tsp. salt
- ¼ tsp. freshly ground black pepper

Pound the slices of meat with a mallet to tenderize. (A friend of my mother's, who taught her this recipe, used very wide slices of meat, 10" wide, which would require using two eggs in the stuffing. Mom preferred a smaller width of meat, 6" or so, that required only one egg and fit easily in her sauce pot … and makes an individual portion.)

Spread 8" long pieces on a flat surface. In a bowl, mix the breadcrumbs, cheese, parsley, garlic, oil, salt, and pepper. (Some people add raisins to the mixture.) Divide the mixture evenly among the slices. Spread out. Place one hard-boiled egg at the shorter side of the meat and gently roll up, jelly-roll style. Tie the rolls securely in several places with kitchen string and tuck in sides.

Heat a small amount of olive oil in a Dutch oven, and brown the meat on all sides. Should take about 6 to 8 mins.

To this, add your tomato sauce (or start your tomato sauce in this pot) and slowly cook, simmering gently for 1 to 2 hours until the meat is tender to the probing of a fork. Do not overcook, for meat will fall apart.

One way to serve is to remove string, slice into 2" slices, and serve with sauce and pasta. Another way (and the one I liked because I could see the egg surprise in the center revealed as they were sliced) is to bring the platter of braciole to the table separately and either serve one per person or slice the amount wanted there at the table. Youngsters will be duly impressed.

Two variations

- Chop the hard-boiled egg and include it in the stuffing mix.
- Place ham slices on the meat and then stuff and roll.

Sliced Biscotti

(These are the ones now popular in all the coffee bars. They're crunchier and great for dipping. The word *biscotti* means twice-baked.)

- ½ lb butter or oleo
- 2 cups sugar
- 6 eggs
- 6 cups of flour
- 6 tsp. baking powder pinch of salt
- 2 tsp. anise seed (You can also add 2 teaspoons vanilla extract to the eggs if no anise)
- 1 lb. or less walnut halves (or almonds which have to be baked and skinned, or pistachios; you can also add some chopped-up cherries.)
- ½ cup milk (maybe)

Cream butter and sugar well in mixer. Add the eggs one at a time and beat well. Sift the flour, the baking powder, and salt, mixing it well and then add to the egg batter. This is a very sticky dough and a thick one, so you may want to mix it by hand. Remember not to over mix. Add the anise and nuts or whatever else you want to the mixture. If the dough is too stiff and can't be worked, add a little of the milk at this time till it's right. (If you want a smoother dough, add a tablespoon of Crisco or canola oil) Form the dough by rolling with your hands into loaves about 1½" in width. They will double in size when baked. Your cookie sheet will indicate the length of the loaves. You should be able to get three loaves onto a sheet. Experiment so that you get the size cookie you want. The above recipe should make 6 loaves, three to a sheet. Flatten the loaves to about an inch in height.

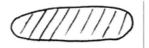

Bake the loaves until they brown in a 350° oven for about 25 mins. Remove from the oven, and while still hot, slice them at a slant so that you get a longer cookie, about an inch in width. Return to the oven, with a space between the sliced cookies, so the sides can now brown. Watch them!

(The anise seed in America is a poor relation to what is available in Italy. When my mother and father made their second and last trip back to Italy, to my father's hometown, they brought back a quarter pound of anise that cost twenty dollars American money but that was worth its weight in gold. It entailed a bit of work to get. A cousin had to call someone in a town up in the hills. And then Mom and Dad had to journey up there to retrieve the anise. It seems to be a flavoring you have to know someone to get. The reason for the expense and the mystery is that each flower has only three tiny anise seeds, which have to be harvested by hand and entails a great deal of work for a very small amount. And the anise in Italy is black, not tan like the one found here in stores. Mom treasured that ½ lb. for twenty years.

Easter Baskets or Cuzzupe Di Pasqua

Mom made these every Easter. The egg, an ancient symbol of fertility and of new beginnings and new life, is used in many different forms. Here it is used to make a basket or ring out of cookie dough. Placed in the middle of the table for a centerpiece, they add a very festive touch to the holiday. I loved seeing them appear every Easter because they were so pretty and were obviously only meant for a special occasion.

Mom used the same dough that she used for her simple Italian cookie.

Roll the dough out into foot-long strips 1" thick. Bend in half and braid twice. Place an uncooked egg in the middle of the braid, continue the dough around the egg, and then braid twice on the other side, pressing the ends of the dough together. You can be creative here and create your own basket shape, even cutting a square of the dough, making a deep impression in the center, placing an egg in it, and then fashioning a handle for the basket out of a braided strip of dough.

Cover the egg with two thin rolled-out strips of dough in a cross, pinching the ends into the dough at the sides.

Bake in a 350° oven till golden brown for 20 to 22 mins. (Use a slightly greased cookie sheet.) Use the powdered sugar icing and sprinkle with colored sprinkles. (Or glaze with ½ cup of confectioner's sugar and 1 to 1½ tsp. water, adding water slowly till glaze is spreadable.)

Or try this beautiful circle with five or more eggs. Just

continue the same braiding as above going around the eggs till you have a circle. Another method is to roll out three lengths of the dough, allowing yourself enough length to complete the circle, and plait the three lengths into a circle, pinching the ends together. Then in this circle, place your eggs at an aesthetic distance from each other. Top the eggs with the crossed thin strips of dough.

Note: Some people use colored hard-boiled eggs. It makes a very pretty ring. My mother decided one year to skip the hard-boiled step (the eggs were overcooked) and just used raw eggs, which cooked along with the dough. That worked out well.

Fig-Filled Cookies

There were always some of these at the holidays. Called *cucidate* or *Petrali*, they also satisfied an ancestral yearning, being rough and rustic. There are many different variations. Mom used her basic biscotti recipe for the dough. For the filling she used the following:

- 2 cups black figs
- 2 tbs. flour
- 1 cup water
- 2 tbs. lemon juice
- 1 cup sugar
- a little grated lemon or
- ½ cup chopped nuts
- orange rind

Chop the figs, add water and sugar, and cook for 10 mins. Add flour and cook until very thick, stirring constantly. Add lemon juice and grated rind. Add chopped nuts. Cool slightly before using. (You can try adding a small amount of raisins. Or orange juice instead of the lemon juice.)

Roll the dough into a square 1/8" thick. Place a tablespoon of filling into the bottom half of square. Dip fingers in water and roll the edges of the bottoms and the tops, squeezing them together. Prick tops with a fork.

In a 400° oven, bake for 25 or 30 mins. or until lightly browned.

(Mom would make a few different shapes of these. Sometimes in a roll that could be sliced ... but mostly in the individual size.)

Struffoli

(Neapolitan Honey Clusters)

These delightful mounds of tiny pieces of fried dough drizzled with honey and then covered lightly with colored sprinkles usually appeared at Easter and Christmas and made a lovely centerpiece for the holiday table, if you could keep the kids from pulling the pieces off and eating them before dessert. In Calabria they are called *Cicirata* and are believed to be of Greek origin.

Beat together:
- 3 eggs
- ¾ cup sugar
- ½ cup vegetable oil

Add to following, mixed together:
- 1 tbs. vanilla
- 3 ½ cups sifted flour
- 2 ½ tsp. baking powder
- ½ tsp. salt

Mix all together and let rest for 15 mins. Then turn out onto a lightly floured board and cut a piece and roll out like a thick pencil. Cut into 1/2" pieces. Fry in deep fat (360°) until light and golden brown. (You can add one tablespoon of freshly grated orange zest and one of lemon zest for a bit more flavoring.) Dry on paper towels.

Form into a pyramid shape, and drizzle with warmed honey and then the colored sprinkles.

Or you can drop the dough balls into a warmed honey-and-sugar mixture and then, with a slotted spoon, place in a mound on a plate.

To-tos

(the round chocolate iced ball)

- 1 cup sugar
- 1 tsp. each of:
- 4 eggs
- cinnamon
- 4 tbs. cocoa cup milk
- cloves
- 4 tsp. baking powder
- ginger
- 2 tbs. Spry or Butter
- nutmeg (or if you'd like 1 tsp. allspice)
- 4 cups flour
- 1 cup raisins
- 1 cup chopped walnuts

Cream shortening, add sugar and well-beaten eggs. Add cocoa, milk, and allspice. Add flour and baking powder and mix well. Add raisins, nuts, and mix. Grease hands, shape walnut-sized balls. Place on greased cookie sheet. Bake 10 mins. in 375° oven. Cool and frost.

The icing my mother always used (and which can be used for all cookies):

- 1 cup powdered sugar
- 1 tbs. butter
- juice of one lemon
- a dash of vanilla

Coat cookies.

Or you can make an icing with powdered sugar and water. Place cookies in a bowl and cover with icing. Let cookies stand in bowl until dry and glazed.

Wandi

(There are many names for this fried, pastry strip, classic. I heard "angels' wings" and "fried ribbons," among other names. My mother called them "Wandi" (a regional dialect version of *Guanti*, gloves? Or a reference to their shape? I don't know.) By whatever name they are a wonderful light treat and great for the holidays, eaten just after being made.)

- ¼ lb. butter
- 1 cup sugar
- 6 eggs, beaten
- 1 tsp. vanilla (or other flavoring)
- 4 tsp. baking powder
- sifted flour

Melt butter, add sugar, and beat in eggs. Add flavoring, baking powder, and enough flour to make a soft dough. Roll on a slightly floured board ¼" thick. Cut into 3" triangles. Make a slit in center and twist one long end through. Or cut rolled sheets of dough into 3-by-5 pieces on which make 4 lengthwise cuts 4 inches long. Or cut sheet of dough into ½-by-6-inch pieces and form into bows or knots or after cutting a 1-inch slit in the center, twist slightly. Fry in hot fat until delicately brown. Place on paper towels when done. When ready to serve, sprinkle with sifted powdered sugar.

Almond Crescents

(My all-time favorite Christmas cookie and, of course, the richest.)

- ½ lb. butter
- ¼ lb. nuts (walnuts, almonds, or pecans)
- ¼ cup powdered sugar
- 2 cups flour (with nuts stirred in)
- 1 tsp. vanilla

Cream butter, add powdered sugar, flour. and nuts.
Mix and form into crescents.
Bake for 20 mins. at 350°.
When cool, sprinkle with powdered sugar. (Try a bit of cinnamon in the powdered sugar.)

Another Method
(This recipe refrigerates the dough)

- 2 cups unsifted all-purpose flour
- 1 cup butter or margarine, softened
- 1 cup ground pecans or hazelnuts
- ½ cup unsifted confectioners' sugar
- ⅛ tsp. salt
- 1 tsp. vanilla extract
- 4 tsp. almond extract

Vanilla Sugar:
- 3" strips vanilla bean, cut up
- 2 cups sifted confectioners' sugar

1. In a large bowl, combine flour, butter, nuts, 1 cup confectioners' sugar, the salt and extracts. Mix, with hands, until thoroughly combined. Refrigerate, covered, for one hour.
2. To make vanilla sugar, in electric blender, combine cut-up vanilla bean and 4 cups confectioners' sugar. Cover, blend at high speed for about 8 secs. Combine with remaining confectioners' sugar on a large sheet of foil.

3. Preheat oven to 375°.
4. Shape cookies by forming dough into balls, using 1 tbs. dough for each. Then with palm of hands, form each ball into a roll 3" long.
5. Place, 2" apart, on ungreased cookie sheet. Curve each to make a crescent. Bake for 12 to 15 mins. or until set but not brown.
6. Let stand for 1 min. before removing. With spatula, place hot cookies in vanilla sugar; turn gently to coat both sides. Cool completely.
7. Store in tightly covered crock or cookie tin in a cool, dry place.
8. Just before serving, coat with additional sugar if desired.

(Makes about 3½ dozens)

CPSIA information can be obtained at www.ICGtesting.com
232764LV00004B/76/P